37463

CENSORSHIP & THE CONTROL OF PRINT

in England and France 1600-1910

CENSORSHIP & THE CONTROL OF PRINT

in England and France 1600-1910

Edited by

Robin Myers and Michael Harris

ST PAUL'S BIBLIOGRAPHIES

WINCHESTER

1992

© 1992 The Contributors

First published 1992 by
St Paul's Bibliographies
West End House
1 Step Terrace
Winchester
Hampshire SO22 5BW

British Library Cataloguing in Publication Data
is available from The British Library

ISBN 1 873040 16 4

Cover illustration: from Francis Bugg, *The Pilgrims Progress from Quakerism to Christianity,* 1700.

Typeset in CG Times by Ella Whitehead, Munslow, Shropshire
Printed in England by St Edmundsbury Press, Bury St Edmunds

Contents

Introduction

WHO CONTROLS SOCIETY? How is power achieved and sustained? Any attempt to answer these large questions, whether at the level of personal relationships or within the public spheres of politics and religion, inevitably leads into a new set of questions about the means of communication. Who controls the media and who has access to it? How is the material it transmits constructed? What are the interests that intervene at the different stages of production and distribution? These are the questions which are considered in this volume mainly in relation to print but also with reference to the various forms of manuscript and verbal exchange. With the invention of printing the lines of access to information and comment of all kinds were gradually extended. Print gave to the material it expressed a greater formality and, potentially at least, a greater force than could be directed through alternative channels.

The printing press, like all the later technologies of communication, was ambiguously placed. Its capacity to reinforce the existing order and at the same time to initiate change was in balance and the mechanism itself was increasingly seen as both a threat and a promise. As gatekeepers to the primary instrument of communication, printers and booksellers assumed a role equally fraught with ambiguity. Over time, the English trade, though always driven by commercial imperatives, developed a structure which reflected many of the opposed interests within society at large. By constructing its own clearly identified and carefully monitored London establishment, a sector of the trade lined up with other top-down metropolitan organisations becoming, in many respects, the natural ally of religious and political authority. At the same time, the creation of a centre of power based on the Stationers' Company excluded many individuals whose interests became identified with those of other outsiders whose opinions ran counter to the dominant forms of ideology. This was still only part of the picture. Different forces came into play as print and other media forms were projected across society. Defining the permissible was never a one-way process and readers, as consumers, applied notions of social acceptability through diverse mechanisms such as library subscription lists.

Within this complex system it is always difficult to identify the way in which the forms of control, explicit and implicit, were mediated. The ebb and flow of interpretative analysis has done something to blur the picture and, as Sheila Lambert shows in her perceptive account of the historiography of censorship in the 17th century, the evidence continues to provide material for academic skirmishing. While it was increasingly true that print marked out the frontier along which authority and dissent were ranged in various embattled postures, violent confrontation has not, in the main, been the way in which the issues of control and access have been resolved. Print has provided the locus for a series of complex, obscure and sometimes highly ominous negotiations involving the shifting networks of interest which extended widely through society.

In the present collection of essays a number of leading scholars investigate this print-centred process which has helped to determine the cultural form of European communities over the last three centuries. Sheila Lambert takes a fresh look at the way in which Tudor and Stuart governments engaged with print. Through a close examination of all the evidence, she shews how the book trade and government interacted in a less formal and confrontational way than is usually assumed by those who have relied too heavily on the data provided by the Stationers' Company records. Print was still, in the early 17th century, a medium with restricted range and impact, and she explains how the booksellers and printers of the Stationers' Company were dominated by self-interest in executing the restraints demanded by Government, diverging from it according to a variety of specific circumstances. Her picture, which is both intricate and convincing, is shared by the perspectives of both David Hall and Alison Shell, whose essays are concerned with the representation in print of religious groups on the frontiers of respectability. David Hall shews how Quaker self-censorship concerned itself with its image in the community as well as with questions of literary taste until changes in the attitude of society at large led to the cessation of such direct control by the Morning Meeting; while Alison Shell's essay gives a masterly exposition of the manipulation of print to increase the anti-Catholic phobia of a Protestant, xenophobic society. Taking a wider, European view, as we stand on the threshold of cultural and scholarly integration, Anne Goldgar investigates the mechanism of censorship in 18th-century France. Through a reading of material in the Paris archives, she develops a highly original analysis in which the notion of state control is substantially modified by the pragmatic intervention of the writers themselves. She demonstrates how journalists working for the state were, in fact, applying the informal principles of the international community of authors often described as the Republic of Letters.

Her representation of what was essentially a form of self-censorship chimes with the picture which emerges in the last two essays in the collection. These are primarily concerned with the wider interaction of print with readers. Michael Walsh describes the way in which the Roman Catholic Index was constructed and applied in the long-term attempt to keep a range of materials out of the hands of believers and others. He focuses on the Index of Leo XIII, which represented the major reconstruction of the 19th century. The shortcomings of the Index in both its centralised and local form appear to have made it far less effective than the controls achieved through the English library system during the same century. Nicholas Hiley investigates the way in which the leading circulating libraries established and exercised a pragmatic control over the distribution of books from the 1890s to the outbreak of the First World War. In his account the interlinked pressures of commercial interest and reader response emerge with unusual clarity.

The attempts which have been made to describe and analyse the control of print over the last three centuries have always been dominated by politics and by the activities of central authority. They have seldom, if ever, acknowledged the complexities of the interventions centred on the book trade and the essays in this collection represent a substantial contribution to the untangling and identifying of the submerged elements in the process. They were originally read at the 13th annual conference on booktrade history at the Birkbeck College Centre for Extra-mural Studies, University of London, 30 November and 1 December 1991.

Robin Myers and Michael Harris
London, April 1992

Contributors

ANNE GOLDGAR received her PhD in 1990 from Harvard University for her study 'Gentlemen and scholars: Conduct and community in the republic of letters', which is to be published by Yale University Press. She is currently Research Fellow at Clare Hall, Cambridge University.

DAVID HALL is currently working on the history of Quaker publishing and also of the Library of the Society of Friends. He is an Under-Librarian at Cambridge University Library.

NICHOLAS HILEY has held research posts at Cambridge, London and at the Open University. He has worked extensively on the history of propaganda and censorship in Britain between the 1880s and the 1920s and is presently writing a book on the origins of the modern mass media for the Cambridge University Press.

SHEILA LAMBERT is editor of the *House of Commons Sessional Papers of the Eighteenth Century*. She has written extensively on parliamentary history in the 17th and 18th centuries and is the author of *Bills and Acts: Legislative Procedure in Eighteenth Century England*.

ALISON SHELL has recently completed a doctorate at St Hilda's College, Oxford University on 'English Catholicism and Drama, 1578-1688'. She worked with Robin Myers at Stationers' Hall for several years and is currently Curator of Rare Books at the RIBA.

MICHAEL WALSH has made a special study of the printing press of the English Jesuits in St Omers, 1608-1753, and has written a history of the English Catholic weekly *The Tablet*. He is currently planning a history of English Catholic printing and publishing. He is Librarian of Heythrop College, University of London.

List of those attending the Conference

Jean Archibald
Librarian

T.A. Birrell
Teacher (retired)

Dr Alistair Black
Lecturer

Lynda Brooks
Librarian

Gillis Burgess
Charity Officer

Jackie Canning
Librarian

Tom Colverson
Publisher/Librarian (retired)

Andrew Cook
Archivist

Dr Karen Cook
Map Librarian

Robert Cross
Publisher

Sarah Dodgson
Librarian

Mary Doran
Reader, British Library

Colston Hartley
Librarian

John Hewish
Librarian

P.A. Hopkins
Historian

A.W. Huish
Librarian (retired)

Arnold Hunt
Research student

G.P. Jefcoate
British Library

B.C. Johnson
British Library

Beverley Kemp
British Library

Vincent Kinane
Librarian

C.L. Lee

Anthony Lister
Lecturer (retired)

Adam Lyons
Student

Giles Mandelbrote
Publisher

G.T. Mandl
*Upper Warden, Stationers'
Company*

Charles Parry
Assistant Librarian

Margaret Payne
Librarian

Michael Perkin
Librarian (retired)

Richard Price
British Library

Gill Ridgley
British Library

Henry Rosenberg
Lecturer/Librarian, University of Surrey

Susanna Reid

David Stoker
University Teacher

Tone Urstad
Research Fellow

Tony Watts
Publisher/Printer

Mrs E.C. Wilkinson
Researcher

Sandra Williams

I.R. Willison
Librarian (retired)

R.B. Woodings
Lecturer in Publishing

P.K.J. Wright
Lecturer (retired)

Williams Zachs
Lecturer

State control of the press in theory and practice: the role of the Stationers' Company before 1640

Sheila Lambert

ATTITUDES to censorship have always been to some extent a matter of personal and political predilection, coloured by the intellectual climate of the time. Writers who wish to champion the underdog and take the part of those who strive against authority find censorship everywhere, while those who prefer law, order and a quiet life are inclined to belittle the importance of occasional instances of repression, however ferocious these are shown to be. Legal historians tell us, quite rightly, that punishments in Star Chamber were no more brutal than those of the common-law courts; that torture was never used as a punishment, and could not be ordered by Star Chamber. Even the use of torture can be palliated: we are told that its use was confined to London so it could not be used for private vengeance in the counties, and the Peacham case is dismissed as a personal vendetta by King James as though that was sufficient explanation.[1] Yet on the whole the notion that there was strict state control of the press continues to win the day, because it is such a useful concept, to be invoked to cover everything from poor standards of printing, to failure to look with sufficient care for evidence of dissent.

The idea that an all-pervasive censorship, which successfully prevented all expression of unorthodox opinion, was intended by the autocratic and repressive governments of James I and Charles I, was a necessary part of the liberal account of the irresistible march of liberty and also of the Marxist version of events. Since not too much overt evidence seemed to be found in historical sources of public demand for a new political order, it had to be assumed that such opinions existed but were suppressed. Over-emphasis on the role of parliament in liberal historiography went hand in hand with the belief that it was only in parliament that something like freedom of speech was possible. Here the influence of American scholars, seeking their democratic roots, has been predominant. One source of a major theme in Wallace Notestein's influential lecture, 'The Winning of the Initiative by the House of Commons', was a study of this kind and Notestein went on to

1

inspire several major editions of the parliamentary debates of the period.[2] American influence has also been crucial in the realm of censorship, for in the United States the question of the origin and interpretation of the first and fifth amendments to the constitution has remained a live political and legal issue.[3] It was as a contribution to this question that F.S. Siebert, in 1930, wrote the book that has become the standard text for the history of censorship, used alike by historians and literary scholars on both sides of the Atlantic.[4]

It is only natural that historians of the newspaper press, believing that 'the battles for a free Press are a part of the march of democracy', should seek to emphasise the extent to which the journalistic profession has triumphed over great odds. At the turn of the century, the author of the first modern British account of the rise of the fourth estate attributed to the Tudor and Stuart governments the principle that anything not specifically permitted was forbidden. A proclamation of 18 May 1544 suppressing publication of military rumours was cited as evidence that a licence had to be obtained before any news could be published. At the same time, the supposed existence of a patent granted for publication of foreign corantos was construed as evidence that no licences were ever granted for domestic news; no such ban and no such patent ever existed, and yet the idea persists.[5]

Edward Arber not only transcribed the Stationers' Register, but also interspersed a variety of documents, including the two Star Chamber decrees of 1586 and 1637, intended to emphasise the risks and penalties to which the Stationers were subject. The 'dual system of control' of the press through the state and the church on the one hand and the Stationers' Company on the other, was a concept flattering to the Company and welcome to bibliographers. The lamentable standard of printing in England in the early 17th century needed a scapegoat, which could be found in Arber's evidence of the 'extremely rigorous' Star Chamber decree of 1586, followed by 'a long series of attacks by the government upon the trade' culminating in the 'even more severe' decree of 1637.[6] McKerrow took a calmer view in 1928 but his first opinion has prevailed despite the fact that the opening of the rest of the records of the Stationers' Company in the 1950s cast considerable doubt on the possibility that a couple of hundred squabbling small tradesmen could have been an effective arm of government; Cyprian Blagden's exposition of the records is in danger of being ignored.[7]

In order to cope with the large amount of writing that actually did reach print, it was assumed that any appearance of anti-establishment literature indicated that the censor was momentarily nodding or that the whole system was near to breakdown. If, as even McKerrow allowed, 'during the reign of James I the book-trade does not seem to have been treated with anything like the same severity' as under Elizabeth, this was because Elizabeth had 'bequeathed a tottering system' to her successor; 'the elaborate structure erected by the Tudors for the control of the press was being subjected to stresses which it could not long withstand'.[8] Faced with the outburst of political pamphleteering of the early 1620s, Godfrey Davies used a series of proclamations which actually had very disparate roots as evidence of an attempt to stem the tide and 'suppress all criticism', thus bringing forward in time the intensification of censorship always associated with the accession of Charles and the rise of William Laud, and which culminated in the Star Chamber decree of 1637. However, 'Drastic as this decree was, it practically remained a dead letter'; 'As vainly did Mrs. Partington with her mop try to keep out the sea'.[9]

Because the evidence for the theatre is a good deal better than that for the printed word, students of the drama have always known that the censorship was not all-pervasive. Careful analysis of the official record of censorship kept by the Master of the Revels has shown some thirty instances of censorship, few of them political, as against some 2,000 plays written between 1590 and 1642. For the period 1622 to 1642 we have only an 18th-century transcript of part of the record which shows some 15 plays criticised for one reason or another (including profanity, concerning which the Master had no discretion, for profanity on stage had been made a statutory offence at the insistence of the parliament of 1605-6), as against well over 100 licensed for performance without any objection. 'The simplest and commonest action of the Master when he was brought a manuscript, ... was to read the script, find nothing objectionable, and write his allowance at the end'.[10] It is true that many plays have been lost, but not 'because they could not obtain the licence necessary for publication': we know of the existence of the 'lost' plays in most cases only because their titles are found in the records of the Master of the Revels or the Stationers' Company; that is because they were in fact licensed at least once and in some cases twice, for performance and then for publication.[11]

At the turn of the century Sir Sidney Lee took a beneficent view of authority's attitude to the arts, pointing out that one of James's first acts as king was to grant a patent to Shakespeare's company, to which he after-wards added many favours. When Phoebe Sheavyn cited his work only to pick out the instances of censorship, Lee went much further, asserting that 'literature on and off the stage enjoyed in practice a large measure of liberty'. For Sheavyn, Shakespeare's lament that art was 'made tongue-tied by authority' was clear proof that 'writers were intimidated, and that some were reduced to silence'; while to Lee this was no more than 'the casual expression of a pessimistic mood'.[12] Sheavyn moved also into the non-dramatic canon and in describing the 'paralysing influence' of censorship, produced a list of 23 authors whom she believed must have concealed their real opinions in print; her analysis held the field, embodied in the *Cambridge History of English Literature*.[13] Half a century later Edwin Miller, whose views on the political background to the period were clearly much influenced by the historical writings of Wallace Notestein and J.E. Neale, as mediated through the work of Louis B. Wright, refused to accept such self-censorship as an adequate explanation of the behaviour of the authors of his highly-romanticised Elizabethan age. Although he accepted Sheavyn's thesis of decline in private patronage, he elected the 'publisher' not the censor as the bogeyman of literature, and, in a rare criticism of Siebert's account, denied the intention and effectiveness of censorship, deriding Sheavyn's view of its pervasive effects. But Miller was able to do this only by concentrating on supposedly 'puritan' demands for moral censorship and regarding political censorship as an acceptable fact of life, its restraints having even a beneficial effect upon the artist.[14]

Then Christopher Hill joined the fray and began to elaborate the thesis which reached its full statement a quarter of a century later. The ending of ecclesiastical control in 1641 is 'the most significant event in the history of seventeenth-century English literature', liberating authors for the first time from the overwhelming need to conceal their true opinions in print.[15] And so the fight goes on. Sir Keith Thomas joins Professor Hill in finding that licensing 'had a deeply inhibiting effect upon printed publication'.[16] Professor Aylmer picked a middle way through the morass: although he relied on Siebert for the 'severe' censorship 'enforced' by the 1637 decree. When he surveyed the historical background for an inter-disciplinary course for students in 1980, Aylmer found no such pervasive effects on literature in general and has continued to maintain that the period was 'no tyranny'.[17] Lately, with the popularity of ideas of coalition, confederation, contract and community, these have been found both by historians of parliament and by those interested in cultural history. The 'revisionist' approach to parliamentary history views the parliamentary debates, not as the forum for the expression of opposition to the crown, but as the scene of an endless search for consensus of opinion.[18] The revisionist case has already brought reaction from the new Whigs who wish to restore the notion of widespread, principled, opposition to the Crown, and have sought more successfully than their predecessors to find evidence for it by greater use of the pamphlet literature and by exploiting a much wider range of manuscript evidence which is presented as proof of an underground network of opposition, beyond the government's control, operating through correspondence and the circulation of manuscript treatises.[19] One difficulty here is that subversive messages are now being found in such number and variety, both in the drama and in printed pamphlets, that the theory of overwhelming censorship looks likely to collapse under the weight of its own proof. It has to be suggested that courtiers were too stupid to understand the allusions found in the court masques.[20] Edwin Miller's beneficent discipline of censorship becomes, in the hands of Annabel Patterson, 'the central problem of consciousness and communication' and produces a theory of 'functional ambiguity'; an 'implicit social contract between authors and authorities' whereby, so long as the former successfully 'encoded their opinion' within the existing conventions, no interference would or did occur.[21]

But the notion of coded discourse is too fragile a concept to elucidate the growing mass of evidence and in any case what purpose can be served by codes that everyone can easily understand?[22] Francis Bacon employed the classical allusions that reinforced the self-conscious superiority of educated men. Robert Burton helpfully translated almost all his Latin quotations, giving less learned readers a nodding acquaintance with the works of Paracelsus, Tycho Brahe, Kepler, John Dee, and others, not forgetting some interesting passages from Aretine, which must greatly have assisted the popularity of his book.[23] The biblical codes were open to all, to the extent that contemporaries would not have regarded them as any sort of concealment. Although the meaning has to be spelled out to modern readers, no one at the time thought it at all necessary to explain what was meant when Henry Walker threw the text 'To your Tents, O Israel' into the King's coach after Charles's attempt to arrest the five members in 1642.[24] This was a generation that simply had a fondness for mystification. They looked for symbols everywhere – in scripture, astrology, anagrams and emblems. And, like the emblem books, with their elaborate allegorical pictures and equally elaborate explanations printed alongside, the symbols were meant to illuminate, not to deceive.

Another and greater difficulty arises from the idea that authors who refrained from printing could express themselves freely. There was no reason for an author to refrain from print for fear of the consequences, for a book that remained in manuscript was safe only from pre-publication censorship, not from prosecution. The most notorious case is that of Edmund Peacham, who was one of the five men who suffered torture in the reign of James I, and who was subsequently sentenced to death for treason on the basis of a draft sermon found in his study, which he had neither delivered nor attempted to print.[25] It is certain that no author could hide behind his printer if a work was questioned as seditious, for printing was quite irrelevant to that issue, and indeed in several notorious cases, notably the Histriomastix charge, the printers were not punished but acquitted as mere hirelings.[26] There was opposition to Crown policies from many quarters (how far that opposition was principled or in any sense organised is another question). This was a free society, growing in size, wealth, education, and political awareness, but one which was not yet print-dependent. The printed word formed only a tiny part of the activities that the state sought to control, direct or manipulate, which fall under the general heading of censorship. The sermon, the stage-play, the proceedings of courts, the public meeting are all, in the 17th century, more important than the printed word to the spread of ideas. The most important means of circulating ideas at a more sophisticated level did not involve the use of print: the tradition of manuscript circulation, or 'scribal publication' as it is now called, remained powerful until the end of the 17th century.[27] This is a point which can never be overstressed.

There was, of course, self-censorship. The articulate class, gentlemen and intellectuals, lived in a small society, known to one another in county oligarchies, connected with (or members of) the court, and often personally known to the king. They lived, most importantly, in a monarchy, if one somewhat less autocratic than its European counterparts, yet one in which the mere whim of one man could mightily affect one's fortunes for good or ill. Caution and secrecy were natural attitudes even in the highest ranks of this society, for there were frequently deep disagreements within the court itself. In the first decade of the century, the Earl of Northampton, at the height of his power and influence as first minister, was asking the King to burn his letters. Archbishop Laud once implored King Charles not to carry a particularly sensitive letter in his pockets, but to burn it or return it at once – even the royal pockets were not safe from picking by spies.[28]

Just as the concept of opposition is seen as almost impossible in the early Stuart parliaments, we are told that the age did not have our concept of censorship, nor any organised means to exercise it.[29] It is true in one sense that the age did have a different concept of censorship, for the polemical manners of the time required that an author should set out his opponent's argument fairly and at length. Thus the texts even of books that were burned might be preserved, the burning being practically as well as theoretically merely symbolic.[30] It is also certainly true that the age did not have the Western liberal idea of free speech; what we find is comparable to more recent attitudes of groups who demand full freedom of expression for themselves, while denying any such right to their opponents. The threat to the English system from powerful Catholic interests meant that not only 'puritans', of whatever shade of opinion, would not only agree but demand that popish proselytising of an ignorant and superstitious people be prevented; the parliaments of the early 17th century made such demands at every meeting. Most gentlemen would have seen millenarian influence as an equal danger, for all of them knew the risks of stirring up discontent amongst the lower orders, especially in a time of considerable economic hardship. Robert Burton, his Utopian message influenced by Bacon's New Atlantis, laid about him in all directions concerning the wrongs of the state, from he who has a kingdom 'and knows not how to rule it', to 'our priests (who make religion policy)' and 'domineer over princes'; from 'so many lawyers ... so little justice', to unlearned patrons who read only Amadis de Gaul, yet his remedy for puritanism was 'burn their books, forbid their conventicles'.[31] The number of men who would have advocated full freedom of speech and writing for their enemies is tiny and Milton is not amongst the number. His 'principled' plea for freedom from 'pre-publication censorship' has to be described with such tortuous care because he was certainly not advocating freedom of the press.[32] After the world had turned upside down and Milton sat in the censor's chair, that 'early hero of the struggle for economic freedom and freedom of the press', Prynne's bookseller Michael Sparke, found himself calling powerfully for censorship again, in language that now echoes in our ears: he wished to see 'all blasphemous books of conjuration, and the Turkish Alcoran and all heretical, schismaticall, ranting, scandalous and libellous books with bawdry and scurrility to be consumed by this second Beacon set on fire by Scintilla'.[33]

I think it is simplest, and not simplistic, to believe that the governments of Elizabeth, James and Charles did have a concept of censorship and a means of exercising it, and that the machinery did what it was expected to do (that is so far as any machinery of government functioned efficiently in those days). What it was not expected to do was to suppress all expression of opposition to the Crown. Francis Bacon recognised the principle of censorship when he lectured his sovereign on the application of it, noting that it was often best to ignore seditious libels 'For the despising of them many times checks them best; and the going about to stop them doth but make a wonder long-lived'.[34]

The simplest proof that the government never intended full control of everything that was printed is that no attempt was ever made to control the import of paper. No paper for printing was made in England, not because of monopoly, but because neither the technology nor the raw materials were available.[35] It would have been entirely in keeping with Jacobean ways of doing business to have granted to some courtier a monopoly of importing paper, and a short step thence to inventing the Stamp Act of 1712 a century before its time. A totally obscure widow could see the possibilities of such a scheme and proposed in 1606 not only that her son, who was the Earl of Salisbury's godson, should operate it, but that he should hold a post of overseer of the press, similar to that held by Roger L'Estrange after the Restoration.[36] Yet this plan went no further and no such project was ever contemplated in government circles, so far as we know. On the contrary, the Crown more than once granted monopolies, that is patents to protect an infant industry, for the manufacture of paper in England, but the patentees made little progress, and the printing trade contentedly relied on imported paper.[37] One of the contributors to Sir Thomas Smith's *Discourse* specifically mentioned paper as one of the luxuries whose import should be banned in order to boost home production, to which the reply was that the Crown would never agree to lose the customs duty on the imports.[38] But the imported paper was not heavily taxed; even when the charge was doubled by the imposition of 1608, printing paper was rated at only 5*s* per ream, meaning a tax of 3*d.* a ream, and since paper, even including all kinds of wrapping paper, formed a minuscule proportion of total imports, the political advantage would surely have far outweighed the loss of revenue if the government had had total censorship in mind.[39]

The primary concern of the Crown was to maintain the integrity of its foreign policy. The principal domestic duty of the Crown was to maintain the peace; that is, to preserve public order, which involved, amongst other things, being alert to nip sedition in the bud. The dangers of sedition were real, not only at the turn of the century when the succession to the Crown was in doubt, but throughout the period; there are some hints that seizures of papers under Charles still related to worries about evidence concerning James's legitimacy. The Scottish problem remained, and the discontented attached themselves to reversionary interests, first Prince Henry, then Princess Elizabeth, then Prince Charles, then Queen Henrietta. Internal and external risks were related, for all discontents were fomented by foreign powers. Just as, in economic policy, 'the maintenance of public order was among the primary ends of government action', and yet action was almost always 'stimulated by the urgent demands of a period of short-term (if recurrent) dislocation' usually caused by events abroad, so the most notorious incidents of censorship or repression come in intermittent bursts, often in response to the requirements of the diplomatic situation.[40] The connection of puritanism and sedition was not an invention of King Charles and William Laud. King James and Archbishop Abbot pursued separatists with equal or greater enthusiasm, and both kings wished to confine discussion of church polity to the universities. While the Crown, left to itself, might have been content to let the weight fall only on writings that seemed likely to disturb the peace of church or state, or actually personally libelled the monarch, other men could use libel actions as they did other forms of litigation, simply as a means of causing difficulties to their enemies. The vast majority of cases in the 'prerogative' courts of High Commission and Star Chamber were not brought by the Crown but by private individuals,[41] and many of those who fell victim to state prosecutions in Star Chamber did so not because of the activity of state informers but because they were reported to authority by a close acquaintance on whom they had incautiously relied, either out of goodwill to the cause, simple malice, or hope of personal advantage.

The evidence for all this cannot be encompassed in a single paper, but some of the points can be exemplified in a demonstration that the Stationers' Company played no very significant role in enforcing state control of the press. As we have seen, and it cannot be too often stressed, the printed word played only a small part in the dissemination of political ideas; any role the Company did play could be only a small part of the whole question of relations between Crown and people.

John Selden remarked in 1629 that there was 'no law to prevent the printing of any books in England, only a decree in Star-chamber'. He went on to propose that 'a law might be made concerning printing: otherwise, he said, a man might be fined, imprisoned, and his goods taken from him, by virtue of the said decree; which is a great invasion upon the liberty of the subject'. Selden on this occasion was making a debating point at the Commons' grand committee for religion.[42] He knew very well that there was legal basis for both licensing and censorship of books. Even if Selden meant to refer only to Statute law (an uncommon usage at this time), and without going back into the history of Tudor legislation, there was in fact one act, passed in the aftermath of the Gunpowder Plot, which prohibited the printing of popish books, and which the House of Commons quite frequently demanded should be better enforced.[43] The Master and Wardens of the Stationers' Company had power by their Charter of 4 May 1557 to discipline members by seizure of goods, fine or imprisonment for breach of company regulations; powers of this kind were common to all the City livery companies and were fully recognised at law.

In the case of the Stationers' Company the regulations included the prohibition of printing any book belonging to another member of the Company, and this covered books to which the Crown had granted exclusive rights by letters patent. At the time of Selden's speech these patent rights had been recognised by Statute just five years earlier when the Monopolies Act of 1624 had exempted all patents concerning printing from its operation.[44] The ecclesiastical commissioners, whose authority was statutory and who became known as the Court of High Commission, exercised the residual prerogative of the Crown to regulate what was printed. The commissioners, who always included privy councillors, leading politicians and civil lawyers as well as clerics, had power from the first, amongst many more important and far-reaching duties, to enquire after seditious books as well as heretical opinions, and possessed their licensing powers long before the Star Chamber decree of 1586 to which Selden referred.[45] When foreign policy or domestic upheaval called for additional wariness, and usually brought with it a crop of tendentious literature; when political circumstances required practical changes in the membership of the commission; when the Stationers' Company sought new privileges; or simply when an energetic new broom decided to sweep cleaner, new formal documents emerge, but many of the regulations adumbrated in them remained dormant for much of the time, as the quite frequent repetitions of them and other evidence indicates.

The incorporation of the Stationers' Company in 1557 was fully described by Graham Pollard who dealt comprehensively with the idea that the Company's Charter was any kind of master-stroke of government policy intended to facilitate control of the press.[46] The powers granted by the Charter were not materially different from those granted to the other livery companies, upon all of which, under the general umbrella of City regulations, central government relied to help maintain orderly development of social and economic life.[47] The Crown kept in its own hands the power to grant licences for approved publications. The injunctions for religion of

1559 which covered the whole government of the church, provided for licensing by the Privy Council, the bishops or the ecclesiastical commissioners of all books, pamphlets, plays and ballads (except standard school and university text books).[48] These injunctions remained the basis of all licensing. The role of the Company was to prevent the printing of works not so licensed, and to use its powers to search for unauthorised publications and punish the printers thereof, but although it was convenient to the Company to claim that it did so when it sought additional help from government, the Crown by no means relied entirely on the Company for these purposes, nor was it likely that this would be the case.

From the beginning, the Crown did not use measures which might have made control through the Company effective. For instance, the injunctions of 1559 included a requirement that the names of the licensers should be 'added in the end of every such work for a testimony of the allowance thereof', yet this was very rarely done; the requirement was renewed by Laud's order on 11 January 1632 and repeated by clause 4 of the 1637 Star Chamber decree, and still was not observed.[49] The injunctions specified that ballads were to be licensed, yet Laud was to say in 1632, 'There was a parish clarke chosen to view all the ballets before they were printed, but he refuseth to doe it, let it be ordered that he shall undertake it by commaundement from the Court. This is not worth the sentence of the Court'.[50] So much for Laud's extreme diligence and sensitivity in the matter of licensing. The injunctions of 1559 referred further measures, particularly with regard to imported books, to the commissioners who produced ordinances on 29 June 1566 providing that all stationers, booksellers, importing merchants, bookbinders, as well as printers, might be required to give bond for good behaviour.[51] Yet there is no sign that the bonds were given in 1566 and the clause was dropped from the 1586 decree, even though the investigating council commissioners had recommended in 1583 that printers, at least, should be bonded; bonding of printers was required by 1637 decree but again we have no evidence that it was insisted on.[52]

The injunctions of 1559, as Pollard observed, did not show much faith in the Stationers' Company as an arm of government: the Stationers were accused of printing anything for money, and were specially required to be obedient to the regulations.[53] The Company had power by its charter to search the premises of any Stationer for books printed contrary to statute or proclamation, as well as to company regulations, yet not 15 months later the Lord Mayor, not the Master and Wardens, was ordered to search 'in as secret a manner as he can' the premises of John Kingston and of Thomas Marshe, one of the founding members of the Company, for illegal books.[54] Both before and after the Charter the livery companies in general were enjoined to give information about particular seditious publications and the foreigners who might vend them.[55] The Bishop of London was given full authority in January 1565/6 to appoint searchers to watch the ports for illegal books and we know the state's organisation was active, but although a similar authority was given to the Stationers' Company by the ordinances of June that year, we hear nothing of this activity of the Company, and the provision was dropped from the search powers of the 1586 decree.[56] In the later 16th century 'at times of crisis rosters of searchers had been appointed' by the Company to make weekly searches of members' premises, and indeed the Company complained of the burdensome cost of these activities when they sought the privilege of printing the Grammar and Accidence in 1582, but later we hear no more of regular searches, while the ecclesiastical commissioners were specially empowered to search and to seize books and presses by the new commission of 1611.[57]

In 1583 a council commission, headed by the Bishop of London and including Thomas Norton, author of *Gorboduc*, Remembrancer of London and counsel to the Company, made a report which was the basis for the 1586 decree, embodying proposals made the previous year by Christopher Barker, the Queen's Printer, in an attempt to cope with protests made by members of the Company who had blamed shortage of work on the existence of patents for printing.[58] Such complaints were not particular to the Stationers but were voiced in all companies; patents were resisted by the City authorities and frequently objected to as grievances in parliament.[59] In the Stationers' Company, grants of exclusive rights to print individual books began in the 15th century and continued in the 17th as a form of additional copyright protection; this was a legitimate form of the patent for protection of a new invention, just as the patents for paper-making were legitimate forms of protection for an infant industry.[60] The complaints related to grants to whole classes of books which, like patents of various kinds in other trades, were given as an inexpensive form of reward to courtiers or their clients or were part of a habit of farming any potentially profitable enterprise. A patent of any kind was not a guarantee of wealth, but rather a speculative investment purchased in the hope of profit that might well not be forthcoming. The government had a legitimate paternalistic interest in ensuring that books for the instruction of children, and those containing the rudiments of the faith, should be reasonably accurate; at least the commandment 'thou shalt not steal' should not be omitted and then misplaced as an afterthought. The books published by the protesters Roger Ward and John Wolfe, the commissioners found, contained many such gross errors, and they agreed with Barker that the best method of prevention was to defend the exclusive rights of known and responsible patentees.

The Company had grown by this time to about 175 members of whom between 20 and 30 at any one time were master printers — the fluctuations in themselves suggest small men going in and out of business. The commissioners also accepted Barker's argument that if printers were to be prevented from engaging in ultimately self-destructive free-for-all competition, the small size of the market for English books, which were 'uttered no where else' demanded that the number of printing houses be reduced from the existing 23 to somewhere nearer Barker's ideal that '8 or 10 at the most would suffise for all England, yea and Scotland too', the number of presses being worked must be restricted, and the number of journeymen entering the trade must be reduced. They also made the ingenious suggestion that every printer should deliver in a specimen type sheet; this (alas) was not adopted.[61] These recommendations became the provisions of the Star Chamber decree of 1586, for which the patentees made the final petition, and for which the patentees, not the Company, most thankfully paid the costs.[62] Two other steps were taken to overcome the criticisms and provide extra work. The journeymen were placated by the recognition of restrictive practices, an important feature of which was the limitation of editions, except in the royal printing house, to 1,500 copies of any one setting.[63] This had the advantage of enlisting journeymen in the prevention of piracy, for editions larger than this were required only for patent books and successful piracy thereof was impossible without such economies of scale. In addition the patentees released some of the titles they held to the Company as a whole, to be allotted for printing in the unprivileged houses; these books became the basis of the English Stock of the Company.[64]

The ordinances of 1566 laid down penalties for breach of the injunctions of 1559 which were increased by the decree of 1586. The only real novelty in the latter was a declared intention to reduce the number of printers and printing houses, to which end printers who had newly set up within the last six months were forbidden to continue (clause 3); the existing printers were required to certify their presses to the Master and Wardens (clause 1, which they did); and the Company's regulations concerning the number of apprentices permitted to each member were reinforced (clauses 8 and 9).[65] However, the requirement (clause 5) that in future no new printers might be appointed until the Archbishop and Bishop of London should so signify, and that the men chosen should submit themselves to the commissioners for approval (either the Archbishop or Bishop being present), a provision which has been thought to put 'an especially powerful weapon in the hands of the Archbishop', was not used at all in the manner intended.[66] The Company took early advantage of the decree to demote Anthony Hill, who had registered his press in accordance with its provisions, for breaching the Day patent for the *Psalms in Metre*.[67] But the Archbishop's interventions were not in a direction to ensure a small and well-ordered body of printers. In March 1588 the Court prevented Thomas Orwin, an apprentice of Thomas Purfoot who had obtained John Kingston's presses by marriage, from printing on his own account unless he was formally admitted, but Whitgift did give permission to Orwin, a man, Marprelate complained, who 'wrought popish bookes in corners', and when Orwin's press was seized by the Company in 1591, the Archbishop intervened to have it restored to him.[68] Simon Stafford had been apprenticed as a printer to Christopher Barker the Queen's Printer, while both were still members of the Drapers' Company, and took up his freedom in that Company in 1586 but continued to work as a printer. In 1597 he began printing on his own account, apparently with the permission of the Archbishop, relying on the Custom of London which permitted any freeman to work at any trade, but when the Stationers' Company seized his press, allegedly because he had pirated the Grammar and Accidence, the Council gave way to the Stationers' insistence that if Stafford was to continue printing he must translate to their Company.[69] Thus on at least two occasions, the number of printers was increased, not diminished, by the action of the authorities, and since prerogative action had proved unavailing, or even counter-productive, the Company attempted in 1604 to enforce the restriction of numbers by statute; it was no use relying on the decree if the Council or the Archbishop would break it by favouring outsiders. A committee was appointed to promote a bill intended to reduce the number of master printers to 14 and prohibit any printing by others. The bill against 'seditious, popish, vain and lascivious books' was introduced in the Lords where it was given some high-powered attention and rapidly laid aside; we do not know how much of the printers' original proposals remained in the new bill introduced by the Council and lost after long but ill-documented disputes in both Houses of Parliament. When that attempt failed, the Company managed to hold the numbers down by their own efforts until patronage reared its head again in the 1620s and we find Archbishop Abbot showing favour to George Wood, George Wither's printer, a man who was a thorn in the flesh of the City as well as the Company. In the 1630s, it was found that only seven of the 19 masters who had been working in 1628 had been formally admitted as required.[70]

The injunctions of 1559 remained the basis of all licensing: the Star Chamber decree of 1586 simply rehearsed that books should be 'allowed ... according to the order appointed by the ... injunctions'; that is, the injunctions were taken as read by the decree. Although the Archbishop and Bishop of London were the only licensers named in the decree (except for law books), no one could have imagined they were to do the whole job themselves, especially since the number of titles printed annually increased by over 50 per cent between 1560 and 1580.[71] Two years after the 1586 decree, the Company was notified of the names of Whitgift's panel of licensers, yet in 1596 while the Council was preoccupied with collecting Ship Money, pressing seamen and raising troops for the Earl of Essex's expedition to Cadiz, Whitgift signed an order of High Commission which ignored the decree, but which announced a determination 'to sett down and establish for future tyme ... That from henceforth' nothing was to be printed unless 'first subscribed and allowed to pass the press under the hand writing' of the Archbishop or Bishop of London. And yet the decree remained in force and the licensers of 1588 continued to act, while this order was not mentioned again, despite the instruction that it was to be 'published and intimated to all your companie' and 'enrolled and registered in your hall'.[72]

The Crown's mistrust of the Company is manifest in the stern wording of Whitgift's order, which referred only in vague terms to existing regulations notwithstanding which 'divers copies books or pamphletts have been latelie printed and putt to sale, some conteyning matter of Ribaldrie, some of superstition and some of flatt heresie, By means whereof the simpler and least advised sorts of her majesties subjects are either allured to wantonness, corrupted in doctrine or in danger to be seduced from that dutifull obedience which they owe unto her highness'. The Master and Wardens were not to 'consent unto or wink at the printing of any such book ...'; clearly winking at least was suspected. The Company did not prove an effective ally during Bancroft's time at London or Canterbury. They did not prevent the publication of the 'vain and lascivious' books he found so offensive in 1599. One of their number, William Jones, actually offered a bill of complaint against the Bishop in the parliament of 1604 and had gone on to print a whole variety of objectionable puritan tracts, including *The Argument of Nicholas Fuller* against the use of the oath ex officio in High Commission, and Bancroft had been left to find the culprit himself, although the Company well knew that Jones continued to print without authority.[73] After the Restoration the Crown again found the Stationers' Company a distinctly feeble arm of government; the Master and Wardens were found to be feathering their own nests rather than enforcing the regulations.[74]

Robert Cecil set out a proposal to appoint additional licensers in 1604, which suggested that King James, very early in his reign, intended to reform the system, and included a suggestion that even the licensing of divinity was not being properly handled by the Bishop's licensers, but the scheme was not proceeded with. In the row over Cowell's *Interpreter*, in 1610, the King again said he would set up a new licensing commission, but again nothing was done, and in response to another parliamentary complaint that year, the King reformed the High Commission.[75] George Abbot succeeded Richard Bancroft as Archbishop of Canterbury in April 1611 and on 29 August the new ecclesiastical commission gave power not only to enquire after, but to search for, heretical and seditious books, and to seize both the books and the presses involved. Two years later, the next reissue of the commission extended the powers to 'all other books, pamphlets and portraitures offensive to the state or set forth without sufficient and lawful authority' and added the power to destroy the offending presses, with the proviso 'restoring nevertheless the materials in such case as they may not afterwards be so abused or otherwise the value of them to the owners thereof'.[76] This little domestic detail, taken over from the provisions of the 1586 decree, indicates that the Stationers' Company at this time surrendered whatever role it had ever had in enforcement of political regulations. The Company continued to deal with offences against their own regulations but political searches became the business of the messengers of the King's Chamber who acted as pursuivants also for the High Commission. These were the men who were to seize Prynne's books in 1634 and two of them became so familiar with the workings of the Stationers' Company that they attempted that year to take over George Wither's patent for *Hymns and Songs of the Church*.[77] Also, hereafter it was no longer Star Chamber, as it had been in the days of Wolfe and Stafford, but the High Commission which was the court that heard disputes between party and party within the Stationers' Company, and even disputes concerning piracies between non-members of the Company. This new arrangement, which William Laud was to inherit 20 years later was put in place by King James and Archbishop Abbot before Arminianism became an issue and long before Laud began his climb to power.

The establishment of the English Stock by the patent of 29 October 1603 marked 'just about the peak of the Company's power and prosperity', before the Civil War.[78] Thereafter, as the various King's Printers' syndicates began to sink into disarray and internal strife following the death of Christopher Barker in 1599, printing abroad began to be almost as great a problem as illicit printing at home. By way of justification of the title of the 1604 bill, and an additional inducement to pass the measure, the Company had tacked to their very short and practical proposals, a fourth clause providing 'that none may bring any seditious or hereticall Bookes from beyond the seas, such as Missals, Breviaries, Ladie-psalters, and the like'. The popish threat was a common-form excuse for any activity; if the Company was really interested in this point, the Gunpowder Plot brought the desired provisions as part of the draconian anti-Catholic legislation of 1606. The import of Catholic liturgical literature was quite irrelevant to the limitation of presses and presented no competitive threat. The Company was indeed about to become very concerned about importing, but the books involved were not vain, lascivious or even popish, but the standard school books and Protestant religious texts. Although the ostensible object of the Latin trade was to bring in not only foreign-language works but all scholarly books including recent publications on medicine and science which, being required in small numbers, could not be produced economically in England, there is some hard evidence and many more hints that booksellers engaged therein also commissioned the printing abroad of books that could and should have been printed in England. It is very much a question how far apparent foreign 'piracies' and smuggled books in general (whether seditious or not) are really what they seem. Publishers saw the advantages of printing overseas where prices were lower, paper was cheaper, and had to be imported anyway, press-men worked longer hours and produced a much higher daily stint than English workmen, imposing no restriction on edition size. In 1611 Nathaniel Butter lost his share in the English Stock for having arranged for the printing of great quantities of primers by George Waters of Dort, against the interests of the Stock in which he was himself a partner. In 1615 the Company bought in from 'Mr. Corden keeper of the English House at Middleborough' 55 reams of Primers printed there, but who the culprit was this time does not appear.[79] There are a good many more examples.

The 1603 patent had given the Company control over children's first readers, but had done nothing to solve the problem of the various patents affecting school books which had been from the first one of the chief bones of contention. The Company had shown an interest in taking over the Grammar from the royal patent for Latin, Greek and Hebrew in 1582, tying the request on to the cost of Company searches, and the patentees were unable to defend the grant without Company help, as was shown in 1598 when they asked the Court of Assistants to join suit against Stafford and Barley.[80] But although they did not own the Grammar patent, the Company was bound to defend it, for the importing of any pirated privileged books was the not so thin end of a very unpleasant-looking wedge. So the Company turned to Parliament again in 1614 and got very short shrift from the House of Commons.

The 1566 ordinances had prohibited importing against letters patent (which had then been relatively few in number), but the 1586 decree had nothing to say on this topic. Both these directives were now long in the past and the City, the Company and the trade were a great deal larger than they had then been. The Stationers did not rely on these prerogative measures for their bill in 1614 but went right back to 1534 to revive the act prohibiting the sale of imported bound books 'Anie Custome or usage to the contrary Notwithstanding'. The bill added an adaptation of the provisions of 1566 into a prohibition on importing of any books previously printed in England, and their lobbying brief stressed that they were particularly concerned with 'Grammers, Accidences and Almanacks and such like, being mixt of English and Latine,' which 'are disorderly brought by stealth in great numbers from beyond the seas, both bound and unbound, without any knowne owners, and are by our owne fugitives secretly dispersed in corners, to the utter impoverishing of the poore of our whole Company'. They did not this time add a religious dimension to their propaganda but attempted to head off criticism by pointing out that they would be bound by the provision of the Henrician act from raising the price of books. This was probably a mistake, for having it drawn to their attention members seized on this point, disbelieved the Company's professions, and threw out the bill.[81]

While the Stationers might legitimately insist, and might expect the support of the government in so doing, that printers must belong to their organisation, and might try to keep control over publishers by confining entry in the Register to Stationers, although this could never be wholly effective, there was little hope of help to impose control over simple bookselling.[82] The Company possessed a sanction of sorts against Butter, but one which could be used only once; when books that were in themselves entirely unexceptionable were printed abroad, very little could be done to prevent the market being flooded by pirate editions sold by non-Stationers. Nothing could prevent retailers selling books, imported or not, along with other wares in London where all trades were open to all freemen. However the Company found a friend in the Archbishop of Canterbury, who at least made the attempt, in defence of the new powers of High Commission. The Council had havered about interfering with the Custom of London in the Stafford case, even when a printer was involved, but Abbot went into action against it in 1615 when two non-stationers, William Nethersall and Richard Peirce, were found with stocks of the Grammar and appealed to the City against the seizure of the books by the High Commission. Archbishop Abbot wrote to the Lord Mayor, Sir Thomas Hayes, 'in the behalf of the Stationers' insisting, most politely, on the rights of the commission against the complaint by Nethersall and Peirce that the commissioners had seized books from them 'and that our messengers' had thereby 'infringed the Liberties' of the City. Abbot pointed out that the King had committed to the commissioners 'all questions and differences concerning printing and selling of books, and there be ancient orders of starchamber from time to time renewed concerning that matter'. He went on 'whether our pursuivants shall execute our mandate ... I hope your Lordship will not now dispute'; the commissioners 'cannot order any thing ... unless that our messengers ... may ... perform these things'.[83] Six weeks later the Court of Assistants required the partners in the Grammar to pay £60 'towards the charges ... about searching for the Grammar and accidence and maintaining the priviledge thereof'; so it looks as though the Company found paying for the High Commission's pursuivants a good deal more costly than searching for themselves.[84] Nor was the High Commission particularly successful in preventing piracy either at home or abroad; indeed it really had very little interest in such commercial problems.

The Company then took steps to get the importing trade into its own hands. In January 1616, 112 stationers set up a Stock to import all books with a nominal capital of £4,800, which carried on the trade of importing books at first in competition, and then in agreement, with John Bill. The failure of this Stock, which finished up owing £800 to Bill, is attributed to the war in Europe, the production of upper-school books in England, and some mismanagement on the part of the stock-keepers. The war was no doubt the most important factor.[85] With the failure of the Latin Stock the Company was thrown back on prerogative again.

We now come to a period of intense interest in foreign affairs, which has resulted in the Company's next attempt to cope with the importing problem being viewed as part of an attempt to tighten censorship in the face of an unprecedented pamphlet campaign. We have the paradox that the decade that saw the beginning of regular newsbook publishing should also be seen as a time in which the censorship was gradually tightened by a series of proclamations. The proclamation of Christmas Eve 1620 against licentious speech of matters of state said nothing at all about printing; drafted by Francis Bacon, it was so obscurely worded that it is difficult to see it having any effect. Indeed it included an echo of the essay 'Of Seditions' in the statement that 'in our own nature and judgement, we do well allow of convenient freedom of speech, esteeming any over curious or restrained hand carried in that kind, rather as a weakness, or else over much severity of government, than otherwise'.[86] The purpose of this and the other similar proclamations was only to assure the Spanish Ambassador that the state was doing its best, as in duty bound, to give him proper protection.[87] There is no general tightening of censorship here, and the proclamation of 1623 is certainly not in this category.

In February 1622 the Company appointed a committee to obtain a proclamation of which Bonham Norton and John Bill were to pay half the cost. Internecine strife between different importing interests within the Company was now being compounded by the growth of the Cambridge University Press, and after considerable wrangling in which both sides appealed both to parliament and to what patronage they could muster, it may be that the Company did not get all it wanted by the proclamation that finally emerged, but its terms make clear that it was a private proclamation intended for purposes of trade, not censorship, although it included the usual common-form anathema against Popish and seditious books.[88] The proclamation against 'disorderly printing, uttering, and dispersing of books' of 23 September 1623 recited the Star Chamber decree of 1586 and the 1566 ban on importing seditious, schismatical and scandalous books. There was nothing new in this, but the proclamation was much more than a restatement of the decree.[89] Its importance is that it forbad the import of any works covered by existing privileges. Its whole thrust is not against sedition but against piracy overseas of 'such allowed books, works and writings, as have been imprinted within this realm, by such, to whom the sole printing thereof by Letters Patents or lawful ordinance or authoritie doth appertain'. It prohibited the import of any books printed contrary to the decree of Star Chamber 'though lawful or allowed to be printed by such to whom the printing thereof doth belong'. Once the purpose of the 1623 proclamation is recognised, we see that the early 1620s do not demonstrate a tightening of censorship, but show only the normal course of politics in a time of tension over foreign policy.

In 1624 the House of Commons insisted on a proclamation against popish books, and James improved the occasion by adding seditious puritan books to the banned works.[90] Thomas Scott's name has been connected with this proclamation simply because he is the most prolific identified author of the year, but the timing suggests that the King was thinking rather of John Reynolds's *Votivae Angliae*. To accuse the King of being an unnatural father was going a bit far, whatever the motive; any man might resent being publicly lectured about his private affairs in the way that Reynolds did. Moreover Reynolds was Lord Feilding's tutor.[91] Reynolds spent two years in gaol, and it was said that the King was told the printer had made £1,000 from the venture – a sum quite impossible as profit and far too great to be a bribe – and consequently fined him that sum and gaoled him into the bargain. The story rests only on hearsay, and times changed, for the two Reynolds works were included in the nonce collection of the works of Scott which Michael Sparke gave to the Bodleian Library three years later.[92] Thomas Scott, whose biography is very obscure, published two works in 1622 and four in 1623 of which three may have been printed in Holland, but there is no evidence that they were smuggled thence 'at grave risk'.[93] It was in 1624, a year far more favourable to such enterprises, that 15 of the works attributed to Scott were printed, and most of them were probably printed in London, at least four of them by Nicholas Okes, whom the authorities could undoubtedly have found if they had wished. The first of these certainly caused a stir in official circles, for when the Lord Keeper, Bishop John Williams, was faced with Scott's *Boanerges*, he found 'Every leafe is stuffed wth false and scandalous untruths', and proposed a new remedy. The name of the licenser should be 'printed upon the first page of the Booke, as it is, in all other Christian ptes of the world'. So that not only the authors, printers and booksellers, but also the buyers of any such books might be severely punished in Star Chamber. Williams thought 'This course, is no way offensive, but will meete, with all Libels against the State, printed here & beyond the Seas, all popish bookes brought over from Doway & Lovayne, all Brownists bookes, printed at Amsterdam, and doe (in my poore opinion) much good, evrye waye, wthout the least Inconvenience'. There is certainly a comprehensive concept of censorship here – Williams's remedy went further than anything proposed by Laud – but although Williams used the King's name it is not clear that James knew anything about this case and no action was taken.[94] Williams suggested employing John Bill to trace the type on this occasion and there are a good many hints that the Crown relied on the King's Printer, rather than the Company as a whole, to be their watchdog of the press until the collapse of the old King's Printer families and the rise in their place of the group known as the Flesher syndicate.

When Laud became Bishop of London, he became active in Company affairs and at his trial took responsibility for the Star Chamber decree of 1637 but there is no doubt that it was sought for by the Company and met their requirements.[95] The only clause to which the Stationers objected at the time was clause 18 requiring re-licensing of new editions. The Clerk of the Company, Henry Walley, put in a memorandum to Sir John Lambe, declaring the clause unworkable because the quantity of such reprinting was too great for any number of licensers to cope with, and unnecessary, because publishers had no intention of interfering with the sale of old stock by promoting new editions, however desirable these might be in themselves; the company won the point and were required only to present alterations for re-licensing.[96]

Clause 5 required catalogues of imported books, clause 6 provided for searches at the ports, clause 7 extended to all legitimate copyrights the protection against imports granted to privileged books by the proclamation of 1623, and to all works in learned languages by a proclamation of 1636. Clause 8 extended the requirement of the injunctions of 1559 and Laud's order of 1630 by requiring the names of authors and publishers, as well as printers, to be given in every book.[97] The real novelties in the decree were clause 10 which forbad haberdashers and others not free of the Company to sell books at all, and clauses 11 and 12 which forbad the import of any English-language books whatsoever, and prohibited any importing by aliens. Clause 10 was a lost cause from the beginning: in dealing with a case against Michael Sparke and Philip Chetwynd for binding *Bibles* without Speed's *Genealogies*, the Council recognised that Chetwynd, a Mercer, who had married into the Company, would continue as a bookseller in St Paul's Churchyard. The next year Chetwynd was in litigation in High Commission with another non-Stationer, John Leaver, concerning the import of 1,000 pirated copies of that well-known best-seller Lewis Baily's *Practice of Piety*, and after the Restoration Chetwynd was still publishing Shakespeare titles from the old Allot list.[98] Clauses 11 and 12 fared little better, as we see from litigation against David van Hooganhuisen and Adrian Vlack, with whom Cornelius Bee was involved. Bee was a wealthy Haberdasher, who remained a member of that Company all his life and brought up apprentices to that trade, yet, without ever making an entry in the Register, was an important publisher throughout the middle period of the century. In the course of the Vlack litigation, the 'booksellers for the Latin trade' thankfully acknowledged Laud's 'endeavours for the good of their profession' and the decree which he had 'intended for their good'. If one wants another proof that the decree was made for the Company's benefit, it is to be found in a petition from the bookbinders, just a month later, asking for similar regulations for their trade, in particular a ban on sending books in quires unbound into the country, and restriction of the number of apprentices.[99]

We know that the restriction of the number of master printers was not observed after 1637 any more than it had been after 1586, the number of presses in use increased from 33 in the 1620s to at least 46 after 1637 and young men continued to flock to join the trade. The number of titles produced annually rose steadily from 259 in 1600 to 577 in 1640, a percentage increase far greater than any estimate of the increase in population, even of London; and the 1630s are littered with failed publishing ventures.[100] The increase in the quantity of printing that occurred after 1640 is by no means so great as is often imagined, or as the crude figures would suggest. The idea that only 22 titles were published in 1640, and that the high figure for 1642 was than 'maintained for the next decade' are mistakes derived from Siebert.[101] In the peak year, 1642, the vast majority of titles are rubbishy single-sheet pamphlets whose whole paper content would not have made more than seven or eight books of reasonable size, going some distance towards fulfilling the prediction of the commissioners in 1583 that in the absence of regulation, the small size of the market for books in England meant that 'onelie pamfletts, trifles and vaine small toies should be printed'. The Stationers identified their problem in their petition of 1643: 'few men bestow more in books than what they can spare out of their superfluities'.[102]

References

1. Thomas G. Barnes, 'Star Chamber mythology', *Amer. Jour. Legal Hist.* 5 (1961), pp.1-11; 'Due process and slow process in the late Elizabethan – early Stuart Star Chamber', *AJHL* 6 (1962), pp.221-49, 315-46; *idem*, 'Star Chamber litigants and their counsel, 1596-1641', in J.H. Baker (ed.), *Legal Records and the Historian* (1978), pp.7-28. John H. Langbein, *Torture and the law of proof* (Chicago, 1977), pp.89-90, 136-8, 139.
2. J.F. Jameson, 'The origin of the standing committee system in American legislative bodies', *Pol. Sci. Qu.* ix (1894), pp.246-97. Wallace Notestein, *The winning of the initiative by the House of Commons* (1924); *cf.* J.H. Willcox, 'Some Aspects of the early history of Committees of the whole House', *Parliamentary Affairs*, vii (1954), pp.409-19; Lambert, 'Procedure in the House of Commons in the early Stuart period', *English Historical Review* 95 (1980), pp.753-81.

3. Leonard W. Levy, *Legacy of Suppression: Freedom of Speech and Press in early American history* (Oxford, 1960); see the preface to the much revised edition for some fascinating sidelights on the subject of patronage and self-censorship: *Emergence of a Free Press* (Oxford, 1986). Levy found similar difficulties with the publication of *Treason against God. A history of the offence of blasphemy* (New York, 1981).

4. Fredrick S. Siebert, *Freedom of the Press in England 1476-1776* (Urbana, 1952), hereafter cited as Siebert. A preferable account is given by Lyman Ray Patterson, *Copyright in Historical Perspective* (Nashville, Tenn., 1968).

5. F.S. Siebert, *The rights and privileges of the press* (New York, 1934), p.vii. J.B. Williams [J.G. Muddiman, pseud.], *A History of English Journalism* (1908), p.2; Siebert, p.50. The proclamation of 18 May 1544, is found only in MS: P.L. Hughes and J.F. Larkin (eds), *Tudor Royal Proclamations* (3 vols, New Haven, 1969), hereafter H&L, no.229; for the effect of the false news abroad, see *Letters & Papers Henry VIII*, XIX pt 1 (1903) preface, p.xxvi. See S. Lambert, 'Coranto printing in England', *Journal of Newspaper and Periodical History*, 8 (1992), 1, pp.3-18.

6. Christopher Hill, 'Censorship and English Literature', *The collected Essays of Christopher Hill. Volume One. Writing and Revolution in 17th Century England* (Brighton, 1985), p.33. Edward Arber, *A transcript of the Registers of the Company of Stationers of London 1554-1640 AD* (5 vols, 1875-94). *A Dictionary of Printers and booksellers ... 1557-1640*, ed. R.B. McKerrow (1910, reprinted 1977), pp.xiv-xvi. H.R. Plomer, *A Short History of English Printing* (1900, 2nd edn, 1915), pp.139, 146, 149.

7. McKerrow, *An Introduction to Bibliography for Literary Students* (2nd edn, Oxford, 1928), pp.141-2. Cyprian Blagden, *The Stationers' Company: a History 1403-1959* (1960).

8. McKerrow, *Dictionary* (1910), p.xv. Siebert, pp.87, 103.

9. Godfrey Davies, 'English political sermons 1603-1640', *Hunt. Lib. Qu.* 3 (1939), pp.5-7. Plomer, *Short History* (2nd edn, 1915), p.150. McKerrow, *Dictionary*, p.xvi. *A Dictionary of Printers and booksellers ... 1641-1667*, ed. H.R. Plomer (1907, reprinted 1977), p.xii.

10. G.E. Bentley, *The profession of Dramatist in Shakespeare's time, 1590-1642* (Princeton, 1979), ch.VII and p.153. The 18th-century scholars Edmond Malone and George Chalmers, who made the transcript, seem to have been, if anything, intent on recording instances of censorship: Joseph Q. Adams, *The dramatic records of Sir Henry Herbert* (New Haven, 1917), pp.vii, 10-11, 18-39. Other fragments of the record which have since been found tend to confirm that they did not miss much of importance: N.W. Bawcutt, 'Craven Ord Transcripts of Sir Henry Herbert's Office-Book in the Folger Shakespeare Library', *English Literary Renaissance* 14 (1984), pp.83-94; *idem*, 'New Revels Documents of Sir George Buc and Sir Henry Herbert', *Rev. Engl. Studies* 35 (1984), pp.316-31. Jerzy Limon talks of 'severe censorship' but his only case is one of profanity: *Dangerous Matter: English drama and politics in 1623/24* (Cambridge, 1987), p.6; the act is 3 Jac.I, c.21 (1605-6). Martin Butler added the very doubtful case of The Valiant Scot (1639), on which see Bentley, pp.180-1: *Theatre and Crisis*, 1632-1642 (Cambridge, 1984), pp.135, 234. See also Richard Dutton, 'Patronage, Politics, and the Master of the Revels, 1622-1640: the case of Sir John Astley', *Eng. Lit. Ren.* 20 (1990), pp.287-319.

11. Hill, 'Censorship', pp.35, 39. W.W. Greg, 'The bakings of Betsy', *The Library*, 3rd ser., 2 (1911), pp.225-59.

12. Sir Sidney Lee, *A Life of William Shakespeare* (1898), pp.230-34; *idem*, (rev. edn, 1915), pp.127, 377-86. Phoebe A.B. Sheavyn, *The literary profession in the Elizabethan Age*

(Manchester, 1909; I cite 2nd edn revised by J.W. Saunders, Manchester, 1967), p.60. This work appeared originally as two articles in *The Library*, n.s., 7 (1906).

13. Sheavyn, *Literary Profession*, pp.39, 61. A.W. Ward, 'Some Political and social Aspects of the later Elizabethan and earlier Stewart period', in *The Cambridge History of English Literature*, ed. A.W. Ward and A.R. Waller (Cambridge, 1910), v, pp.370-71.

14. Edwin Haviland Miller: *The professional writer in Elizabethan England: A study of nondramatic literature* (Cambridge, Mass., 1959), esp. chs 5 and 6. Louis B. Wright, *Middle-class culture in Elizabethan England* (Chapel Hill, 1935; reprint 1958).

15. C. Hill, *The Century of Revolution* (Edinburgh, 1961), pp.98-9; *Intellectual Origins of the English Revolution* (Oxford, 1965), pp.32, 177-9, 271; *Milton and the English Revolution* (1977), pp.64-5; *Some Intellectual Consequences of the English Revolution* (University of Wisconsin Press, 1980), pp.48-9. 'Censorship', *passim* and p.40.

16. Keith Thomas, 'The meaning of Literacy in Early Modern England', in Gerd Baumann (ed.), *The Written Word: Literacy in Transition* (Oxford, 1986), pp.119-20.

17. G.E. Aylmer, 'The historical background', in *The Age of Milton*, ed. C.A. Patrides and R.B. Waddington (Manchester, 1980); *idem*, 'Collective Mentalities in mid-Seventeenth Century England: III Varieties of Radicalism', *TRHS* 5th ser. 38 (1988), pp.1-26; *idem*, *The Personal Rule of Charles I, 1629-1640* (1990).

18. Conrad Russell, *Parliaments and English Politics 1621-1629* (Oxford, 1979), pp.38-41. Russell has since distanced himself from the idea: *Unrevolutionary England, 1603-1642* (Hambledon, 1990), pp.x-xv, xxvi. For a critique see R.P. Cust and A.L. Hughes, 'After Revisionism' in (eds), *Conflict in Early Stuart England* (1988), pp.1-13. For surveys of recent work see Glenn Burgess, 'On Revisionism. An analysis of Early Stuart Historiography in the 1970s and 1980s, *HJ* 33 (1990), pp.609-28; *idem*, 'Revisionism, Politics and Political Ideas in Early Stuart England', *HJ* 34 (1991), pp.465-78.

19. Richard Cust, 'News and politics in seventeenth-century England' *P&P* 112 (1986), pp.60-90. Cust & Hughes, 'After Revisionism', p.13. T.C. Cogswell, *The Blessed Revolution. English politics and the coming of war, 1621-1624* (Cambridge, 1989); *idem*, 'England and the Spanish Match', in *Conflict in Early Stuart England*, pp.107-33.

20. For instance Martin Butler, *Theatre and Crisis, 1632-1642*; Cogswell, *The Blessed Revolutiion*, pp.20-50, 281-301; Philip J. Finkelpearl, '"The Comedians' Liberty": Censorship of the Jacobean Stage reconsidered', *Eng. Lit. Ren.* 16 (1986), pp.123-138; Kevin Sharpe, *Politics & Ideas in Early Stuart England* (1989), pp.9-39; A.B. Worden, 'Literature and Political Censorship in Early Modern England', in A.C. Duke and C.A. Tamse (eds), *Too Mighty to be Free. Censorship and the press in Britain and the Netherlands* (Britain and the Netherlands, vol.9, Zutphen, 1987), pp.45-62. C. Hill, 'The pre-revolutionary decades', *Essays* I, 7, citing Graham Parry, *The Golden Age Restored: The culture of the Stuart Court* (Manchester, 1981), p.63 n.13, p.152.

21. Annabel Patterson, *Censorship and Interpretation: The conditions of writing and reading in early modern England* (Univ. Wisconsin Press, 1985), pp.17-18. See Worden, 'Literature and Political Censorship'.

22. The point is made by Lois Potter, *Secret Rites and Secret Writing. Royalist literature, 1641-1660* (Cambridge, 1989), pp.209-10.

23. Hill cited two passages to demonstrate that Burton made his 'riskiest points ... by means of quotations from classical authorities', ('Censorship', p.56) but the first of these is simply the original story of Hippocrates and the reason for Democritus's mirth, told to explain Burton's stance as 'Democritus junior', unusually there is not one word of Latin

in four pages of text; the second passage applies the story to the contemporary scene with no holds barred: *The Anatomy of Melancholy* (Everyman edn 1932, reprinted 1961) I, pp.48-51, 61-4; II, pp.48-58, 95-7; III, pp.108-16, 121, 124-5, 130, 138-9.

24. Walker's pamphlet must have been a half-sheet folio of which probably very few copies were pulled off, but the text is not lost, for according to the economical habits of printers at that time, it was reused to fill up the length of a single-sheet quarto newsbook: *VII Articles Drawen up against Lord Kimelton*. Printed for W.R. 1642 (Wing S2736, LT E131(3)); cf. E. Sirluck, '"To your Tents, O Israel": A Lost Pamphlet', *HLQ* 19 (1955-6), pp.301-5.

25. John H. Langbein, *Torture and the law of proof*, case no.77. Peacham was not charged with libel nor tortured by or tried in Star Chamber. He was tortured by Council order, and tried at Taunton assizes: J.S. Cockburn, *A history of English Assizes from 1558 to 1714* (Cambridge, 1972), pp.115, 227; cf. Finkelpearl, '"The Comedians' Liberty"', *Eng. Lit. Ren.* 16 (1986), pp.123-4. However, it is not true that anyone was sentenced to death for translating a pamphlet from the French. This statement results from a misreading of the evidence concerning William Philips printed in W.W. Greg, *A Companion to Arber* (Oxford, 1967) pp.222-3: Jerzy Limon, *Dangerous matter*, p.8; the story was told correctly in J.B. Williams, *A history of English journalism*, p.27.

26. Cf. Stanley Morison 'The origins of the Newspaper' (1954) in *Selected Essays on the History of Letter-Forms in Manuscript and Print*, ed. David McKitterick (Cambridge, 1980), p.330; Hill, 'Censorship', p.33; Worden, 'Literature and Political Censorship', n.19. Several examples are given by David Loades, 'Illicit presses and clandestine printing in England, 1520-1590', in A.C. Duke and C.A. Tamse (eds), *Too mighty to be free* (Britain and the Netherlands, vol.9, Zutphen, 1987), pp.13, 14, 17, 19-20. J. Rushworth, *Historical Collections*, II-1, p.234.

27. *English Manuscript Studies 1100-1700*, ed. Peter Beal and Jeremy Griffith, vol.I (Blackwell, 1989), preface. Harold Love, 'Scribal Publication in seventeenth-century England', *Transactions of Cambridge Bibliographical Society* 9 (1987), pp.130-54. D.F. McKenzie, 'Speech-Manuscript-Print', *Library Chronicle* 20 (1990), pp.87-109. Lambert, 'Richard Montagu, Arminianism and Censorship', *P&P* 124 (1989), pp.62-3.

28. Linda Levy Peck, *Northampton: patronage and policy at the court of James I* (1982), p.235 n.3. W. Scott and J. Bliss (eds), *The Works of William Laud* (7 vols, Oxford, 1847-60), iv, pp.475-6.

29. Worden, 'Literature and Political Censorship', p.45. Kevin Sharpe, *Criticism and Compliment. The politics of literature in the England of Charles I* (Cambridge, 1987), pp.36-7; *idem, Politics & Ideas*, p.9.

30. Charles H. McIlwain, *The political works of James I* (Cambridge, Mass., 1918, reprinted New York, 1965), p.lxxxi. Elizabeth Read Foster, 'The Journal of the House of Lords for the Long Parliament', in Barbara C. Malament (ed.), *After the Reformation. Essays in Honor of J.H. Hexter* (Univ. Penna Press, 1980), p.140.

31. *The Anatomy of Melancholy* (Everyman edn), respectively II, p.190; III, p.331; I, pp.62, 320; III, p.378. H.R. Trevor-Roper, 'Robert Burton and the Anatomy of Melancholy', *Renaissance Essays* (1985), p.251. Lambert, 'Richard Montagu', pp.61, 68 and n.117.

32. Hill, 'Censorship', p.34. On Milton, Siebert (as often) is inconsistent: Milton wanted the press to be 'free and uncontrolled', p.3; he wanted 'universal freedom', p.192; but Siebert quite correctly explains Milton asked for no such thing at pp.195-7. See Worden, 'Literature and Political Censorship', pp.45, 47.

33. Hill, 'Censorship', p.64 n.27, citing Leona Rostenberg, *Literary, Political, Scientific and Legal Publishing, Printing and Bookselling in England, 1551-1700: Twelve Studies* (New York, 1965), pp.11-12, 161-202. Siebert (describing Sparke as a printer, which he never was), equated him with Milton and declared that 'No man of his time waged such persistent warfare against the regulation of the press', pp.140-1. *A Second Beacon fired* (1652. S2259). Sparke was undoubtedly the author of *A Second Beacon*; however Siebert's assertion (p.168n) that not Sparke but George Wither was the author of *Scintilla* (1641) is worth serious consideration.

34. Bacon, *Of Seditions*. Written 1612, published in *Essays*, 3rd edn, 1625, STC 1147; cited from James Spedding, *Works* (14 vols. 1857-74), vi, p.407. The passage was quoted at Charles, almost verbatim, by the Scots in *The Remonstrance of the Nobility* (1639 STC 21907), p.16.

35. Hill, 'Censorship', p.34. See D.C. Coleman, *The British Paper Industry, 1495-1860* (Oxford, 1959), pp.1-54. Hill includes the alum patent, for which see W.H. Price, *English Patents of Monopoly* (1906), ch.7 and Anthony F. Upton, *Sir Arthur Ingram* (Oxford, 1961), ch.5.

36. Katherine Thomson to Salisbury, c.1606, HMC *Salisbury (Cecil) MSS*, Addenda 1605-68, xxiv, pp.108-9; since there are two letters, Cecil evidently took the plan sufficiently seriously to ask her to elaborate on the proposal.

37. Joan Thirsk, *Economic Policy and Projects. The development of a consumer society in Early Modern England* (Oxford, 1978), pp.52-7. Philip Gaskell, *A New Introduction to Bibliography* (2nd imp., Oxford, 1974), p.60.

38. Mary Dewar (ed.), *A Discourse of the Commonweal of this realm of England. Attributed to Sir Thomas Smith* (Charlottesville, Va., 1969), p.66.

39. *The Rates of Marchandizes* (1608.STC 7691); I am grateful to D.J. McKitterick for assistance with this point. Thirsk, above, Appx I, pp.181-5; C.G.A. Clay, *Economic expansion and social change: England 1500-1700* (2 vols, Cambridge, 1984), ii, pp.38-9.

40. Barry Supple, *Commercial Crisis and change in England 1600-1642* (Cambridge, 1959), pp.226, 228, 230.

41. The vast majority of the hundreds of cases of defamation found in T.G. Barnes (ed.), *List and Index to the proceedings in Star Chamber for the reign of James I* (3 vols, Chicago, 1975) are not charges of seditious libel brought by the Crown, but private suits: cf. Finkelpearl, p.123.

42. 11 Feb. 1628/9 in W. Notestein and F.H. Relf (eds) *Common Debates for 1629* (Minnesota Studies 10, Minneapolis, 1921), p.58; cf. Hill, 'Censorship', 40.

43. For the early history see D.M. Loades, 'The press under the early Tudors', *T. Cambs Bib. Soc.*, 4 (1964), pp.29-44; *idem*, 'The theory and practice of censorship in sixteenth century England', *TRHS* 5th ser., 24 (1974), pp.141-6; *idem*, 'Illicit presses and clandestine printing', pp.9-27. Act 3 Jac I, c. 5. 1605-6, clause 15; repealed 1844 by 7&8 Vic c.102. For the various petitions on religion see Lambert, 'Richard Montagu', pp.52-3; *idem*, 'Committees, Religion and Parliamentary Encroachment on Royal Authority in Early Stuart England', *EHR* 105 (1990), pp.81-5.

44. Monopolies Act 21 Jac. I, c.3, clause 10.

45. The commission was originally 19-strong but grew to 90 in the 17th century. G.W. Prothero (ed.), *Select Statutes and other constitutional documents ... of Elizabeth and James I* (4th edn, Oxford, 1913), pp.227, 232, 235, 424. For the names see Roland G. Usher, *The rise and fall of the High Commissiion*, (ed. Philip Tyler, Oxford, 1968),

pp.345-61; Leland H. Carlson, 'The Court of high commission: a newly discovered Elizabethan letters patent, 20 June 1589', *HLQ* 45 (1982), pp.295-315.

46. H.G. Pollard, 'The Company of Stationers before 1557', and 'The early constitution of the Stationers' Company', *The Library*, 4th ser., 18 (1937-8), pp.1-38, 235-60. The charter is printed in full with his own translation, in Arber I, xxviii-xxxii, see Greg, *Companion*, cal. no. 10; Loades cites the English summary given in *Cal. Patent Rolls*, P & M III, p.480, but misdates it March 1557: 'The press under the early Tudors', p.45; *idem*, 'The theory and practice of censorship', pp.152-3.

47. Steve Rappaport, *Worlds within worlds: structures of life in sixteenth-century London* (Cambridge, 1989), pp.184-93.

48. The injunctions were proclaimed before 19 July 1559 and the whole text is printed in H&L no.460; see their note ii, p.129 n.7, correcting Arber, who printed only the clause (6) requiring the setting up of the Bible in churches and the licensing clause (51), and dated the document before 11 Nov. 1559: Greg, *Companion*, cal. no. 20, Arber I, pp.xxxviii-xxxix. Siebert's account of the licensers appointed by the injunctions is thoroughly confused; the 'ordinary' is not 'an ecclesiastical judge above the rank of archdeacon', the term means the bishop of the place concerned: Siebert, p.56.

49. H&L ii, p.128; McKerrow, *Dictionary*, p.xii. William A. Jackson (ed.), *Records of the Court of the Stationers' Company, 1602-1640* (1957), p.234. Blagden was mistaken in saying the requirement was omitted from the decree: *Stationers' Company*, p.119. See Lambert 'Richard Montagu', pp.66-7.

50. S.R. Gardiner (ed.), *Reports of Cases in the Courts of Star Chamber and High Commission* (Camden Soc., n.s. 39, 1886), p.314; see Lambert, 'Coranto printing'.

51. Blagden, 'Book Trade Control in 1566', *The Library*, 5th ser., 13 (1958), pp.287-92. The black-letter version of the ordinances, here printed by Blagden, added to clause 2 of the text as previously known, which directed three months imprisonment for printing or importing illegal books, a provision for an additional fine of £10 for offenders who had not entered into recognisances as specified in clause 6.

52. Bonds were occasionally required from individuals after some misdemeanour, see below on Simon Stafford; another instance is the letter from Whitgift ordering the restoration of Edward Allde's goods on condition of a bond for good behaviour, Liber A, fo. 68r, 6 June 1597.

53. Pollard, 'The Company of Stationers', pp.31-2.

54. *A[cts of the] P[rivy] C[ouncil]* vi, 346, 13 July 1558; see also a search of John Cawood's premises, September 1557, in Pollard, 'The Company of Stationers', p.32.

55. Instances 1554, 1555, 1569 in Rappaport, *op. cit.*, pp.189-90.

56. SP12/39/18 and Lansdowne MS 84/29 in Greg, *Companion*, pp.114-15, 152.

57. Blagden, *Stationers' Company*, pp.65-6, 70, 72, 120. Greg, *Companion*, cal. nos. 69, 118, Arber II, pp.41, 42. Lansdowne MS 48/83, in Greg, *Companion*, pp.116-17; see also below.

58. Barker's report, December 1582, Lansd. MS 48/82 fo. 189ff, Greg, *Companion*, cal. no. 90, Arber I, pp.114-16, 144. Report of commissioners to Privy Council, 18 July 1583 from John Aylmer, Bishop of London, Alexander Nowell, William Fleetwood, John Hammond, Thomas Norton SP12/161/(III) in Greg, *Companion*, pp.130-31. As so often, the relevant documents are miscalendared in the State Papers, and Greg's long and valuable survey of the background and the other patents involved, with corrections to Arber, is somewhat confused on this point: *Companion*, pp.117-22. A letter from Aylmer

to Burghley of 1 June 1583, SP12/161/1, Greg cal. no. 99, Arber I, pp.246-7, has attached to it as Annex I a list of 23 printers with 53 presses, Greg, cal. no. 98, Arber, I, p.248. Annex II is a petition from the wardens to Aylmer which was enclosed in his letter of 1 June together with a printed 'toy' that has not survived, Greg, cal. no. 97, Arber, I, pp.247-8. Annex III is the report of the commissioners, Greg, cal. no. 104, text pp.126-33. Although Greg noticed that the list of printers, Annex I, was mentioned in the commissioners' report, he followed the *Calendar of State Papers* in assuming it had been enclosed in Aylmer's letter: Greg, pp.29, 30, 121. In fact, the commissioners' covering letter of 18 July (SP12/161/37, Greg, pp.125-6, also Arber II, pp.783-4) says that it encloses their report, while the report itself (Greg, p.130) says it encloses the list of printers. Siebert said the list of printers came from Barker's report and gave the false reference Arber I, p.218: Siebert, p.69. Gerald D. Johnson, 'The Stationers versus the Drapers: Control of the press in the Late Sixteenth Century', *The Library*, 6th ser., 10 (1988), p.3, refers to the report as from the High Commission; since the ecclesiastical commissioners now numbered more than 60, almost anyone eligible for a duty of this kind would already be a member of that body and all but Norton were so. For Norton's political career see M.A.R. Graves, 'Thomas Norton the Parliament Man: An Elizabethan M.P., 1559-1581', *HJ* 23 (1980), pp.17-35.

59. George Unwin, *The gilds & companies of London* (4th edn, 1963), chs 15 and 17. Joan Thirsk, *Economic Policy and Projects, passim*. Ian Archer, 'The London lobbies in the later sixteenth century', *HJ* 31 (1988), pp.29-34.

60. The patents from 1539 to 1635, taken from Rymer's *Foedera*, are listed in Thomas E. Scrutton, *The Laws of Copyright* (1883), pp.293-8; the later patents are also listed in James Harrison (ed.), *Printing Patents. Abridgement of Patent Specifications relating to printing. 1617-1857* (1969).

61. Greg, *Companion*, pp.130-1; Arber I, p.144.

62. 4 May 1586, Lansd. MS 48/74 fo. 174, Greg, *Companion*, cal. no. 123, Arber II, pp.804-5. P.M. Handover's account of the glee with which the decree was received by the patentees may well be right in spirit, though it is not fully borne out by the mundane entry in the Court Book: *Printing in London* (1960), p.41; W.W. Greg and E. Boswell (eds), *Records of the Court of the Stationers' company, 1576-1602*, p.19.

63. 4 Dec. 1587, Greg & Boswell, *Records*, p.25; Greg, *Companion*, cal. no. 131, Arber II, p.43; Blagden, *Stationers' Company*, p.72 n.2; Gaskell, *A New Introduction to Bibliography*, pp.161-3.

64. 8 Jan. 1583/4, Lansd. MS 905, fos. 282-4, Greg, *Companion*, cal. no. 108, Arber II, pp.786-9; Blagden, 'The English Stock of the Stationers' company', *The Library*, 5th ser., 10 (1955), pp.163-9.

65. The text of the decree is printed in John Strype, *The Life and Acts of John Whitgift* (3 vols, Oxford, 1822), iii, pp.160-5; Greg, *Companion*, cal. no. 125, Arber II, pp.807-12. Clause 4 of the decree increased the penalty for unlawful printing from three to six months imprisonment; clause 5 changed the penalty for the sale of such books from the (very heavy) fine of 20s per book to three months imprisonment. Return of presses, July 1586, Liber A. fo. 51, Greg, *Companion*. cal. no. 126, Arber V, lii; Greg says, wrongly, that there are 24 names – there are 25 including Christopher Barker.

66. Siebert, p.137. Loades, 'The theory and practice of censorship', p.155.

67. 22 Oct. 1586, Greg & Boswell, *Records*, p.20. Cyril B. Judge, *Elizabethan book-pirates* (Cambridge, Mass., 1934), pp.65-6.

68. 4 March, 3 June 1588, Greg & Boswell, *Records*, pp.27-8; McKerrow, *Dictionary*, p.208. 30 Aug. 1591, Liber A, fo. 64, Greg, *Companion*, cal. no. 142, Arber V, li.

69. Judge, *Elizabethan book-pirates*, pp.112-40, 160-81; Gerald Johnson, 'The Stationers versus the Drapers', *The Library* (1988), pp.1-17. Stafford's first independent work was Nicholas Breton's *A solemne passion of the soules love* (STC 3696): Breton was not one of the authors whose works were called in in 1599, indeed Judge (p.124) treated Breton's name as a guarantee of respectability in the eyes of authority; cf. Hill, 'Censorship', pp.34, 35.

70. Abbot's order 2 Dec. 1622, Jackson, *Records*, pp.378-9. Lambert, 'The Printers and the Government, 1604-1637', in Robin Myers and Michael Harris (eds), *Aspects of Printing from 1600* (Oxford Polytechnic Press, 1987), pp.3-4, 7-11.

71. Greg made the point that the bishops could not be expected to license personally, but thought the reference in the decree to the 1559 injunctions was a polite way of brushing them aside: *Some aspects and problems of London publishing between 1550 and 1650* (Oxford, 1956), p.9. Edith L. Klotz, 'A subject analysis of English imprints for every tenth year from 1480 to 1640', *HLQ* 1 (1937-8), pp.417-19.

72. 3 June 1588, Greg & Boswell, *Records*, pp.28-9; Greg, *Some Aspects*, pp.52-4. 20 March 1595/6, Liber A, fo. 67v.

73. Liber A, fo. 67v. It seems possible that Bancroft had this order in mind when he issued his directive of 1 June 1599: Arber, III, pp.677-8. Mark H. Curtis, 'William Jones: Puritan Printer and Propagandist'; *The Library*, 5th ser. 19 (1964), pp.38-66; Lambert, 'The printers and the government', n.7, pp.22-3. Jones was allowed an apprentice on 28 Jan. 1613 on condition that he did not 'employe him in printinge till he himselfe be a mr printer by laufull & orderly meanes': Donald F. McKenzie, *Stationers' Company Apprentices 1605-1640* (Charlottesville, Va., 1961), nos.306, 1693.

74. Blagden, *Stationers' Company*, p.173; J. Walker, 'The censorship of the press during the reign of Charles II, *History* 35 (1950), 236-38; John Hetet, 'The Wardens' Accounts of the Stationers' Company, 1663-79', in *Economics of the British Book Trade 1605-1939*, ed. Robin Myers and Michael Harris (Chadwyck-Healey, 1985), pp.32-59.

75. Draft letter from Cecil to the Stationers' Company, 1604, HMC *Hatfield MSS*, xvi, p.427. J.F. Larkin and P.L. Hughes (eds), *Stuart Royal Proclamations* (Oxford 1973), hereafter L&H, no.110. E.R. Foster, *Proceedings in Parliament 1610* (2 vols, New Haven, 1966), ii, pp.263-5, 294. Richard Montagu had heard of another plan for a new system in 1625: Montagu to Cosin, 31 Jan. 1624/5, G. Ornsby (ed.), *The Correspondence of John Cosin.* (2 vols, Surtees Soc., lii, lv, Durham, 1869-72), i, p.51.

76. Translation of extracts from the patent rolls 9 Jac, pt 18, 29 August 1611 and 11 Jac, pt 15, 21 June 1613, with the changes made in the latter shown in italic, are printed in Prothero, *Select Statutes*, p.427, extract of this clause in Siebert, p.139.

77. S.R. Gardiner (ed.), *Documents relating to the proceedings against William Prynne* (Camden Soc., n.s. 18, 1877), p.54. Robert Crosse and Toby Knowles applied for Wither's patent: Greg, *Companion*, pp.215-17.

78. Blagden, 'The English Stock of the Stationers' Company', *The Library*, 10 (1955), p.177; *idem*, 'The English Stock of the Stationers' Company in the time of the Stuarts', *The Library*, 12 (1957), pp.167-8; *idem*, *Stationers' Company*, ch.vi, pp.92-4. It is not the case that in 1603 the Stationers' Company was 'reorganized by James I into five sections': Natascha Wurzbach, trans. Gayna Walls, *The rise of the English Street Ballad, 1550-1650* (Cambridge, 1990), p.19.

79. Lambert, 'The printers and the government', pp.6, 16-17. Lucien Febvre and H-J Martin, trans. David Gerard, *The Coming of the Book* (1976), pp.39, 42-3, 131-2. Jackson, *Records*, pp.344-5, 26 Oct. 1611; *ibid.*, p.79, 4 Dec. 1615.

80. See above, Greg, *Companion*, pp.116-17. 27 Jan. 1597/8, Greg & Boswell, *Records*, p.60.

81. Act 25 Hen 8 cap 15 of 1533-4. HL Main Papers 2 May 1614. STC 16786.2; the brief is printed in civilité type thus neatly evading the Commons' rule of 20 April 1610, which stated that 'no brief or reasons' should be offered in print, C[ommons] J[ournals] i, 419. A diarist noted 'it could not pass, for those books which were made here would then be sold at their own price by hindering that traffic between other countries and us': Maija Jansson (ed.), *Proceedings in Parliament, 1614* (Mem. Am. Phil. Soc. clxxii, Philadelphia, 1988), pp.118, 126, 293.

82. Order of 19 Jan. 1597/8 against 'printing for foreigns': Greg & Boswell, *Records*, p.59. Pollard, 'The English market for printed books', *Pub. Hist.* 4 (1978), pp.19-20, pointed out that the monopoly was never quite complete, mentioning Joseph Moxon and Richard Chiswell. William Barley is an early case in point: G.D. Johnson, 'William Barley', *The Library*, 6th ser., 11 (1989), pp.19-20. See also below.

83. 8 Feb. 1614/5, Liber A, fo. 85a, Jackson, *Records*, p.349; Blagden, *Stationers' Company*, p.120.

84. 22 March 1614/5, Jackson, *Records*, p.74.

85. H.R. Plomer, 'Some notes on the Latin and Irish stocks of the Company of Stationers', *The Library*, n.s., 8 (1907), pp.286-97. H.G. Pollard and A. Ehrman, *The distribution of books by catalogue to 1800* (privately printed, Cambridge, 1965), ch.4. Pollard, 'English market', p.13.

86. 24 Dec. 1620, L&H no.208. Jonathan Marwil, *The trials of Counsel: Francis Bacon in 1621* (Detroit, 1976), p.23.

87. 8 April, 21 July 1621, 8 March 1623/4, L&H nos.216, 218, 250. See Lambert, 'Coranto printing'.

88. Jackson, *Records*, p.142. 23 Sep. 1623, L&H no.247. Cambridge certainly got what it wanted two years later by another private proclamation which specifically prohibited the import of piracies of any Latin works previously printed at the Universities: 1 April 1625, J.F. Larkin, *Stuart Royal Proclamations* (Oxford, 1983), no.5.

89. The proclamation has long been regarded as a reissue of the 1586 decree: Prothero, *Select Statutes*, pp.394-5; John P. Kenyon, *The Stuart Constitution*, (2nd edn, 1986), p.115; Siebert, pp.142, 154.

90. 15 August, L&H no.256; the alterations are shown in Greg, *Companion*, pp.226-9.

91. *Votivae Angliae*, (1624. STC 20946.2) sig. Aiii r. Jerry H. Bryant, 'John Reynolds of Exeter and his Canon: A Footnote', *The Library*, 5th ser., 18 (1963), pp.299-303. Limon thinks James oversensitive to criticism because he refused to sit quietly through a play which suggested he had murdered his own son, prince Henry: *Dangerous Matter*, p.11. Cogswell, *Blessed Revolution*, pp.289-91.

92. Thomas Locke to Sir Dudley Carleton, 11 July 1624, SP14/169/41, in Greg, *Companion*, p.225, wrongly given as SP14/159/41. L&H no.256 n.2 states wrongly that it was 'the supposed author' who was fined, as does Limon, *Dangerous Matter*, p.8, and Cogswell, *Blessed Revolution*, p.290. William Jones printed Reynolds's *Vox Coeli* (1624. STC 20946.4-8) and may also have printed *Votivae Angliae*. Sparke's collection, which suggests he had something to do with the original publications, is STC 22064.

93. Simon L. Adams, 'Captain Thomas Gainsford, the "Vox Spiritus" and the Vox Populi', *BIHR* 49 (1976), pp.141-4. The works of 1622 are *Newes from Parnassus* (STC 22080), and *The Belgick pismire* (STC 22069); the latter was reprinted by John Dawson the following year (STC 22082). The works of 1623 are *The Projector* (Dawson, STC 22081), *Digitus Dei* (STC 22075), *The high-waies of God* (STC 22079) and *Vox Dei* (STC 22097a). C. Hill, 'From Marprelate to the Levellers', *Essays* I, p.78.

94. *Boanerges. Or the humble supplication of the ministers of Scotland, to the High Court of Parliament in England.* Edinburgh [i.e. London], 1624, STC 3171.3. Williams to Conway, 15 Feb. 1623/4, SP 14/159/40.

95. Laud, *Works* iv, p.264. Blagden, *Stationers' Company*, pp.117-25. The decree is printed in Rushworth II-2, Appx, pp.306-15 and Arber IV, pp.528-36; draft SP16/376/15.

96. SP16/376/17 and 18. Nevertheless, Walley raised the issue as a grievance at Laud's trial; there was undoubtedly an element within the Company opposed to Laud: Laud, *Works* iv, p.264.

97. For the proclamation of 1636, Larkin no.219, see Lambert, 'The printers and the government', p.16 and n.48. The list of printers, SP16/175/45 and the order of 23 November 1630 are wrongly attributed to Abbot in *ibid.*, p.5 and n.11.

98. Blagden, *Stationers' Company*, p.120; PC2/48, pp.438-9, 6 Dec. 1637; Jackson, *Records*, pp.286-7, 294; Arber IV, pp.387-8; SP 16/378/24; William P. Williams, 'Chetwin, Crooke and the Jonson folios', *SB* 30 (1977), pp.75-95.

99. Greg, *Companion*, pp.310-18; Leo Miller, 'Milton and Vlack', *PBSA* 73 (1979), pp.174-81; Lambert, 'The printers and the government', p.17; Tanner MS 67 fo. 195, endorsed 28 Nov. 1638, printed in Plomer, 'More Petitions to ArchbishopLaud;, *The Library*, 3rd ser., 10 (1919), pp.133-5. SP16/365/15 endorsed 2 Aug. 1637.

100. Lambert, 'The printers and the Government', p.11; *idem*, 'Journeymen and master printers in the early seventeenth century', *Jour. Printing Hist. Soc.* (forthcoming). Klotz, 'Subject analysis of English imprints', *HLQ* 1 (1937-8), pp.417-19; Maureen Bell and John Barnard are producing much higher figures from the second edn of *STC*. I mentioned two of the many failed ventures in 'Richard Montagu', pp.65-6.

101. Hill, *Milton*, p.65; *idem*, *Some Intellectual Consequences*, p.49; *idem*, 'Censorship', p.40; R.C. Richardson and G.M. Ridden (eds), *Freedom and the English Revolution* (Manchester, 1986), p.3. Siebert, p.191 n.71; Siebert misused the count of titles given in Fortescue's deplorable catalogue of the Thomason tracts.

102. Commission report 1583, Greg, *Companion*, p.127. Fortescue's count showed 692 titles in 1644 and 694 in 1645: G.K. Fortescue, *Catalogue of the pamphlets ... collected by George Thomason, 1640-1661* (2 vols, 1908), p.xxi. Stationers' Company petition of 1643, Arber I, p.587.

Catholic texts and anti-Catholic prejudice in the 17th-century book trade

ALISON SHELL

THERE HAVE BEEN certain commonplaces associated with 16th- and 17th-century censorship in England. It is deemed to have been primarily a political weapon, with a restrictive absolutist government — usually with the lineaments of Archbishop Laud — attempting to curb an opposition associated with puritanism and radicalism. It concerned itself with sensitive topical references and inflammatory ideas, Hobbes's *Leviathan* or the excisions to plays demanded by successive Masters of the Revels. Mutilation of books or of authors, bonfires of Wycliffe's New Testament or the cropped ears of Prynne, combine with bibliographical evidence of an erasure, a damasking, a cancel. That a book has been censored automatically makes it interesting, and 'subversive' has replaced 'radical' as a synonym for 'worthwhile'; in an essay by Christopher Hill, 'heresy' is used as a term of approval.[1] Recently, too, attention has focused on the textual strategies by which censorship was circumvented and subverted, entry codes which signal a covert meaning to the initiate. Literary critics, self-styled initiates, have found this an imaginative challenge. Using the twin metal-detectors of inexact analogy and polyvalent meaning, the most unpromising ground can be found to conceal references — of a sort — to the Overbury murder or the Spanish marriage.

This is, of course, something of a caricature. It presupposes a government not only totalitarian but monolithic, whereas — as many recent studies have shown — the picture of censorship even under the Laudian ascendancy is intermittent and spasmodic, and before that, subject to very varying controls under the tripartite system of church, crown and city. It puts into the foreground the early 17th century, whereas much useful work has been done on periods before and after. But it is certainly true that censorship is still thought of primarily in political terms, as an instrument of power. Considerations of religious reasons for censorship, the prevention of heresy or schism, have been subsumed to this: a Machiavellian model, and one which eliminates the altruistic factors that are inseparable from

33

religious censorship in an age of faith. Nevertheless, the binary structure of government versus opposition is compelling, has been influential, and because of this has one overriding danger: that the shibboleths on which both government and opposition agreed may not be seen in terms of censorship at all. Anti-Catholicism is one such shibboleth.

The paradigm of the Catholic text in Protestant England poses questions as to the limits of free speech. In an illustrated catalogue of a recent exhibition at the New York Public Library, title-pages from Galileo's *Dialogo* and an *Index Librorum Prohibitorum* are juxtaposed with that from Milton's *Areopagitica*. The implication is obvious, borne out by the caption to the latter: 'Published during the Civil War, this is the English-speaking world's first great statement urging freedom of expression'.[2] Yet, turning to *Areopagitica*, it makes no concessions to 'Popery, and open superstition, which as it extirpates all religions, and civill supremacies, so it self should be extirpat ...; that also which is impious or evil absolutely either against faith or maners, no law can possibly permit' (p.565)[3]. Analogies between *Areopagitica* and the Index are, of course, far from exact: one was implemented and one was ignored, one has a monolithic and the other an agonistic conception of truth. Because of the latter there is also, perhaps, a slight difference of emphasis in the two sides' conception of the religious other. To the Catholic hierarchy, heresy was a germ to be studied by the few and sterilised for the many; and Catholicism, to Milton, was so egregious a cheat that it was unfit to take part in an open contest. Both advocate censorship, and both do so out of fear and horror.

Areopagitica's definition of press freedom does not spring fully formed from Milton's head, but is arrived at through the contest of dialectic: largely through his intense conviction that the papal system of indexes and imprimaturs must be wrong. The Stationers' Company had, in April 1643, petitioned Parliament for the reinstatement of press restrictions following the abolition of the Star Chamber, and had argued that 'to give Papists their due' they were more careful than Protestant Englishmen to preserve their form of religion from alterations.[4] Milton is responding to this when he demonstrates that papal censorship is an historical innovation and utterly unjustifiable: and hence, that any similar system of licensing is borrowed from popery. To those that argue that the invention may be good even though the inventors are bad, he has this to say:

Yet this only is what I request to gain from this reason, that it may be held a dangerous and suspicious fruit, as certainly it deserves, for the tree that bore it, untill I can dissect one by one the properties it has. (p.507)

In effect he is asking the reader to hold the pro-censorship argument tainted almost before it has been considered; in craving his audience's indulgence Milton relies on their anti-papal prejudice.

A good deal has been said about Milton's anticipation and shaping of the free press; and when such discussions touch on his treatment of Catholic writing, they tend to resolve themselves by invoking the prime dogma and paradox of liberalism, the need to restrict the freedom of those who want to restrict the freedom of others. This paper aims to strike out sideways, and to do so by stressing the intense religious implications of truth. To the polarised Catholic or Protestant, to Milton or to Paul IV, who issued the first index, there was no doubt about the falsity of the religious other: it was outside the arena of legitimate questioning, and its danger was palpable. This paper is to do with Protestant censorship, and does not aim to make any reflections on the censorship in Catholic countries at the time: but a distinction can perhaps be drawn between the Catholic orthodoxy of imposition as against Milton's orthodoxy of limitation.

Like Milton, England wished in general to extirpate Catholic books. Importation of them from English and foreign continental presses was forbidden; illicit Catholic presses and caches of books were searched for and destroyed by government pursuivants; bonfires of them and of other popish artifacts were a common cautionary demonstration; Catholic texts were expurgated where they impugned Protestantism; the legislation regulating the book trade had profound implications for the distribution of Catholic texts. In contrast, the area with which this paper is more concerned is that where censorship shades into conditioning: where some areas of knowledge are cordoned off from inspection, others are blackened, and a consciousness of popery leads to apology, or satire, or caution, or − in the case of Catholic writers − placatory self-censorship and censorship of tradition: where, in short, a Catholic text is presented in a way that predetermines the response of the audience to it. The difference between the conventional picture of popery and that given in this paper is that between repression and oppression. Blair Worden has said that to extend the term of censorship beyond banning, burning and expurgation to boundaries of thought is to widen the term to the point of uselessness, and perhaps the discussion of what an era takes for granted is better called epistemology than censorship: for the purposes of this particular paper, the two are not the same. But Worden's implied model leaves out a whole category of responses that occur when censorship dilutes into censoriousness: a sneer, a footnote, an apology, or an image.[5]

The first illustration (fig.1) shows four Jesuits grouped around the order's founder, Ignatius Loyola. It serves as the frontispiece to Edward Stillingfleet's *The Jesuits Loyalty* of 1677; and in a number of ways it exemplifies the phenomenon on which this paper will be concentrating. Its conception and its workmanship seem to suggest a Continental provenance: a Catholic one, judging by the lack of caricature in the portraits and the straightforward depiction of Loyola as a saint. But the names engraved under the subsidiary Jesuits are all ones which the Protestant Englishman knew that he should hate: Francisco de Suarez and Juan de Mariana, authors respectively of one of the most influential Catholic attacks on Anglicanism and of a justification of regicide; Henry Garnet, whose likeness miraculously appeared on straw at his execution to be greeted by Catholic veneration and Protestant mockery; and Robert Persons, chief polemicist among the Elizabethan Catholics and founder of numerous Catholic schools and seminaries on the Continent. The lettering is different for these inscriptions, and clumsier; the signs of re-engraving are clear. This implies a block for a Continental Catholic work finding its way into England to serve ultimately as decoration for an anti-Catholic tract: rubbed down, re-engraved, and topped and tailed with condemnatory epigraphs. Catholic texts — as it might be the books above the figures in the picture — are subject to similar defamatory rewritings.[6]

An icon is explicated by its context: good Jesuits become evil Jesuits when picture comes into bibliographical unity with print. This was not the only typographical stratagem with which prejudice about popery was inculcated. Often these were signalled: *The Popish Courant* of 14 March 1679 explains the printing in black-letter of an excerpt from an ancient Catholic homily by saying that they are presenting it 'in the very Antique Pseudography' as a 'work of Supererogation'. The typographical satire is double-edged: 'pseudography' can mean either the writing of words falsely, not according to sound or usage, or by analogy it can be used for false argument (*OED*). In *The Spirit of Popery Speaking out of the Mouths of Phanatical-Protestants* (1680) the names of Catholic murderers are rubricated in 'Letters of Blood ... as it is fitting to set forth the horror of such a Murder' (p.63).[7] Printers' devices and ornaments could purvey similar messages. One shows the pope in the company of the world, the flesh and the devil, providing the customer with a casual validation of the contents before he even opened it; another, the pope, the devil and prelates puffing at an immovable globe; and a third printer's ornament includes

Illud unum sciant Reges, nihil magìs cordi esse Pontifici & ejus affeclis, quàm ut Regiam potestatem vilem reddant, infirmam, imbecillem & abjectam. Spalat.

Let Kings take notice of this, that the Popes and their followers make it their business, to lessen the Authority of Princes, and to make it as weak and contemptible as they can.

SUAREZ | MARIANA | S. IGNATIVS LOYOLA SOCIETATIS IESV FVNDATOR | GARNET | PARSONS

Optabilior est Fur quàm Mendax assiduus, utriq; verò Perditionis hæreditatem consequentur. Eccles 20 vers 25

A thief is better then a man that is accustomed to lie : but they both shall have destruction to heritage. *Eclus.* 20. 25.

Fig.1.   Frontispiece to Edward Stillingfleet, *The Jesuits Loyalty* (1677). Reproduced by permission of the Syndics of Cambridge University Library

Fig.2. Printer's ornament: see J.A. Lavin, 'Three 'Owl' Blocks: 1590-1640'. *The Library* (5th ser.) XXII (1967) pp.143-7.

Fig.3. Printers' device or ornament: no.391 in Ronald B. McKerrow, *Printers' and Publishers' Devices* (London 1913)

Fig.4. Another, from the title-page to *A Full Narrative, or a Discovery of the Priests and Jesuites* (1679)

flatulent monkeys and an owl in a cardinal's hat.[8] Unlike the putti playing with pontifical impedimenta in Counter-Reformation decorative schemes, the motive behind this ornament is anti-Roman and deadly serious: cardinals exist in spiritual darkness as owls do in physical.

The appearance and understood significance of a text, rather than its illustration, could also be used to anti-Catholic effect as in the pope-burning processions which numerous towns held during the Popish Plot years. The priest in the procession held in London in 1679 held out bulls, pardons and indulgences to the passers-by; at Aberdeen indulgences were distributed free: while at Abergavenny the papal officers offered them at lower and lower prices 'till at last they were proffered for four pence a Dozen, but no body would buy any'. In London in 1680 the Pope's typographer carried and was dressed in bulls, pardons and indulgences; text can become vestment, and Protestant printing subvert Catholic image.[9]

A number of fallacies have been bred from the polarisation of Catholic image and Protestant word, but just as it is a truism that the rise of Protestantism is ineluctably bound up with the printing-press and literacy, it scarcely needs saying that part of Protestant propaganda, from an early date, was indeed to stress this truism. John Foxe's call to arms in *Acts and Monuments* is well-known:

The Lord began to work for his church; not with sword and target to subdue his exalted adversary, but with printing, writing and reading.... How many printing presses there be in the world, so many block houses there be against the high castle of St. Angelo; so that either the pope must abolish knowledge and printing or printing at length will root him out.[10]

But satire is more complicated than the binary oppositions of polemic, and these ornaments and effigies at pope-burnings link text and image in the spirit of a pasquinade. Pasquinades were anonymous social comments attached to the defaced statue of Pasquil in Rome; being frequently anti-papal, they gave the impetus to Protestant satirists across Europe and − to some extent − were how the Protestant printer saw himself.

Anti-popery certainly stimulated the rivalry between printers: and the *locus classicus* of this is the slanderous emphasis on personalities of the Popish Plot. Doubt was cast from all sides on Sir Roger L'Estrange's suitability as Surveyor of the Press because of his supposed popish sympathies, while the satires and fantasies of the Whig news-sheets, published by Benjamin Harris and Langly Curtis depended on the presumption that certain printers and booksellers − usually Benjamin Tooke, John

Gadbury or Nathaniel Thompson — were popish fifth columnists.[11] For instance, in the advertisement column of Benjamin Harris's *The Weekly Discoverer Strip'd Naked* (23 February 1681) there appears, mixed among genuine advertisements, this message:

> If any Person hath occasion for Popish Cobwebs spun out of the Bowels of Roman-Catholick Spiders, ingeniously contrived and excellently designed for the catching silly Protestant Flies, Let them repair to the famous Catholic Merchant Mr. *Benjamin Tooke*, at his Warehouse, at the *Ship* in *Paul's* church-yard, where they may be furnished with several sorts, and very cheap, with directions how to use them.[12]

Here is the basic assumption with which not only Catholics but those Anglicans, like Tooke, more liberal towards Catholic books had to contend. Popish books are a locus of disgust and horror because they are false, and because that falsity is designed as a snare. A traditional polarisation is used, the bee gathering honey versus the spider spinning webs: the Catholic writer excretes false matter obtained from man's inward inventions, with the intention of catching unwary Protestants in the pathless toils of adhesive heresy. Catholic pamphlets are generated from corruption, and betoken in their turn a corrupt fertility. The polemical Latin play *Risus Anglicanus* [1614-1625], is plotted around the assumption that Catholic pamphlets are begotten by demons on papists and composed in a creative stupor: it gives a solid imaginative substance to the act of textual controversy, that may be summed up by the anti-Protestant polemicist within the play who describes himself as egg-bound with books.[13] What inspires the Protestant pamphleteer, though, is the notion that the web may be swept away, or the egg broken, by the brush of a godly hand or the tilt of a pamphlet: holy wars are waged with textual missiles. There is nothing subtle or complex about this idea: what this paper is about is its ubiquity.

It was the supposed ubiquity of Catholic texts, in contrast, that was a source of concern to 17th-century England. This demands some chronological qualification. Catholics are, if not on the Continent then certainly in the British Isles, usually thought of as having responded slowly and ineffectively to the first Protestant onslaught. A few names are cited under the Marian regime, notably Miles Hogard and the almanac-writer Anthony Askham; and more importantly, an emphasis on response fails to take into account Catholic survivalism, or the numbers of Catholic texts undoubtedly still in circulation from pre-Reformation times.[14] But during Elizabeth's reign polemicists marshalled themselves for the intellectual end of the market, and, of a few decades later, Margaret Spufford also quotes John Rhodes's complaint (1602) that a number of Catholic pamphlets 'together with other like Romish wares' are being widely distributed by pedlars and chapmen; and Tessa Watt, in a recent book, has stressed how the conservatism of the consumers of cheap print kept a number of images in circulation beyond the time when they would have been acceptable to the Protestant purists of the later 16th century.[15] But it is the books imported from Catholic countries in Europe, and polemical texts produced at expatriate centres abroad or secret presses in England, that become and remain the chief concern in the Elizabethan era and beyond.

This primary model of polarised Catholic and Protestant texts needs moderating. For practical purposes there was a continuum between the two, and the emphases in this paper mean simply that texts were susceptible to polarisation for polemical purposes, rather than perpetually existing with battle-lines drawn up. But even within the controversial tradition, there are paradoxes. The first, and an obvious one, was that it was often those most firmly Protestant that were responsible for distributing Catholic texts. Central to pamphlet dialectic – and Catholic-Protestant controversy is no exception — is the detailed refutation of one's opponent by dint of extensive quotation from him, extensively countermanded. There was a rationale to this: though contemporary pamphlet collections demonstrate that both sides of a controversy were often collected together, it did not necessarily follow that the reader would have access to the one while reading the other.[16] With Catholic pamphlets, in particular, there would be the difficulty that they were clandestine. The Catholic author of *Why are You a Catholique?* [n.d.] is sensitive to this, saying in the preface that

He is not ignorant that this fashion of writing *Controversies Dialogue-Wise* is oft obnoxious to exceptions, and not unjust suspicions of partiality and prevarication, For indeed we sometimes see *Dialogues*, in which the *Authours*, (who may make their pretended *Adversaries* to speak as they themselves please) do put foolish *Answers* into their mouths, and then laugh at them, presuming thereby to have gained a Victory. (A4)

Catholic manuscript distribution was a widespread phenomenon, and in some cases a pamphleteer would claim to be refuting a Catholic manuscript: John Shaw's *Origo Protestantium: or an Answer to a Popish Manuscript (of N.N's)* (1677), for instance, is allegedly answering a Catholic manuscript sent to him privately. Its London printing seems to have been financed by the Mayor and Corporation of Newcastle-upon-Tyne, to whom the book is dedicated (*DNB*), and is clearly seen as a local corrective to an urgent local danger: '... the Romanists in these parts grew every day more insolently active to bring more Grist to their own mill, and list more men in the Popes Service, not only by Printed Books, but by private *Letters* and *Manuscripts*' (A3r). Shaw promises to animadvert other similar manuscripts as part of 'scouring these northern Coasts' for popery (A3v). But the enigmatic attribution of the manuscript to 'N.N', initials often used as a cloak for anonymity, highlights the problem faced by the researcher of how to determine the authenticity of the original document. Were Shaw's suggestions of identity in the preface as they seem, or strategies of authentication?[17]

Sometimes a Catholic text would be printed in full for purposes of refutation. Stillingfleet's *The Jesuits Loyalty* (1677) juxtaposes three Catholic with three Protestant texts on the subject of allegiance to the Crown, placing the Protestant texts last in each case to emphasise their unanswerability. Less clear-cut, though, are the motives behind the translation of a work of Justus Lipsius's printed in 1688, *Miracles of the B. Virgin*: the date — perhaps still under the Catholic James II — and the lack of any imprint invite the question as to whether the brief and perfunctory denunciation of Catholicism in the Epistle to the Reader should not be seen as a smokescreen. Adrian Morey suggests that this was a recognised means of gaining access to Catholic books.[18] Smokescreens of this nature, though, did not go unpenetrated by the contemporary opposition: *The Reclaimed Papist*, a dialogue in which the papist — despite the title — has the best of the argument, is listed as a Catholic book in the sale catalogue of Richard Maitland, 4th Earl of Lauderdale (p.128).

Texts by Catholics were expurgated to purge them of offensive references — as one would expect — but also as a response to the uncontrollable circulation of those same texts. Edmund Bunny's edition of Robert Persons's *Christian Directory*, which had a dedication to the Archbishop of Canterbury, gave as a reason for publication in the preface that so many people were reading the book that it seemed wise to produce an expurgated edition.[19] At the other end of the scale Catholic or supposedly Catholic texts, such as the numerous books of instruction for Jesuits, undoubtedly had their infamy retouched, though a Catholic book could sometimes be issued unexpurgated and — except for the tone-setting introduction — unsophisticated, if it was thought the contents were sufficiently damning. Edward Gee, issuing Robert Persons's *Jesuits Memorial* in 1690, claimed that the publication was 'doing a greater service to the Protestant Interest against Popery, than I was ever able to do by any thing I wrote against Popery during the Controversie in the late Reign' (A3v).

Perhaps the most conspicuous act of anti-Catholic textual publicity was the catalogue of popish books, or Protestant Index.[20] Serving a function analogous to the cheap printed anti-Catholic diagrams of the era, showing rosaries, paxes and Agnus Deis, they alert the Protestant reader to the names and conformations of popery. The fiction is consistently that the innocent need to be educated in these matters; but given the sheer weight of information on the topic available, one can imagine that the reader, like the prude of Restoration comedy, was to some extent colluding in the display of shock on cue. The best-known of these catalogues is John Gee's vividly written *The Foot out of the Snare* (1624); after an autobiographical account of his temporary apostasy to Catholicism, it offers the reader a deprecation of the times and a call to action, a censuring of books and of people that invites censorship. Jesuits were often compared to the locusts of the Apocalypse, and Gee applies the topology both to them and to their literature: 'Witnesse the swarmes of their books, which you may heare humming vp and downe in euery corner both of City and Countrey' (p.21). Popish books are listed in some detail, sometimes with authors and value-judgements – Anthony Clerke's *The Honour of God* is called 'An idle frothy booke, by a brayne-sicke man, a concealed Priest' (O3v) – notorious priests and Jesuits are also named and in later editions the names are added of those prepared to disperse, print, bind and sell popish books. In all, *The Foot out of the Snare* ran to four editions in a year and a sequel, *New Shreds of the Old Snare*. The book's progress is chronicled by Gee in marginal notes: undercutting its status as best-seller he declares in the second edition that the papists must certainly have bought up all his first edition in order to burn it: 'the first impression, consisting of 1500, is vanished in a week, and now I sweat under the Presse againe' (H1v). His charges are unprovable, but *The Foot out of the Snare* is certainly detailed enough to be used, at least, as a directory by both sides.

Gee's complaint is consistently that not only are Englishmen going the high way to hell by obtaining these books, but that they are paying over the odds to do so. 'And how doo they by this meanes put their poore Disciples vpon the Tenters, selling that book for forty or fifty shillings, which they might affoord for eight or ten; & that for ten, which they might afford for one?' (pp.21-2). In the case of a number of books by John Sweet he complains that 'containing but some sixe sheetes of paper, either of them are sold ... for two shillings or half a crowne apiece' (O3r), though the logic of even postulating a reasonable price for such pernicious books is dubious. Because of the costs involved in their importation and the risks of distribution, there is certainly plenty of evidence that Catholic books were unusually expensive. Much prejudice against them centred on this fact. *The Pragmatical Jesuit New Leaven'd*, an anti-Catholic closet drama of the 1660s written by the Catholic apostate Richard Carpenter, contains a scene with one Fr. Robert, a Catholic bookseller. Agrippa, a magician, asks him:

A   -   What Books have you?
R   -   Books of devotion, Sir: you may take your choice of English or Latin.
A   -   Are you a Bookseller?
R   -   Yes, Sir, a poor one: but my Books are not sold publickly.
A   -   Your Books, I see, belong to t'other side of the great Pond.
R   -   They do, Sir: therefore they bear the higher price here. (p.63)[21]

The aggregation of evidence given by a Protestant Index could be used for political ends. In the 1650s a group of Presbyterian sympathisers, headed by Luke Fawne, inaugurated a controversy with the pamphlet *A Beacon Set on Fire*, pleading with the government of the Interregnum to reinstate censorship for the purpose of stamping out popish and other seditious books: it was answered speedily by *The Beacons Quenched*, the initiative of a group headed by Thomas Pride. In a spirited exploitation of the confrontational titular rhetoric of the period, Fawne and his allies retorted with *The Beacon Flameing with a Non Obstante* and *A Second Beacon Fired*.[22] The presence in England of popish books is seen as a tactical counter: for Fawne and his colleagues an unarguable reason why censorship should be placed in the hands of men of proven godliness, and for Pride, a cause for some caution which nevertheless does not compare with the Presbyterian threat.

A Beacon Set on Fire estimates that at least 3000 popish books have been printed in England – probably in London – in the three years previous to the pamphlet, and argues that the 'Act now depending concerning the Company of Stationers and Printing' should make allowance for this. Three main charges on this subject are brought in *A Beacon Quenched* that are answered in *The Beacon Flameing*. Firstly, the danger of popery is held to be a smokescreen behind which the Presbyterians are laying traps. This *A Beacon Flameing* treats with silent disdain. Secondly, those very presbyters are alleged to be profiting from Catholic books in both Latin and English, and even, Pride says, 'to have a Factor in Rome it self' (A2v). Fawne responds to the second half of the charge that he has no need to send to Rome for popish books, there already being too many in England, and to the first half, that such books are sold by none of them 'except very rarely to a learned pious friend whom they know to be sound in the faith, and able to handle the snake without being stung: which manner of selling may very

well stand with a zealous desire that such books might never be published'
(p.4). This somewhat contradicts the earlier declaration in *A Beacon Set on
Fire* that the stationers concerned have a 'just fear ... lest Popish and
Blasphemous Books should grow so numerous, as to become a considerable
(if not the greatest) part of our Trade, and so we be tempted to be Venders
of such Loathsom Ware, or else necessitated to leave our Callings to keep
our Consciences pure' (p.3).

The third point relates as directly to confessional difference as it does
to press control. Pride points out that Fawne included the anti-episcopal *The
Christian Moderator* among popish books because it 'holds forth an absolute
incoertion in matters of inward beleef' (B2v) – as so often in the 17th
century, 'popish' is used as a generalised term of abuse – and that, anyhow,
popish books wisely read may do more good than ill:

> The greatest part of them only hold forth Morall Divinity, as they call it, with
> exhortation to, and rules of good life; ... and if these books have 19 parts of good
> Matter, and the 20th part Popery, it were great pitty the much good should suffer for
> the little evill.... (B3r)

This is an attitude similar to that which William Crashaw had declared 40
years previously in his compilation *Manuale Catholicorum* (1611), that 'it
is no small point of wisdome, to seeke out gold out of mire and clay' (F7v-
8r). Fawne's retort to Pride, however, highlights the difference between the
moderate and the hard-liner, between the advocates of personal expurgation
and those of banning: if Pride's argument were true 'it would prove it pity
and folly to throw away a whole gile of beer that hath a gallon of strong
poyson in it' (p.20).

The poison of popish books is a bargaining counter essential to the
Presbyterian interest: admission that a judicious reading of them could do
no harm would have obviated the perceived need for censorship. The two
planks of Fawne's case are that many booksellers and printers do not qualify
as competent and able judges of a text, and that by the time the state has
caught up with a 'popish, Blasphemous, Treasonable Book' it will have
already been printed, sold and read: 'when the Steed is stolen you'l shut the
Stable door' (p.8). The issue is one of the rights and judgemental abilities
of the individual conscience, and the problem of Catholic texts serves as a
paradigm. But Fawne's learned pious man and Pride's wise reader both
serve as exceptions to the general rule: either that popish books may not be
read, or that much of a popish book should not be attended to. Definitions
of wisdom are polarised, but both sides are agreed in their desire to restrict

reading of popish books to the wise. In effect, too, Fawne and his allies are aiming to set up a system hardly different from that which prevailed at Lambeth Palace, echoing the earlier Puritan critiques of Archbishop Whitgift's suggestions for press control which suggested substituting four divines and four lawyers for the Archbishop of Canterbury and the Bishop of London. The only difference – and perhaps it is not large – is between an episcopacy and a godly elite self-styled responsible.

Libraries were a mechanism for allowing the perusal of dangerous matter by appropriate readers. Anti-popery was a factor behind the Henrician dispersal of monastic libraries; but a generation later, it was often the impetus for amassing post-Reformation libraries, and influenced their composition.[23] William Crashaw described his motives for Protestant antiquarianism as 'to gather up such Antiquities though they be scattered and almost lost in these old worme-eaten Manuscripts wherein they lie buried, which ... Gods providence hath delivered from the force and fury of the inquisitors fire'; he says nothing, though, about the pillage of the Henrician reformers.[24] Thomas James, the first keeper of the Bodleian, had as a strong motive for accepting the job the possibility of refuting Romish error by collating manuscripts of the Church Fathers and comparing them with corrupt Catholic editions; this prompted him to acquire a number of patristic MSS and a comprehensive printed theological collection with a number of Catholic books. In pamphlets of his such as *A Treatise of the Corruption of the Scriptures* (1611) he makes his charges of corruption more explicit, expressing fears that papists have elevated false prophets to patristic status, corrupted the true fathers, introduced even into their Bibles 'sundry varieties and contrarieties' (*2r) and travestied censorship with the Papal Index: the remedy is seen to be pamphlet warfare. In the Appendix to the Reader opinion modulates into hearsay and prejudice: James tells of men in the Vatican Library who 'it is to be feared' imitate ancient script:

In copying out of bookes, they doe adde, and take away, alter and change the words.... And so these transcripts may within a few yeares, (by reason of their counterfaicting the auncient hands) be auouched for very old Manuscripts; deluding the world with a shew of Antiquitie. The danger is the greater, because there may be an *Index Expurgatorius* (for ought that wee know) for purgeing the Manuscripts, as well as the Printed bookes. (A4r)

The qualifications are significant, and to do with a perennial Protestant preoccupation in the area of patristics; wishing to prove that their church had an existence before Luther, affirmative evidence for Protestant beliefs from antiquity was assiduously sought in an attempt to prove that it was only

Protestantism that could be justified by history. James is not relating fact, but expressing a distopian fear that under Catholic regimes history – and more importantly theology – may be rewritten. The Bodleian thus assumes a greater significance as a fall-out shelter of truth.[25]

Protestant libraries could also be conceived as potentially having refugee status, textual equivalents to the Marian exiles canonised by John Foxe. At the other end of the 17th century from Thomas James, Dr Williams, in setting up the library that bears his name, provided that in the event of a state reversion to Catholicism his estate given over for charitable purposes should pass at once to the magistrates of Glasgow and Edinburgh: as P.L. Heyworth points out in *The Book Collector*, 'That Scotland might lapse was unimaginable to him'.[26] Archbishop Bancroft too, when setting up the library at Lambeth Palace, provided for his books to be given to Chelsea College, James I's projected academy for Protestant learning and polemic, if the Lambeth foundation failed.[27]

The need for a repository of popish books to consult for authoritative refutation was obvious. The first contradiction that arises – that these were books that could be and were confiscated from ordinary people – is explained to some extent by the militaristic metaphors employed about them. Thomas Fuller described the library at Lambeth Palace in martial terms, 'a spiritual garrison, with a magazine of all books for that purpose, where learned divines should study and write in maintenance of all controversies against the papists'.[28] Perhaps an even better analogy is that of a dispensary, where poisonous substances are issued but carefully controlled. It was possible for a reputable polemicist like William Crashaw to write to government officials and ask them for confiscated books to use in his refutations, and to build up a large personal collection of Catholic books and manuscripts to supplement official sources, which in his will he was to distribute to centres of learning around the country.[29]

Archbishop Bancroft's and his successor George Abbot's library catalogues have an impressively large collection of Catholic texts – vulgates, missals, works of scholarship and of polemic by English and foreign Catholics – and Bancroft's catalogue, at least, seems to imply separation of Catholic works from Protestant by shelf-arrangement.[30] This has obvious practical implications, but also a symbolic and eschatological significance: sheep are divided from goats. The idea of separating orthodox books from heretical also figures in an anti-Catholic fantasy, the 'Treatise touching some … Studies and Practjses of the Jesuits' appended to the anonymous English translation of *Aphorismes* (1609). In the Jesuit study sound and unsound writers are distinguished from each other by location and by colour-coded bindings:

> Turne thee to the right side, and thou shalt see a very choice and well furnished library, with all sorts of authors, all the bookes, are bound in leather or very Cleane Vellume, and glitter againe with gold and siluer ... there are no bookes of heretikes ..., for they iudge them unworthy to haue any place amongst the rest: and it may be, that they feare lest they should infect others with some pestilent contagion: wherefore turn thee now to the left side, and there thou shalt see the miserable bookes of heretiks, placed in very mournefull and heavy manner, and the same bound in black leather and foule parchment, & all of them died ouer with blacke and sad Colour. (p.10, i.e. 8)[31]

Junior members of the college, it is claimed, are not allowed to read any book from these shelves until they have written a refutation of it. The dark implications of this fantasy are enlarged upon in another passage, where the collection of instruments of torture in the Jesuit dungeons is referred to as a 'wonderfull library' (p.5). The implication is that the Jesuits' knowledge is all of the refinements of pain, and all their text is wrung from the lips of tortured heretics. It is a literal interpretation of the titles of polemical pamphlets, which often called themselves whips, racks and swords. More importantly, it sets up the Catholic library as a dishonourable alternative to the Protestant garrison: fair fight versus torture-chamber.

The division of Catholic books from Protestant takes a number of forms. As seen above, it can be dualistic, a polarisation of orthodoxy with heresy, though in libraries this is more likely to occur with polemic or sacred texts than in areas such as history. To booksellers Catholic books were a grey area. Andrew Maunsell's 1595 *Catalogue of English Printed Bookes* says primly in its prologue:

> The auncient Popish Bookes that haue beene Printed heere, I haue also inserted among the rest, but the Bookes written by the fugitiue Papistes, as also those that are written against the present gouernment, I doe not thinke meete for me to meddle withall. (π.i 3v)

Notwithstanding this assurance, a number of manuscript copies of an addendum to the catalogue survive. They are almost identical, suggesting a common source − Maunsell himself, perhaps, or some other bookseller − and include a *Catalogus librorum prohibitorum papistarum* with lists of the publications of other groups frowned upon by the state such as Brownists and Familists. The clandestine nature of this bibliography invites a number of questions: did all copies have this addition?; what does it tell us about the regularity with which prohibited texts were available for sale?; did one have to pay more for all prohibited matter on the black market? Most importantly, though, the division between written and printed text confirms rather than challenges the prevailing order. The bookseller who commissioned the manuscript additions was acting illegally but not subversively.[32]

Division of Catholic and Protestant books could also be a judicial act, weighing up each side's store of truth to find the heavier. For obvious reasons, evidence for this sort of procedure comes from the accounts of converts or from personal manuscripts: one records resolution, the other confusion. An example of the latter is the commonplace-book of the Somers family in Cambridge University Library: this records the spiritual struggles experienced by one member of the family as he debated whether to convert to Catholicism or to stay within the Church of England.[33] As part of his impassioned internal dialectic he lists Catholic books against Protestant, roughly equal numbers of each, and compares the experience of reading these controversial volumes with the 'sev[er]all Conferances' he has had with 'diuers men on both sides' (p.17): from the Catholics among whom, one may guess, he may have obtained the clandestine material. The manuscript, sadly, does not relate what Somers' final decision was, but for this purpose it suffices to point out that the polarisation of texts could also be an expression of perplexity.

More often, though, the reading of popish books must have served only to reinforce previously held convictions. Anne Sadleir asserted to her Catholic nephew Herbert Aston in a letter of 1663: 'this advantage I must tell you our Religion haue ouer yours wee haue the Liberty to read all bookes as well as yours though you must read none of ours, but you must confess it as a sin'. One must remember that Sadleir was a Royalist and an Anglican, more likely to encounter latitude in the matter of reading popish books than the Presbyterian discussed earlier. But her later comments suggest that this ostensible freedom conceals a reliably Anglican precon-ditioned response:

I thank allmighty god they haue bin soe far from conuerting me, that they haue more confermed me in my owne, Sum I haue read that I must tell you I stand Amased at ... one of them called the flower of The English Saints, which I take to be but the Romances of those times, but if beleued as truths, then I haue nothing to say but what the blessed apostle has saide before me ... they recaiued not the loue of the truth that they might be saued....[34]

So far the discussion has been largely of controversial texts. Even where Protestant has quoted Catholic the division between confessional sympathies has been assumed to be clear, and with some reason: yet it would mimic the controversy of the time to present too one-sided a picture. Even with religious material there is plenty of evidence of textual traffic between the two sides; the simple tenets of devotional literature, in particular, could be subscribed to equally by both Catholic and Protestant. Yet even where Catholic texts were exploited in England an element of apology was often involved. Emblem books are an example of this. Like the whole genre of the emblem, they were evolved both by Catholic and by Protestant, and the textual give-and-take between countries and faiths can often be charted precisely: partly because of the high cost and continental superiority of emblematic engravings, partly because images are more easily identifiable than ideas.[35] But some nervousness is discernible in Edmund Arwaker's preface to his translation of the Jesuit Hermann Hugo's *Pia Desideria* (1686):

In the fourteenth Poem of the first Book [the author] had a fair opportunity of mentioning Purgatory, he wholly declines it.... And in the twelfth Poem of the third Book he says nothing at all of *Transubstantiation*, tho he had occasion to mention the Sacrament of the Eucharist. And this particularly I thought it necessary to offer, lest some may think I have mis-render'd him in those places, which, if they consult himself, they'll find I have had no occasion for. (A7v)

Uncertainty about Catholic books goes hand in hand with ambivalence about Catholic learning. This is demonstrated particularly well in Thomas Salusbury's 1660 translation of P. Daniel Bartolus's *The Learned Man Defended and Reform'd*. Bartolus was a Jesuit, and Salusbury's epistle to the reader is a masterpiece of rhetorical double-think, justifying the worth of the book while at the same time pouring opprobrium on Jesuitical guile. In the main text he first introduces Bartolus as 'a learned Jesuit' which is immediately qualified by a side-note reading 'If it be not Tautology, where to our shame they are all such'. Going on to praise the book as 'replenisht with *Eloquence*' and for sticking to its argument, Salusbury expresses his hope that he will benefit his countrymen by translating it: '... many are brought to a disesteem of *Learning* ... even by *Learned Jesuits* themselves; who are said in strange disguises ... to wound *Learning* with her own Weapons'. Like any anti-Catholic controversialist he then draws aside the curtain of the preface to reveal the enormity of his subject:

Then, I say, see here the true and undessembled *Pourtraict* of a *Jesuit*, pleading for that same *Human Learning*, which others of the same *Order*, do (with *Designs* aim'd higher than this *Innocent Handmaid*) with so much subtlety in our *Climat* oppose;

thus *Retaliating* upon them, their *Learned Suicide* of *Learning*, with this *Jesuitical Refutation* of *English Jesuitism*. (A8)

The logical switchbacks are dizzying. If the learning of Jesuits is declared to work against learning, then the Jesuit text is at its best turned against itself: the act of Englishing is more praiseworthy than the act of writing, and Protestantism is accorded the text in translation. Salusbury certainly seems to have learnt from somewhere the jesuitical arts of casuistry, defensive ingenuity and *suppressio veri*.

The uneasiness displayed here with the idea of a learned Catholic spills over into reactions to Catholic scholars and scholarly material. Catholic writers, even in such dangerous areas as Biblical commentary, were extensively employed by English scholars.[36] As John Selden said in characteristically outspoken vein in *Table-Talk* (1689), 'Popish Books teach and inform, what we know, we know much out of them. The Fathers, Church [hi]Story, Schoolmen, all may pass for Popish Books, and if you take away them, what Learning will you leave?' (p.9). This was a problem of which Protestant scholars were well aware. William Crashaw was one of many who sought to prove that the church fathers had held doctrines acceptable to Protestants, but had been wantonly misrepresented in later years. The question, as with libraries, is that of establishing dominion over a repository of scholarly truth.

In *Areopagitica* Milton postulates that it is the scholarly man, not the ignorant, who is more likely to be converted by popish books (p.519). To counteract this Catholic scholars were subject to constant criticism, some scholarly and some not. As an example one can take the reaction in England to the works of Cardinal Baronius, the Counter-Reformation historian who codified the calendar of Catholic saints and martyrs in his *Annales Ecclesiasti*. Baronius's work was certainly known in England and the *Annales* read. Selden recommends him for ecclesiastical history; and for certain subject areas, particularly Byzantine history, he was the prime source of modern scholarship. Scholarly criticism of Baronius, pioneered by Isaac Casaubon in his *Excertationes contra Baronium* (1614), was nothing new. But in England he is chiefly conspicuous as the bogey-man of anti-Catholic polemic pamphlets. Though summaries and translations of the *Annales* proliferated in Europe from the start, there has never been an English edition: those who read it in England would have had to have it imported. As a work inspired by the Counter-Reformation, according high praise to the Catholic martyrs of England and emphasising the historical justification for papal supremacy, it was unashamedly partisan and was condemned in equally and opposingly partisan tracts.

The interpretation that Baronius places on historical fact is seen to invalidate the facts themselves. The main line of Protestant argument ran thus: if Baronius wishes to prove that the Catholic church depends on submission to the Pope, 'so likewise the overthrowing of that power is the refutation of all *Baronius*'.[37] William Howel's posthumously published *Institution of General History* (Vol.II, 1685) treating of largely the same area of history as the *Annales*, has a preface that purports to sum up the intentions of the author. It reads at the end: 'In particular, that *supream authority* usurped by the *Roman Bishop* is represented, how, and by what means it was first pretended to, but ever rejected by the whole Catholick Church.' Howel's book is setting itself up, or rather being set up, against Baronius. Thomas Comber's *Roman Forgeries in the Councils* (1689) is also typical in denouncing the unreliability of the *Annales* as an historical abstract. Maligning Roman scholarship in general through Baronius in particular, Comber groups Baronius's methods of falsification under seven heads: quoting forged or spurious tracts and late writers, corrupting the words and sense of reliable writers like St Augustine, suppressing or contradicting authorities, taking his own suppositions as grounds of argument, contradicting even himself in Rome's interest, making false inferences, and displaying a polemic particularity towards the Church of Rome. The idea of methodical, wilful and sophisticated falsification is paramount. Comber further regrets that those interested in ecclesiastical antiquity are 'forced to seek it in the Roman Editions of the Councils, and the Modern Historians of the Church: Where every thing is misrepresented and placed in so False a Light, that its [*sic*] hard to find out what is Truth' (Preface). This genuine apprehensiveness echoes that of Thomas James quoted earlier, and goes right to the core of Protestant fears about the Catholic text: that the textual falsification of the Catholic historian rewrites truth. As the motto on Picture I says: 'A thief is better than a man who is accustomed to lie: but they both shall have destruction to heritage.'

The requirements of polemic are twofold: liberality to one's own side, counterbalanced by draconian standards applied to one's opponent. Historically dubious material, therefore, can also be used as a Protestant weapon. Alexander Cooke's dialogue *Pope Ioane* (1610) is a classic example of how an apocryphal figure could be elevated to the status of fact in the cause of invective. Baronius is taken to task for not giving the female prelate historical validity: (PROTESTANT) '... he brings no other proofe thereof than *teste meipso*, which how ever it may go for proofe among Princes, yet is no proofe among scholers. And, for my part, without proofe, I beleeue nothing, whosoever he be, that speaks it, especially if he be a Papist' (p.43). The message, ultimately, is simple: because papists are liars, mutability and untrustworthiness condemn any text with which they are associated.

How did Catholics respond to this assiduously fostered atmosphere of textual disbelief and hostility? Stray pieces of evidence survive. The book trade could occasion demonstrations: the Spanish noblewoman doña Luisa de Carvajal, who devoted her life to the cause of English Catholicism, staged public anti-Protestant demonstrations at booksellers' shops, tearing up caricatures of the Pope and engaging the proprietors in public debate.[38] In a dialogue performed at St Omer in 1599, the character Indignatio, a personification of Protestantism, declares that Catholics are operating a thriving black market in books to be compared with other forms of clandestine religious operation: 'Our enemies are alive, and sell their writings in safety; their assemblies operate widely in secret, they celebrate masses' (l.118-21).[39]

But it is perhaps appropriate to end this paper with how some Catholics responded to anti-Catholic prejudice with conscious self-censorship; the internal conflicts that took place, pitting confessional and evangelical obligations against the considerations of prudence and practicality, one can only guess at.

Catholics could doctor for a Protestant audience material from an explicitly Counter-Reformation tradition. William Byrd, well-known as a crypto-Catholic who managed nevertheless to be accepted within court Protestantism, published a musical setting of some verses on the death of the martyr Edmund Campion with all the references to Campion excised, and praise of 'the Martirs of auncient times' substituted.[40] Attempts were also made to impose the rulings of the Papal Index on English Catholics. Henry Holden's *Check: or Inquiry into the late Act of the Roman Inquisition* (1662) is, though Catholic, hostile to what he saw as the Jesuit insistence on papal legislation. Objecting to the condemnation of Thomas White's books by the inquisition, he remarks that sometimes books are only prohibited in England for the inappropriate reason that they go against the decrees of the Council of Trent: '... which rules' he says '(though in themselves excellent) are so unsuitable to the present circumstances of *England*, that very few Catholick writers can observe them: so that almost all the Catholick Books in English are subject to the censure of the Roman Inquisition' (p.13).

Censured by their own side and censored by the other, the achievement of recusant and seminarist writers is all the more remarkable; but it is their lack of visibility that has been a constant feature of English literary history. I hope it will not be adjudged too partisan if I end with a bibliographical exemplum of this lacuna, or erasure, in contradistinction to the ornaments with which I began. Some title-pages of the anti-Catholic *Aphorismes: or Certaine Selected Points of the Doctrine of the Jesuits* have the statutory imprint, 'London', neatly cut out – and inked out first on one copy – guying the bibliographical subterfuge of recusant literature.[41] The gap is far more eloquent than text: this is censorship mocking itself, while making the serious satirical point that textual gaps are the norm among the children of the Father of Lies.

Censorship condemns transgressions of the parameters of orthodoxy, and orthodoxy is defined by opposition to falsity. The continual association of Catholics with textual corruption and deceit is easily assimilable into this model, but there is a ubiquitousness to anti-Catholic prejudice that challenges the idea of censorship as incidental and disciplinary. Hyperbolically, perhaps, but provocatively, Roland Barthes has said:

> True censorship, the ultimate censorship, does not consist in banning (in abridgement, in suppression, in deprivation), but in unduly fostering, in maintaining, retaining, stifling, getting bogged down in ... stereotypes.... Just as a language is better defined by what it obliges to be said ... than by what it forbids to be said ... so social censorship is not found where speech is hindered, but where it is constrained.[42]

References

1. In 'Censorship and English Literature', *Collected Essays. Volume I. Writing and Revolution in Seventeenth-Century England* (Brighton: Harvester, 1985), p.60.
2. *Censorship: 500 Years of Conflict* (New York Public Library, 1984).
3. cf. F.S. Siebert, *Freedom of the Press in England, 1476-1776* (Urbana: U. of Illinois Press, 1952), p.197. All quotations from *Areopagitica* are taken from the edition by Ernest Sirluck in *The Complete Prose Works of John Milton*, vol.III (Yale University Press: New Haven, 1959), pp.480-570; see also Sections 5-8 of the introduction, esp. Section 8 concerning Milton's conception of Catholic falsity.
4. *To the High Court of Parliament: The Humble Remonstrance of the Company of Stationers* (1643), A1v.
5. A.B. Worden, 'Literature and Political Censorship in Early Modern England', in *Too Mighty to be Free: Censorship and the Press in Britain and the Netherlands* (Zutphen: De Walburg, 1987), pp.45-62. Among general accounts of the Catholic book trade are Thomas H. Clancy, *Papist Pamphleteers* (Chicago: Loyola University Press, 1964); H.S. Bennett, *English Books and Readers, 1558 to 1603* (Cambridge University Press, 1965),

pp.74-81, 113-28, 134-7, and *English Books and Readers, 1603 to 1640* (Cambridge University Press, 1970), pp.50-1, 88-91, 94; Leona Rostenberg, *The Minority Press and the English Crown* (Niewkoop: B. de Graaf, 1971); A.C. Southern, *Elizabethan Recusant Prose, 1559-1582* (London: Sands, n.d.). See also the introductions to A.F. Allison & D.M. Rogers, *A Catalogue of Catholic Books in English Printed Abroad or Secretly in England, 1558-1640* (Bognor Regis: Arundel Press, 1956), and *The Contemporary Printed Literature of the English Counter-Reformation between 1558 and 1640. Volume 1, Works in Languages other than English* (Aldershot: Scolar Press, 1989); Thomas H. Clancy, *English Catholic Books, 1641-1700: A Bibliography* (Chicago: Loyola University Press, 1974).

6. cf. the ornament to *The Jesuits Character* (1679).
7. *Legenda Lignea* (1652) prints 53 names in red type in the section 'A Legend of Revolters to Rome'.
8. See captions to figs.2, 3 & 4. Fig.2 can also be found on the title-pages of *Texeda Retextus* (1623) and *Hispanus Convertus* (1623); Fig.3 (in addition to the publications cited by Lavin) can be found in *The Reigne of King Edward the Third* (1599) and Isaac Bargrave, *A Sermon Preached before the Honourable Assembly of Knights, Citizens and Burgesses* (1624).
9. See *The Solemn Mock Procession of the Pope, Cardinalls, Jesuits, Fryers, etc.* (1679: engraving); *The Popes Down-Fall at Abergavenny* (1679); *The Solemn Mock-Procession of the Pope Cardinalls Jesuits Fryers &c* (1680: engraving); *A True Account of the Trial, Condemnation and Burning of the Pope at Aberdene* (1689); *The Account of the Popes Procession at Aberdene* (1689).
10. *The Acts and Monuments of John Foxe*, ed. S.R. Cattley (London: B. Seeley, 1837), vol.III, pp.719-20. See Rosemary O'Day, *The Debate on the English Reformation* (London: Methuen, 1986), p.26.
11. See George Kitchin, *Sir Roger L'Estrange* (1913: repr. New York: Augustus M. Kelley, 1971); G.M. Peerbooms, *Nathaniel Thompson: Tory Printer, Ballad Monger and Propagandist* (Nijmegen: N. Sheldruk, 1983).
12. The third note advises those with some popish intelligence to take it to Nathaniel Thompson.
13. See *'Risus Anglicanus': John Hacket, 'Loiola'*, facsimiles ed. Malcolm M. Brennan (Hildesheim: Georg Olms Verlag, 1988). The reference is to 1.478-9.
14. See Bernard Capp, *English Almanacs 1500-1800: Astrology and the Popular Press* (Ithaca: Cornell University Press, 1979), pp.150-1; John N. King, 'The Account Book of a Marian Bookseller, 1553-1554', *British Library Journal* 13.1 (1987), pp.33-57; Robert Whiting, *The Blind Devotion of the People: Popular Religion and the English Reformation* (Cambridge University Press, 1989), ch.10.
15. Margaret Spufford, *Small Books and Pleasant Histories: Popular Fiction and its Readership in the Seventeenth Century* (Athens, Georgia: University of Georgia Press, 1981); Tessa Watt, *Cheap Print and Popular Piety, 1550-1640* (Cambridge University Press, 1991).
16. Bennett (1970), p.90.
17. Another N.N., in *The Arts and Pernicious Designs of Rome* (1680), alleges that he has come to '*think* and *speak* of Things so as I do, either from *their own printed Books*, or from *their private writings* (which I have seen and at times transcribed for them) ...' (A1v). See Nancy Pollard Brown, 'Paperchase: The Dissemination of Catholic Texts in

Elizabethan England', *English Manuscript Studies, 1100-1700.* vol.I, ed. Peter Beal & Jeremy Griffiths (Oxford: Basil Blackwell, 1989), pp.120-43.

18. *The Catholic Subjects of Elizabeth I* (London: George Allen & Unwin, 1978), p.103.

19. *A Booke of Christian Exercise* (1st ed. 1584). Richard Rogers, in *Seven Treatises* (1603) complains that Persons's book has been 'in the hands of thousands' and is all the more dangerous because of its 'pretended shew of godlines', i.e. its superficial resemblance to Protestant counterparts (A6v). The list of popish books in *A Beacon Set on Fire* (1652) mentions '*Parson's Resolutions*, as he first put it forth without *Bunny's* Correction, (p.9).

20. Siebert (1952), pp.44-6, points out that Henry VIII's list of prohibited anti-Lutheran books in 1529 preceded the first continental Index by 15 years.

21. Lewis Owen's *The Running Register* (1626) complains about expatriate printing-presses and the high price of books they issue (p.14).

22. The Stationers' Company — whose court Fawne had challenged earlier in his career — tended to have a vested interest in supporting acts for the regulation of printing. See Cyprian Blagden, *The Stationers' Company* (London: George Allen & Unwin, 1960), ch.8, esp. p.147 re. the Printing Act of 1653; Siebert (1952), pp.226-7. See also Sheila Lambert, *above.*

23. See W.D.J. Cargill Thompson, 'Notes on King's College Library, 1500-1700, in particular for the period of the Reformation', *Transactions of the Cambridge Bibliographical Society* II (1954), pp.38-54.

24. *Manuale Catholicorum* (1611), A7r.

25. cf. William Guild, *Three Rare Monuments of Antiquitie* (1624), pp.10-14.

26. In 'Unfamiliar Libraries XVI: The Forbes Library', *The Book Collector* 19:3 (1970), pp.317-27 (quotation p.322).

27. M.R. James, 'The History of Lambeth Palace Library', *Transactions of the Cambridge Bibliographical Society* III (1959), pp.1-31; Geoffrey Bill, 'Lambeth Palace Library', *The Library*, 5th ser., XXI (1966), pp.192-206; Anne Cox-Johnson, 'Lambeth Palace Library, 1610-1664', *Transactions of the Cambridge Bibliographical Society* II (1954-1958), pp.105-26.

28. *Church History* (1665) X, p.51.

29. See P.J. Wallis, 'The Library of William Crashawe', *Transactions of the Cambridge Bibliographical Society* 3:3 (1956), pp.213-28, 'William Crashaw, the Sheffield Puritan', reprinted with addenda and index from *Transactions of the Hunter Archaeological Society*, VIII, parts 2-5, 1960-63; Kenneth Larsen, 'The Religious Sources of Crashaw's Sacred Poetry' (Cambridge PhD thesis, 1969), p.19; Thomas F. Healy, *Richard Crashaw* (Leiden: E.J. Brill, 1986), pp.16-22.

30. Both survive at Lambeth Palace Library. (I am grateful to Mary Nixon for suggesting these.)

31. Anthony Kenny describes how in his time at the English College, Rome, books on the Index, but in the College library, were marked with a red blob on the spine to show that they could not be read without a dispensation: *A Path From Rome* (Oxford University Press, 1988), p.75. (I am grateful to Tim Pitt-Payne for pointing this out.)

32. Copies at Trinity College, Cambridge (VI, 3.60 (1-2); Lambeth Palace (1595.4). I am most grateful to Arnold Hunt for drawing this, with the material in Notes 19 and 34, to my attention.

33. U.L.C. Dd. 14.25 (3), pp.13-17.

34. Trinity College, Cambridge (MS. R.5.5. (James 699) f.10). Anne Sadleir is quoting 2

Thessalonians 2.10, a favourite chapter with anti-Catholic polemicists for its mention of the mystery of iniquity (v.7) and the man of sin (v.3) identified as being Catholicism and the Pope.

35. Barbara Lewalski, *Protestant Poetics and the Seventeenth-Century Religious Lyric* (New Jersey: Princeton U.K. 1979) ch.6; Rosemary Freeman, *English Emblem Books* (London: Chatto & Windus, 1948), esp. pp.117 ff., 132, 134, 139.

36. Arnold Williams, *The Common Expositor* (U. of North Carolina Press: Chapel Hill, 1958), p.33.

37. Pierre du-Moulin (i.e. Doulin), *A Short and True Account of the Several Advances the Church of England hath made towards Rome* (1680), chapter 13.

38. See *Vida y virtudes de la Venerabile Virgen Dona Luisa de Carvajal y Mendoza, su jornada a Inglaterra* (Madrid, 1632) trans. Lady Georgiana Fullerton, *The Life of Luisa de Carvajal* (London: Burns & Oates, 1873); Michael Williams, *St. Alban's College, Valladolid* (London: C. Hurst, 1986), pp.64-6; Sherrin Marshall (ed.), *Women in Reformation and Counter-Reformation Europe: Private and Public Worlds* (Bloomington: Indiana U.P., 1990).

39. Historical Manuscripts Commission, MSS. of the Marquess of Salisbury at Hatfield, IX, 420. *Brevis dialoguismus* has been translated and edited by Victor Houliston: I am grateful to him for supplying me with a copy.

40. See J.H. Pollen (ed.), William Allen, *A Brief Historie of the Glorious Martyrdom of Twelve Reverend Priests* (London: Burns & Oates, 1908), pp.xix-xx. For Byrd in general, see Peter le huray, *Music and the Reformation in England, 1549-1600* (Cambridge University Press, 1978), pp.229-234; under name in Stanley Sadie (ed.), *The New Grove Dictionary of Music and Musicians* (London: Macmillan, 1980), vol.3.

41. See copies in U.L.C. (Syn.7.60.29[14]) and Jesus College, Cambridge (D.12.15[2]).

42. *Sade, Fourier, Loyola*, trans. Richard Miller (London: Jonathan Cape, 1977), p.126.

'The fiery Tryal of their Infallible Examination': self-control in the regulation of Quaker publishing in England from the 1670s to the mid 19th century

DAVID J. HALL

'FRIENDS, to you all that answers any books or writes forth any papers to be printed, let them be sent to Robert Drings, at Moorfields to be seen and read before they go to the press.' Those words of George Fox, the most prominent of the first leaders of Quakerism, probably come from the mid-1650s.[1] They set the scene for my theme which is dominated by the Morning Meeting's effective control of the greater part of Quaker publishing in England from the 1670s until the early 19th century. The main concern of this paper is the establishment and operation of this system of internal control and the principal source is the administrative records of the Society of Friends in England at the national level. The 17th-century position is already quite well known but some of the examples used to illustrate it may be less familiar and an introductory description is necessary as a foundation for the narrative continuing to 1860.[2] The evidence from the national records can be supplemented with the comments of some critics and some examples of control of the press at the local level.

The first Friends' publications appeared early in the 1650s. In the 1660s they averaged 117 per year or approximately 13 per cent of the national total of publications recorded by Wing; for the 1670s these figures were 65 per year and seven per cent.[3] By the 1700s however the annual average of Quaker publications dropped to six, after something of a brief surge in the wake of the Act of Toleration. These figures are possibly misleading in that they take no account of the relative size of the publications in the sample; it may be that the reduction in the 1670s resulted partly from the activities of the Morning Meeting as well as from external constraints or loss of the initial enthusiasm of the first Quakers. There were, too, some controls before the Morning Meeting's work began in 1673: 'the check, such as it was, upon unwise publications, was not exercised by any public licenser, but by the authority of the leaders'.[4] One Friend was found rejoicing at the end of 1653 that George Fox was to view all books before they were printed.[5]

As the Friends' business meetings evolved at local level they took on some responsibility for the regulation of publishing, not merely for the censorship or approval of suitable texts but also arrangements for printing, proof-reading, finance and distribution. The Somersetshire Quarterly Meeting in 1659 produced a document of nine advices signed by 45 Friends, the ninth of which reads:

> That if a necessity be layd upon any friend or friends to write and printe any booke or books for the service of truth that the Coppys be first tryed and weighed by such persons who are able to judge thereof in the wisdome of God, and the Coppys thereof being allowed by such persons, the charge of printing may be borne by the publique stock so much thereof as shall not be raysed by the booke so printed, and that such books as are or may not be sold shalbe payde for by the publique stocke, care may be taken for the distributing of them to the severall meetings, and for such books as are already printed for the service aforesaid and approved by friends as aforesaid, an exact accompt be delivered in what moneys were disburst for such books, and by whom and how many of them remayne unsold, and that they may be brought forth or be in readiness to be dispersed to every meeting or otherwise as by the generall meeting may be thought fitt, and that such moneys as yett remayne on the charge of any particuler friend for the said service may be satisfyed out of the publique receipts.[6]

That passage also sheds light on the early general arrangements for dealing with Quaker publications once a manuscript was approved, and the degree of organisation demonstrated may help to account for their proliferation.

Constraints on publication imposed from outside the Society of Friends are not directly part of the theme of this paper, though it must be remembered that the earlier publications were in defiance of the law. Quaker publishing had several main aims; defending through the printed word the integrity and existence of the movement, including answering hostile publications; attempting to disseminate the Quaker message in the wider world at home and abroad and sustaining Friends themselves in their daily lives and spiritual journeys. Persecution or adverse comment came from state, church, their local representatives or private individuals – sometimes disenchanted Friends – in a torrent of literature.[7] Quaker enthusiasm had to be curbed too as it became evident that intemperate, inaccurate, repetitive works could discredit Friends, and the early controls attempted to stop their publication and pre-empt attacks while husbanding resources for the publication of useful works. John Hetet suggests that the process began with financial support for publication being sought through the Quaker leaders and then developed into a system for control of the text.[8] His view of early

Quaker publishing is very much concerned with the practicalities of the book trade and he argues that the Quakers 'developed their own press arrangements because of the problems they faced in obtaining a reliable and accurate service from the book trade. Their attitude reflects a certain scepticism towards the motives of the trade.'[9] For a recent account of the political context of early Quaker publishing and of the part played by Quaker literature in the Society's relationship with the state the reader is referred to an article by Thomas O'Malley.[10]

In 1672 the Yearly Meeting of Friends appointed a group of ten to see that books were carefully corrected and that no new book or new edition was printed except by order.[11] This printing committee continued in being until 1679 but its work soon overlapped with that of the Morning Meeting (properly the Second Day's Morning Meeting) set up in 1673 to consider works submitted for publication, to answer adverse publications and to take responsibility for the ministry in the London meetings.[12] This meeting also collected two copies of each book written by Friends and one of any adverse book, thus creating the present library of the Religious Society of Friends.[13] The Morning Meeting minuted in 1673 that: 'when bookes come that are not approved of the sence of the brethren to be signified to the Authors' and then in 1674 regularised the position in relation to the printers used by the Society: 'Agreed upon that hereafter A.S., B.C. nor other print any bookes but what is first read and approved of in this meeting and that the Tytle of each booke that is approved of and ordered to be printed be entred in this booke, and that A.S., B.C. and all others who print for friends receive their books of E.H.'.[14] The Society next set up the Meeting for Sufferings in 1675, a standing executive committee with the prime responsibility of responding to and recording the sufferings of Friends. This meeting dealt with the practicalities of the printing and distribution of Friends' books approved for publication by the Morning Meeting, though the dividing line between the two meetings should not be considered that rigid. Both meetings met weekly for many years and, although it could be argued that the Morning Meeting's deliberations slowed down the publication process, works could be produced very quickly. In 1679 the Meeting for Sufferings recognised that the printing committee was no longer necessary as its members came to the Meeting and agreed: 'That all bookes read at second days morning meeting be presented to ye meeting of sufferings who are to order and direct ye manner and number of books and ye printer thereof'.[15] There are nevertheless regular examples of the Morning Meeting actually deciding the number of copies to be printed.

From time to time the ground rules were modified in the light of experience or reiterated as a reminder. In 1699 Friends were urged to: 'take care to keep to the ancient and General agreement of Friends, That before anything Relating to the Doctrines and Principles of Truth be published It be first sent to the Friends and Brethren of this meeting for their Concurrence'.[16] Then in 1701 the Morning Meeting considered a reminder to Yearly Meeting about answering adverse books, recommending the appointment of local Friends 'in the Severall Countyes' to read them over and to be prepared to answer them.[17] Next in 1702 the Yearly Meeting of Ministering Friends in London issued a series of 21 advices to all Quaker ministers; the 20th was against giving authors of manuscripts 'expectation of their being Printed before they are approved by the 2d days Morning Meeting...'[18] In 1738 the Yearly Meeting issued in manuscript the first attempt at a codification of Quaker rules for administration incorporating guidance on Quakerly behaviour, the *Christian and Brotherly Advices*, generally known as the Book of Extracts. Under the heading 'Books' this repeated the earlier advices and rules concerning the production and distribution of books. It was revised and reprinted in 1783 and then restated helpfully the 1706 rule establishing the Morning Meeting's responsibility to co-operate with the Meeting for Sufferings.[19] Rules or arrangements seem occasionally to have become temporarily forgotten, for example in 1742 the Yearly Meeting had to ask for a copy of the rules on revising, printing or reprinting books though when they received this from the Morning Meeting in 1743 the matter was 'left as usual'.[20]

The official Quaker view of the process of controlling publications thus set up would have been that it was a necessary part of the organisation of the Society. The contrary view of this censorship would be that it restricted freedom of expression. All rule-making and formal organisation within Quakerism can potentially be seen as contrary to the Spirit of the movement's original ideas but Fox himself played a major part in devising the framework of Quaker church government. The organisation went on to ensure the survival of the movement in a period of persecution but some tension between the needs for both freedom of the spirit and organisation continued intermittently throughout the period of this study. O'Malley records some opposition to Quaker publications based on allegations of interference from the central Quaker bodies and it is salutary to see that Fox himself was crossed by the system when a paper of his proved unacceptable. He wrote:

I was not moved to set up that meeting to make orders against the reading of my papers; but to gather up bad books that was scandalous against Friends; and to see that young Friends' books that was sent to be printed might be stood by; ... and not for them to have an authority over the Monthly and Quarterly and other Meetings or for them to stop things to the nation which I was moved of the Lord to give forth to them.[21]

Before going on to look in some detail at the work of the Morning Meeting as described by its own records it may be worth considering some observations by two of its external critics. These will remind us that there was more vehemence in the business of religious literature than the restrained formality of the Morning Meeting's minutes usually indicates. Charles Leslie wrote critically of the editing of Quaker texts for publication in 1696:

let them take time, and put in such Expressions, as oft they please, in the New Edition of G. Fox's Works, according to their Laudable Custom, before spoke of, to chop and change the writings of their Dead Prophets, to answer the Exigency of the Times: Tho', if what they wrote was Dictated Immediately by the Holy Ghost, as they pretend, they are of Equal Authority with the Scriptures; and it must be as great a sin to Add or Diminish in the Writings of the Quakers as in the holy Scriptures themselves.[22]

This observation was part of a lively and broader controversy between Leslie and the Quakers generating a substantial if repetitive literature so that Leslie having published his *Snake in the Grass* came back to its defence more than once.[23] Francis Bugg refers specifically to the Morning Meeting in his *The Pilgrim's Progress from Quakerism to Christianity*: 'that Meeting where Satan dwells and where he employs his archest Emissaries...'[24] Bugg was a former Quaker and he certainly had some understanding of the process:

This Meeting of the Quakers is held every Second-Day of the Week, ... throughout the Year in London; the Members of it are the Teachers of the Quakers reciding in and about London;... This Meeting doth much resemble His Majesty's Privy Council: For the King, by and with the Advice of his Privy Council, can do many things... So can this Meeting; ... they can alter, and change any Message, stop any Prophesie, stifle any Revelation, silence the Voice uttered by the Spirit of the Lord, thro' their most eminent Prophets, in what respect they please, and make it speak louder and more shril, where they think there is most Service, or may be more conducive to their Designs; ... they are the Wheel within the Wheel, which move all the whole Work, yet so invisibly, as few shall know how, and fewer know who; for they are Persons uncertain and accidental, and cannot be chargeable by Name, for any Errour, tho' guilty of every Errour in their Books, so far as Consent, Approbation and Recommendationcan make them: For all Books Printed and Reprinted, pass thro' the fiery Tryal of their Infallible Examination; they Govern, they Rule, they steer the Vessel, but all INVISIBLY; ... their principal Work is, to Approve and License their Books, Printed for the Service of the Truth as they phrase it: But the last being their most principal Verb, I shall the more insist upon it, to shew their most horrible Deceit and Hypocrisie; For, suppose one of their People pretend, he is moved of the Lord, by his Eternal Spirit, to write a Message or Warning to the Inhabitants of Bristol, with this Title; THIS IS THE WORD OF THE LORD, TO THEE, O BRISTOL! Well, this Book is sent up to their Second-Day Meeting, and there they take into consideration; they then will Alter, and Change Words and Sentences, put in, and leave out, what they conceive suit best with the Times; and yet, let it go as THE WORD OF THE LORD ... of this most horrible Deceit I could give a hundred Instances, and find Matter enough for to write a Book by it self...[25]

Bugg goes on to illustrate his case against the editing of texts with the example of Friends' treatment of Edward Burrough's 1656 *A Trumpet of the Lord sounded out of Sion* between its first publication and its reappearance in Burrough's collected works in 1672, *The Memorable Works of a Son of Thunder and Consolation...* The hostile writers argued that if Burrough had written down the word of the Lord in 1656 it should have surely remained constant. The Morning Meeting could have replied that its considered version of the text was arrived at under divine inspiration too. The argument will reappear taken up by later Quaker writers who see things rather as Bugg and Leslie did. Professor McKenzie sums up the position:

The Friends, for example, not only insisted that new texts be orthodox, but they held to a very firm principle that their own old books must be reformed. This of course made reprints a matter of special concern, since the text, as reprinted, had to be wholly acceptable as an immediate and living truth. So when Isaac Penington's works were being reprinted in 1680-81, it was ordered that a number of underscored lines in one text must 'be wholly left out of all Impressions; Ben Clarke to take care therein'. There was no nonsense about the historical objectivity of the original text, but only an over-riding concern for the accurate formulation of truth. This results in the paradox of an extraordinary concern for 'correctness' in the sense of orthodoxy and then, given that, a meticulous concern for accuracy in the mechanics of proof-correction.[26]

Although this was not stated the objection of writers such as Leslie or Bugg was two-edged; not only was it immoral to tamper with the text but by doing so the Morning Meeting tended to remove the most vulnerable areas for their attacks on Friends. The Meeting did after all realise that many critics alleged that the supposed fanaticism or disloyalty of Friends could be proved from their publications.

It is difficult to be sure just how comprehensive the records of the Morning Meeting are. At first sight they seem thorough but references to an author's manuscripts are not always accompanied by a title so that identification of those published after official rejection remains difficult and it is seldom possible to know much at all about rejected titles or the details of the editorial process when the relevant minute is concise. The records of local meetings throughout the country must contain numerous references to manuscripts being sent up to the Morning Meeting or to local arrangements (a few examples will be given later) but they comprise a very formidable body of material from which only a few series have been transcribed and published and those chiefly limited to the 17th century. The account given here therefore is admittedly rather one-sided, and much more work on local records or biographical sources could change its balance. The actual publication of works can of course be checked against Wing or the *Eighteenth Century Short Title Catalogue* in addition to Joseph Smith's quite invaluable *Descriptive Catalogue of Friends' Books*.[27] Many of the Morning Meeting's weekly meetings in the 18th century had the reading of manuscripts as their main or only business and it is clear that a preliminary reading was often followed by reference to a sub-committee or by prolonged section by section consideration over a number of meetings. Later commentators have observed that the Meeting had a substantial workload. Rufus Jones wrote that: 'This work of censorship involved great labour, and resulted in the elimination of many proposed books'.[28] Luella Wright calls the Meeting: 'a long-suffering and superconscientious body of men' and surmises that: 'it is clear that half a day a week would not suffice for accomplishing the work delegated to them, and that many a midnight candle must have burned as the wearied elder perused the crabbed writing of these 17th-century devotees'.[29] Professor Arnold Lloyd wrote that: 'The Morning Meeting read through with scrupulous attention a well-nigh overwhelming mass of manuscript material submitted for publication and rejected gently but firmly a very great deal of unprofitable rubbish'.[30]

A manuscript submitted to the Meeting might encounter a fate varying across a spectrum from unqualified acceptance to outright rejection. My examination of the Morning Meeting minutes still has some way to go but a sample of five years, 1691 to 1695, shows 73 titles accepted, 19 not accepted, and seven where reservations were expressed. Not all the titles accepted were accompanied by a commitment from Friends to secure publication; in some cases the formula was that the author might print the work if he wished. Now, in those five years 236 Quaker publications actually seem to have appeared, 30 of those were reprints or works of non-Quaker content by Friends, but the discrepancy is considerable.[31] Most of the examples quoted below are not of manuscripts considered as straightforward for publication and a more analytical account of the control of publishing ought to take that larger group into account to form a comprehensive picture of the range of acceptable material.

Let us look first at the category of material where the Morning Meeting approved a manuscript for publication but did not recommend that the Society should bear the cost. This was presumably the case with William Bingley's *An Epistle of Love and Tender Advice to Friends in America...* where it was: 'left to him to let what printer he please to print it' in 1689.[32] Rather later the Meeting approved a request in 1758 from John Kendall of Colchester to reprint Isaac Penington's works at his own risk and a substantial two volume quarto appeared in 1761.[33] Kendall was a bookseller, the previous printing of Penington's works was in 1681 and the fact that they were reprinted again in 1684 suggests that Kendall judged his market correctly. In 1763 Abiah Darby was given permission to print and dispense her *Useful Instruction for Children, by way of Question and Answer...* at her own expense, again justified by six 18th-century printings.[34] In one early case the author, Thomas Bayles of Colchester, wanted to have a text approved by the meeting 'printed at his owne Charge and not at the charge of Freinds'.[35] Then there were the titles which the Society's printers were prepared to publish at their own risk. In 1764 Luke Hinde wanted to reprint the 1683 *Counsel to the Christian-Traveller* provided the Meeting for Sufferings would defray the cost of advertising.[36] This was agreed, there were to be 500 copies and it was reprinted four more times with revisions before 1800. In 1772 Mary Hinde obtained approval to reprint eight titles including three by John Woolman, all at her own expense.[37] Sometimes it was decided to print a work only in the quantities required by the local meetings. Many officially issued documents such as the epistles of Yearly Meeting or brief statements of advice on specific subjects, often issued in large quantities, were not for sale.

An important manual of guidance to Friends by Samuel Bownas, first published in 1750, was reprinted in 1767 in complex circumstances. The reprint was agreed by the Morning Meeting and the widow Hinde asked to quote for 500 bound copies (the quotation was £37 10s. or 1s. 6d. per copy in calf, the book is 112 pages in octavo) by the Morning Meeting, not the

Meeting for Sufferings. Enquiry was made of monthly meetings as to the number needed and it was ordered to be printed subject to abbreviating the repetitive introduction.[38] Later in the year the Yearly Meeting sent an instruction to the Morning Meeting:

This Meeting directs that Saml. Bownas's Book, entitled 'Advice to Ministers and Elders', with an abridgement of the Preface as proposed by the Meeting of Ministers and Elders, be reprinted, & that this Impression be subscribed for, and become the Property of Monthly Meetings & be lent out to be read by Ministers and Elders within the same returnable from time to time...[39]

This is a restrictive condition on what appears on the face of it a conventional publication, suggesting strongly that Friends did not welcome wider circulation. Yet another category of the acceptable was when the Morning Meeting took the initiative and suggested that someone else should pay for or even on occasion take the decision to approve a text. In 1770 it looked at a manuscript life of an American Friend, Elizabeth Ashbridge, and sent it to her Monthly Meeting in North America for further consideration.[40] Editions of that title can be found from Nantwich, Cheshire 1774, Liverpool 1806, Philadelphia 1807 and Concord NH 1810 as well as some published later.[41] In another case limited circulation was permitted when the Morning Meeting allowed William Penn to print about 100 copies of *An Account of the Blessed End of Gulielma Maria Penn, and of Springett Penn*, his wife and eldest son, in 1669.[42] Failure to print a work did not prevent its circulation. In 1674 the Meeting decided that Thomas Taylor's epistle *a Loving Seasonable Advice to the Children of Light* should not be printed but: 'spread and read amongst friends in Manuscript where it may be serviceable'.[43] It appeared later in his collected works *Truth's Innocency and Simplicity...* 1697, among 94 previously unpublished writings, mostly very brief. Similarly in 1675: 'John and Margaret Lynams paper was read and freinds did not judge it meet to be printed but corrected and so sent back that they might transcribe it, and dispose of it as necessarily lyes upon them from the Lord...'.[44] These cases probably indicate that the Meeting felt that circulation outside the Friends' community was injudicious though it may perhaps have been that the text was considered of limited value.

Many of the works passed for publication required some editorial work or revision either by Friends appointed for the purpose or by their original author. An early example seems to allow for both processes:

Richard Robinsons paper to the unmarried hath been read And Friends Judgment is that it is unsafe for it to goe as it is, But is the Advice of the meeting he be writt to, that if he will leave it to friends to correct it hee may write his mind therein and Friends may correct it. Friends not being satisfied that he should place soe much upon it as to be a Rule and Law for ever.[45]

This was in 1680; the work appears not to have been published. The reasons for revision could be quite simple. In 1677 two Friends were asked to consider a book by Joan Whitrow and it was: 'desired by this meeting that what is chiefly to her own praise be left out'.[46] The work is probably *The Work of God in a Dying Maid...* printed twice in 1677. The editorial process for George Fox's works was very substantial. Three large volumes resulted – the *Journal*, 1694, *Epistles*, 1698 and *Gospel Truth Demonstrated*, 1706. Their preparation has received some attention from Quaker historians.[47] Fox's *Journal* contained some references to miracles which drew the fire of the violently anti-Quaker polemicist Francis Bugg despite the editorial caution which had resulted in the exclusion of some provocative matter.[48] These references remained in later editions, unlike a couple of other passages in 1694 recounting retribution falling on persecutors, where cancels were issued after initial publication. That arose, not because the fashion had changed, as it would later so that the idea of direct divine retribution falling on the persecutors of Quakers became unacceptable, but because it was felt that the evidence supporting the accounts was inadequate. This interesting editorial initiative from the Morning Meeting was not entirely successful; Cadbury observes that the two new leaves are seldom supplied in extant copies of the book.[49] The Morning Meeting also seems to have quietly suppressed a major work by Fox which has now been reconstructed by Cadbury. In the 1695 manuscript index to the late 17th-century listing of Fox's writings prepared as the groundwork for the three volumes mentioned above, Cadbury discovered about 350 references to a 'Book of Miracles'. Fox had something of a contemporary reputation as a spiritual healer and miracle worker but by the late 17th century doubts had arisen among Friends about the wisdom of making extensive public claims for such gifts. The few such incidents published in the *Journal* played into the hands of their opponents, and the Friends wisely refrained from publishing too many.[50]

Editing required by the Morning Meeting often affected the works of the most important Quaker authors, those whose impact outside the Society might be considerable and whose works in substantial editions might be expected to be consulted over long periods. In the case of William Penn the editors of his select works (1771) omitted a number of references to controversial matters which had been included in the 1726 edition.[51] John

Kendall of Colchester's permission to reprint Isaac Penington's works was subject to his leaving out several sheets. The Dutch Quaker historian Willem Sewel's English version of his *The History of the Rise, Increase, and Progress of the Christian People called Quakers* was considered in detail by the Meeting for Sufferings and a letter survives from Sewel to Theodore Eccleston, who happened to be the Clerk of the Meeting, recounting his trials over the translation.[52] In particular Sewel had presented too openly some of the more extreme events from the earliest Quaker history and his account of James Naylor's trial was replaced by one prepared by an ad hoc committee. The whole process took about six years and it must be said that Sewel was, in general, supported by the Meeting.

The Dutch version of Sewel's *History* had contained some passages not acceptable to English Friends. The problem there was not with the translation but the content. Translation, however, was a major aspect of the control exercised by the Morning Meeting; an unauthorised translation could introduce misleading statements or errors into an acceptable text. The Meeting went to some effort to find good translators and to vet the translations it commissioned or had submitted to it. A translation into High Dutch of Sewel's *History* was sent by the Meeting for Sufferings to Hamburg for review but the only manuscript was lost en route in a shipwreck. The insurance money was used to commission a replacement and after first agreeing the proposal in 1725 the German translation was finally published in 1742.[53] Quaker classics were translated into a number of languages. Barclay's *Apology* appeared first in Latin, then in English, Dutch, German, French, Spanish and Danish before 1800.[54] His *Catechism and Confession of Faith* appeared in Latin, French, Danish and Dutch.[55] William Penn's *Brief Account of the Rise and Progress of the People called Quakers* was translated into French, German, Welsh and Danish.[56] A number of earlier titles were translated into Dutch or (less often) Latin while the emphasis later was on French. The Morning Meeting had to find Friends who were competent to examine translations. In 1675 Richard Richardson had Barclay's translation of the *Catechism* referred to him: 'to compare the Latine with the English and if it be true to print it'.[57] By 1747 enthusiasm for Latin was waning, and a proposal to translate Penn's *No Cross No Crown* was not pursued: 'there appearing at present no demand or use as we know of for the same'.[58]

In 1737 a translation by William Massey of part of *Piety Promoted*, a long-running series of brief biographical accounts of deceased Friends, was brought to the Morning Meeting by John Owen who objected: 'to particular

Expressions as not being in the Style used among friends but the Translator borrowing several terms from Heathen Authors, not agreeable to the Scripture Language nor our holy Profession which book was translated and printed without the knowledge of this Meeting'.[59] Massey came to the Meeting a fortnight later to explain himself but did not convince Friends who returned to the subject after two weeks taken to study his translation:

This Meeting having perused Willm Massey's Translation of Piety promoted, do find that not only the Plainness & Simplicity of Scripture language is Deviated from, and some heathenish Phrases introduced, whereby the Testimony We have to bear in that respect is in degree laid Waste, but also the Doctrine in Translating Misrepresented, and many material Sentences Omitted, Cannot therefore Recommend it to be taught in Friends Schools till a New Impression be made thereof, where in the Language may be restored the Doctrine truly rendred and the Omissions Inserted, according to the Originals, which were printed with the Approbation of Friends.

The Massey episode led to a proposal from the Morning Meeting to the Yearly Meeting that in future they should consider prospective reprints as well as new titles in manuscript.[60] Missionary activity, though not perhaps thought of as a major activity for British Friends in the 18th century, was a spur to a spate of translations into French towards the end of the century. These were dealt with by the Meeting for Sufferings and printed by the Society's printer, James Phillips. Edmond Philip Bridel translated at least eight works for publication in French between 1790 and 1813 ranging from brief texts to new translations of Penn's *No Cross No Crown* and Barclay's *Apology*.[61]

We have seen that the Morning Meeting considered texts already published by Friends as well as manuscripts. If the Meeting disapproved of something printed by one of the printers closely linked to the Society action could be taken to suppress it. Edward Wharton's *New England's present Sufferings under Their Cruel Neighbouring Indians* 1675 brought its printer into deep trouble with the Meeting:

Ordered that the paper (conteyning two letters from E.W.) printed by B. Clerk being a Relation of the Warr in New-England be not dispersed, but brought to John Osgoods there to lye till freindes see meet to deliver them back for waste paper & that B.C. print no bookes for the future but what are first read & approved of by this Meeting.[62]

No reason was given for that decision but the title, not quoted in the minute, may give a clue. Wharton was one of the most prominent of the early much persecuted New England Quakers.[63]

The reasons for the rejection of manuscripts are not always stated or in some cases there is insufficient explanation of the rejection. A text may have been untimely but without an opportunity to study the manuscript we cannot necessarily see why. Those references in the Morning Meeting's minutes that explain a rejection are especially valuable and some examples follow. A manuscript might simply be too long with a worthwhile message obscured by an excess of words, as in Isabel Eston's:

Book called a warning piece ... part read and viewed. Which being not onely large and tedious some things often repeated, But also many Things not clear, Tis not judged meet to bee printed. Tho there be several things, which concern the warning, the light and way of salvation, which are good things and plain. The substance whereof might be abstracted and collected in one sheet...[64]

A work of Abraham Bonifield's at first seemed simply too long — the longest title of the four works recorded after Bonifield became estranged from Friends ran to 184 words. Bonifield was to be told that the work submitted could be used if much reduced but on further inspection the next meeting decided that its tone was not appropriate either: 'his despairing conditions are too much insisted on'.[65] At the same time Thomas Lawrence produced two manuscripts. One was untimely; it was clearly an answer to William Rogers, a Friend who was the author of books hostile to Fox and Whitehead which were being answered by others, probably commissioned to do so. The minute is unusually helpful:

Thomas Lawrence's manuscript read; which friends do not think fitt to print, seeing severall things writ therein setts up too high, and tend to puff up W. Rogers.
But if T.L. have any thing from the Lord to write to W.R. privately, tis left to him, To let him know that there is a large Answer to W.R. coming forth from Thomas Ellwood, & another from Christopher Taylor.[66]

The other was rejected too: 'because the Adversarys will take advantage upon his propositions'. Those examples are all from the early 1680s.

The Meeting did try to let some of its unsuccessful would-be authors down lightly. William Smith was to be written to in 1690 by two Friends: 'to let him know the Labour Friends took in reading ... and tenderly persuade him to let it by'.[67] This book may already have been considered two years earlier:

W. Smith's book read to p.80. And left with Richard Richardson, till W.S. write about it again;and then he may be advised, That many old transient Things, whose service is past, are conteined in it, printing thereof will be chargeable.... In many places the scriptures seem to be made too diminutive, and severall things not safe to be published.[68]

This attitude of tenderness was consistent, the Meeting for Sufferings taking a generous view of a text it wished to reject; in 1760 there is another good example:

Upon considering Jno Fry's Manuscript which appears to be partly an Index and partly an abstract of the Yearly Meetings Epistles, This Committee are of Opinion that at this time, it will not be of general service to make it publick; as the Index to the Collection of Epistles lately Printed at large entirely anticipates the former prt. We have nevertheless a Just Sense of Jno Frys great labour and good intention in that work, which appears to be well executed and might have been of considerable use if the Epistles had not been published at large....[69]

Fry requested a meeting to reconsider this position and the Meeting decided to refer the question to the higher authority of the Yearly Meeting. The work appeared in 1762 with the imprint 'Printed for and sold by the author' so he evidently went ahead at his own expense.

Circumstances could be more extreme. In 1674 a book by Solomon Eccles, *the Soul saveing principle*, was considered by the Morning Meeting: 'freinds have taken three daies to read it & their sense and judgment is that it is not safe to be published, there being many things in it that are to be left out, and others to be corrected, both of which will require much labour and care...'.[70] It was not published and it is clear that contemporary Friends considered Eccles unbalanced; Braithwaite describes him as emotional and William Sewel's defence is telling: 'Altho' some reckoned him out of his wits, yet he was not'.[71] In 1701 the Morning Meeting considered some manuscripts which were read by five Friends:

we doe find by the said papers the author thereof to be much discomposed in his understanding; and the matter contained therein to be not only unsound but very confused: yet we have pitty to the Young Man, and doe propose if this meet that he be Recommended to the Monthly Meet: at the Savoy that some Friends may take care of him and in love and Tenderness Endeavour that the Young Man may be helped for according our Sence of his Condition he had need thereof, and is in very great Danger... And Thomas Arch being now present, who appeared in a Shattered Discomposed Manner, and bt more papers. The Meeting has Compassion towards him, and doe recommend him to the Monthly Meet. at the Savoy's care in Tenderness to Endeavour his preservation and in the meantime doe intreat Gilbt Latey and Jno Vaighton to advise and Councill him...[72]

Typically the minute quoted gives no indication of the content of those unpublishable papers. It is possible that the works by both Eccles and Arch were unintelligible and would have brought discredit upon the Society as well as wasting resources. The Morning Meeting also wished to avoid any washing of the Society's dirty linen in public, so in 1683 it decided against printing papers from Warwickshire criticising the behaviour of some associated with Friends:

But for printing them, we do not see it safe nor convenient, as to so much public notice of them and their dirty actions, as to spread them abroad in print. But rather for friends to keep these papers in record... But as to the world tis best to send a generall abstract in a few lines of friends disowning and testifying against them at sundry meetings, as persons shut out of our society, for their disorderly and loose conversation. We think it not safe to spread particular matters of fact to the world; lest the persons break out into outrage and enter actions of defamation against friends because they cannot swear to the matter of fact charged as some have done in like case.[73]

Principle here is coupled with prudence. Warwickshire Friends were evidently anxious to denounce these dirty actions to the wider world in some detail and research in the local records might shed further light on the circumstances.In 1764 when Abiah Darby submitted the manuscript of her *expostulatory Address to all who frequent places of diversion &c* the Meeting was: 'well satisfied of the Friends good intention in writing it, but not being clear in the propriety of making it generally publick; agree that it be returned to the author'.[74] However she showed the manuscript to Friends at the Monthly Meeting in Shrewsbury in January 1765 and it was clear that the subject was the Card Assembly at Shrewsbury where county families gathered for a winter season. She also showed the address to some attending the Card Assembly and later the Dancing Assembly and also at a similar body in Worcester. Abiah Darby records that she was asked to print it 'for the general benefit'.[75] Smith records two printings, one with no place or date though she used a Shrewsbury printer for other addresses in 1755 and 1769, and another in London.[76]

It was alleged from time to time that the Morning Meeting was conservative. The Meeting in 1769:

having read James Gough 'Memoirs of the life of the late worthy Abraham Richard Hawksworth of Bristol deceased ... are unanimously of Opinion that it would not be proper for this Meeting to adopt the publication, there being no Precedent of that kind, and the making one might be attended with Inconveniences, and be productive of much Uneasiness, as Relations or Friends of deceased Persons hereafter might from such Precedent expect the same Liberty of publishing Testimonials of such who from their Affection for, they may apprehend equally worthy.[77]

The point of this minute is not entirely clear because its next part reads: 'The Testimony concerning Rebecca Smith may more properly come through the Quarterly Meeting to which she belonged'. The implication is that Gough had not followed the proper channels with his proposal and that the Hawksworth text seemed more of a personal tribute. Hawksworth's life received its tribute, published by Farley in Bristol in 1769: *Elegiac and other POEMS, by several hands, gratefully inscribed to the honoured Memory of a late eminently valuable Citizen of the City of Bristol, Abraham Richard Hawksworth, late Treasurer to the Infirmary of the said City, and one of the People called Quakers. Wherein is exhibited a view of his Life, as an accomplished model for the universal imitation of Mankind. To which are added some lines on Rebecca Smith.*[78]

We have already seen some examples of the central, London-based, system being bypassed by local actions. Clearly only a small percentage of the total output of Friends' books was produced outside London and that included straightforward reprints of unexceptional texts and works by Friends with no Quaker content. Sometimes local production may represent an evasion of central control but on other occasions the Morning Meeting will have left it to the author to arrange publication. Local meetings may have initiated printing locally, particularly of reprints, because they could then control it more effectively or because costs were lower than in London. Some publications were no doubt seen as of purely local interest, while occasionally speed of production may have been vital. Local meetings did not ignore the views of the Morning Meeting. In 1692 York Monthly Meeting agreed to buy five copies of each Friends' book published provided that it had the Morning Meeting's approval. On occasion they bought many more copies, 43 of Robert Barclay's *Apology* in 1699 or 350 copies of Middleton's *A Tender and Compassionate Call to Prophane Swearers* in 1736, presumably the Leeds printing of that year.[79] The Yorkshire Quarterly Meeting tended to take a line independent from London on varied issues throughout its history. The Meeting's historian, Pearson Thistlethwaite, observes that this tendency extended to its relations with the Second Day's Morning Meeting in London and to its printer who was thought for example in 1687 to have sent material speculatively that had not even been approved by the Morning Meeting. A similar complaint was made in 1793 and in the meantime in 1763 the Quarterly Meeting had complained to Yearly Meeting about Quaker booksellers supplying books: 'such as plays, loose romances, Novels, books teaching Musick, gaming, and other of evil Tendency'.[80] Thistlethwaite gives several examples of the Quarterly Meeting's own initiatives in publication. The first title considered by the Quarterly Meeting, Judith Boulby's *Testimony for Truth*, was to be vetted by local Friends and printing paid for from local funds in 1670 while in 1673 a text which I assume to have been *A Few words to the Rulers of the Nation* was referred to the Recording Clerk in London.[81] A text from Robert Mainforth was also referred to London in 1688 but in 1690 the decision to print one by George Myers was taken locally because it was thought to be only of local interest.[82] A work by Roger Hebden was first considered by the Quarterly Meeting's committee in 1696 and then passed to the Morning Meeting.[83] The Yorkshire Quarterly Meeting considered a number of other works that evidently passed through the Morning Meeting's system too, for example John Taylor's journal printed by Sowle in 1710 and Samuel Watson's works in 1712.[84] In one case, the Quarterly Meeting felt that an author had acted wrongly in having his work printed without its prior scrutiny.[85] The text of Benjamin Holme's *A Serious Call in Christian Love to all People* discussed must be the 1744 Leeds printing but there were earlier printings of this title from Leeds and Bristol as well as four from the Friends' London printer so it was hardly an unacceptable work. Smith records 21 18th-century printings in English and translations into Dutch, Latin, French and Welsh.[86] Yorkshire acted independently in the case of the Middleton pamphlet against profane swearing mentioned earlier by ordering 3,000 copies from James Lister in Leeds at 4*d.* a dozen but it had been printed first by Sowle in 1710. According to Smith it was reprinted in Dublin in 1736 and in Newcastle in 1735 on another local initiative: 'Reprinted, by order of Durham Quarterly Meeting, and distributed gratis'.[87]

Yorkshire Quarterly Meeting has been used for examples of local endeavour in publishing as much because it has been well written-up, though apparently without reference to Smith's standard bibliography of Quaker works, as because Yorkshire did take a somewhat independent line. In 1699 the Morning Meeting's minutes provide an example from Bristol of similarly independent action: 'a book intituled a Testimony to the Truth of God as held by the People called the Quakers further cleared from mistakes &c printed at Bristoll as We are Informed upon an Emergency for the service of Truth was proposed to be Read in order to be reprinted'.[88] The Meeting in agreeing to that noted: 'it was not first communicated to this meeting according to the Usuall Method' and that it had already been printed.

Nevertheless Friends went on to issue the general reminder quoted earlier that the Morning Meeting should receive anything 'Relating to the Doctrines and Principles of Truth' before it was published. The Bristol Friends' Mens Meeting had had 500 copies printed the previous month and eight local Friends had met to carry out minor corrections, the printer being paid from local funds.[89] Pursuit of more meeting records at the Quarterly or Monthly Meeting level could produce many more examples.

It was possible for a local meeting to take firm action when one of its members published something unacceptable. At the beginning of the 19th century there was a movement towards re-asserting what was thought to be Quaker orthodoxy supported by the writings of Henry Tuke and Joseph Gurney Bevan. There had been a separation in Ireland Yearly Meeting with the Meeting disowning from membership those Friends who did not meet its standard of orthodoxy. In 1804 the Liverpool businessman William Rathbone published his *Narrative of Events that have lately taken place in Ireland among the Society called Quakers*. This expressed doubts about the Yearly Meeting's action, suggested that the elders were too powerful and that a visiting American minister, David Sands, was contributing to the problems. Rathbone's English Monthly Meeting took exception to the book, published without any sanction from Friends, but Rathbone refused to admit that he was in error in writing it. A committee of three was appointed to visit Rathbone and report back while eight Friends examined the text in order to describe the ways in which it was deemed unsatisfactory. The Monthly Meeting generally felt that the book was bringing the Society into wide public discredit. Friends were then appointed to inform Rathbone of the Meeting's view. He wrote back at length raising eight charges against the Meeting. The Meeting finally decided to disown him.[90] All this protracted episode took place at the local level. It is an important prelude to some of the major internal difficulties experienced by the Society of Friends in the 19th century as well as an example of the publishing process and serves to illustrate the tension arising between those who felt that the basic Quaker (and Christian) revelation was complete and those who held as an essential of Quakerism an openness to new light and continuing revelation. Rathbone seems to have shared his approach in some respects with the 17th-century critics of the Morning Meeting.

Returning to the national scene, by the later 18th century the system seems to be less effective and less clearcut in operation, even if neither totally breaking down nor being extensively ignored. When it came to producing *A Collection of Testimonies* 1760 the Morning Meeting was asked by the Yearly Meeting in 1757 to produce a text; a year later nothing had happened and the next Yearly Meeting asked the Meeting for Sufferings to undertake the task.[91] One Morning Meeting in 1756 was described by the prominent minister Samuel Fothergill:

> The Morning Meeting consisted of about six Friends, who asked each other a few questions about their common affairs, then as usual, how were the Meetings attended last week, and put down names for that succeeding: read a few pages in John Richardson's journal, and then broke up. I used my endeavours to have us collected into silence, but in vain. I had a continued chain of hard labour, and principally toward those who ought to be the Head, but are the Tail.[92]

The Meeting for Sufferings seems to have been taking more initiatives in publishing matters by this time. Nevertheless the official role of the Morning Meeting had not changed and in the observations of James Jenkins, spanning almost 70 years of its work, we can see a critical attitude virtually echoed from some earlier anti-Quaker writers.[93] Jenkins was a Friend who wrote substantial memoirs in which an anti-establishment stance is very apparent. In the case of John Richardson's journal his recollection is more colourful than the reality but his comment on the excision of an account of a diabolical encounter goes beyond the quotation given here into language which could have been Bugg's:

> I apprehend, that an *original* copy of this journal is not now to be purchased, for, in subsequent Editions the aforesaid prudent critics of the Morning-meeting have entirely suppressed the account which he left behind him of this uncommon occurrence.[94]

In another example Jenkins recounts the author's surprise at the rejection of a pamphlet by the Morning Meeting coupled with his own feelings about Quaker Elders:

> Jno. Roper wrote a pamphlet which he intendd. for publication, but his literary child was knocked on the head with the critical axes of the morning-meeting. On his way to obtain the Imprimatur he called at Woodbridge, and ... I heard him, and our family converse freely on his book, a portion whereof he afterwards read to them —— it was (I think) a religious, and affectionate address to the Society.
>
> But alack, and alass! poor John brought back, dissappointment, and sorrow to his friends —— 'how came this, (said they) that thou hast not been permitted to publish? Yes, how indeed (he replied) when several Friends expressed their approbation whilst it was reading? —— but, I believe they found some things too *close for themselves.*

What that was, we can only conjecture. From knowing the Author so well; that his mind was of the most liberal cast, without an atom of domineering propensity about it, I suspect, that he had condemned the exercise of that exclusive power —— that uncontollable domination with which our little commonwealth was ruled, by the Elders of that day. Perhaps too highly (in their view) eulogised Christian meekness, and courtesy of manners.[95]

Jenkins sees a conservatism in the Morning Meeting's encounter with James Gough over his translations of continental religious writers. Gough had published several works of this nature beginning in 1772 with a two-volume life of the French Quietist Madame Guyon. None of these were printed in London in his lifetime and Jenkins suggests reasons:

... I understood that James was obliged to desist from this specious of Authorship, by the Morning Meetings refusing (if I may say so) its *Imprimatur*, to more works of that kind —— what was their reason I never knew, but suspect that they were afraid of these new, superseding the good old books we had of our own. Before this time, we had Abstracts from Michael de Molinos – Thos. a Kempis's Christian pattern —— Cambray, & Guyon on pure Love —— and Extracts from all these together, – perhaps the Morning-Meeting thought, if it did not use its restrictive interference, the Society might have been deluged with the pious effusions also of Madm. Teresa Thomas, Francesca Lopas, Falcon, Theophylact 'the illuminated mother of Cantal,' St. Francis of Sales, &c, &c, &c.[96]

The Morning Meeting was not always wrong in Jenkins's eyes, he approved of its rejection of Obed Crooke's account of his late wife: 'that sanction was very properly refused, on account of his book containing anecdotes of pious exercises of mind when in bed with his wife, and her heaviness to sleep "causing her to lose many precious opportunities, by not joining him therein"'.[97]

John Thorp's *Letters*, published in Liverpool in 1820, were evidently not submitted to the Morning Meeting and the passage in which Jenkins comments on this gives a good impression of his views, surely not unique to him:

The perusal of Jno Thorp's Letters, lately published, hath afforded me much pleasure, —— I am pleased also to hear, that the Editor hath *dared to do so*, without having previously submitted them to the over-cautious criticism of the Morning-Meeting. Perhaps they mean well, but their office appears to me, to be that of restraining the press —— the exercise of the *Imprimatur* (let it be printed) —— I feel disposed to grudge them, such a privilidge and to pity the Author who has submitted the offspring of his genius, and labour, to the revision, and expungation of these embodied critics; and this I am induced to do, from what I have known of their sometimes entirely suppressing, and at others of returning works most sadly mutilated.*

I have in my mind compared them to a set of literary and mechanical workmen, with their hatchets, and saws, & bill-hooks, and planes both rough, and smooth of edge, to chop off and shorten, and lop, and pare down to a thin state, whatever comes before them.

In my youth, I used to read with pleasure what (in new Editions) I now turn away from — to mention no more, only see what they have made of Thos. Ellwood, & Gilbert Latey's Journals — They now come to us metamorphos'd, 'an old friend with a new face,' like one of our modern effeminates, in tight-laced bodices — almost entirely divested or their original ease and comeliness. ... Often have I thought, and queried with myself, that if this community of male, and female curtailers were allowed to prepare a new Edition of the Bible, would not the public have returned to them, a poor megre, — a mere skeleton compilation?

*This (a Friend tells me) has been the case with Josh G. Bevan's Letters &c — in critical Chymistry, the *race*, or flavor of the mental soil has evaporated — so that instead of the genius of the Author, it is that of *mechanical revision* which too many of our new books display — they are not (as they ought to be) — 'Warm from the soul, and true to all its fires'.[98]

William Rathbone, who we have seen disowned by his Monthly Meeting on account of a publication, rather shared Jenkins's view of the Morning Meeting. In the 1769 ninth edition of one of the most printed Quaker works of the 18th century, Hugh Turford's *The Grounds of a Holy Life*, a note on a particular passage was inserted. Rathbone comments:

There is nothing objectionable in the note; but, if it was not introduced by H. Turford's *own direction*, the editor was reprehensible for not having *so stated* it. At present, it leads the reader to conclude, that the AUTHOR had deemed it necessary to insert this note, for the purpose of guarding against *misapprehension*.

Cases may *perhaps* occur, wherein additions or omissions, in the works of *authors*, may be justifiably made by *editors*. But as those works are hereby rendered less GENUINE, does it not merit serious attention, whether any unauthorized additions or omissions ought ever to be made in the works, either of living or deceased authors, unless there by some appropriate *notice* thereof, for the *information of the reader?*[99]

A little later he makes a comparison between the *Index Librorum Prohibitorum* of the Roman Catholics and the activities of the Morning Meeting. Referring to the Meeting's terms of reference and the invariable practice of expecting every book 'concerning the principles of Friends' to be read and corrected by the Meeting as reiterated in the 1802 *Extracts from the Minutes and Advices* ... he noted that no sanction was prescribed for non-observance of the rules (nor was it in fact in many other categories) and went on to hope that the regulation would be withdrawn:

There is no injunction to inflict either censure or disownment, upon those who do not comply with the directions of the following minute. And as every RULE requires some sanction for securing its observance, it would seem that the minute ought to be regarded, not as one of the RULES of the society, but as the JUDGMENT or ADVICE of the yearly meeting, held in London, 1801. Even in this point of view, however, it maybe hoped that the good sense of the society will not long continue its sanction to a regulation, so evidently resembling the policy of the darker ages.[100]

Neither Thorp's *Letters* nor Rathbone's *Narrative* had been submitted to the Morning Meeting. This is a symptom of the changing state of affairs in the early 19th century. Changes happened too at the formal level consolidating some of those that had begun in the mid 18th century. The Meeting for Sufferings gradually began to establish specialist committees. In 1806 a committee was set up to respond to attacks on Quakerism made in print, it was to be: 'careful in repelling them where it may seem necessary'.[101] After 1809 this committee reported annually to the Meeting for Sufferings though by 1817 it was not meeting regularly for lack of business and it was laid down in 1819. Then in 1830 another committee was set up to: 'pay what attention they may find needful to publications which may issue from the Press, or be in progress for printing, and to correct any misrepresentations respecting our Society they may find within'.[102] By 1834 the Meeting for Sufferings recognised this as one of three standing committees in the printing and publishing area, the others being the committee responsible for printing and the Society's libraries and the Continental Committee, responsible for printing books in foreign languages.[103] However the role of the Morning Meeting was still formally recognised in the Society's *Rules of Discipline* in 1834 which give an insight into an openness of approach one might not have expected:

This meeting recommends to friends generally, the observance of the ancient and approved practice of our religious society, of submitting manuscripts which relate to our Christian principles and practices to the morning meeting in London.

The said meeting is annually to appoint a committee, with whom those who are concerned to publish works of the above description may consult and advise. And the friends of the said committee are encouraged in brotherly openness to communicate and confer with such authors. The manuscripts thus submitted are to be first presented to the meeting, but not read there; and the committee are to make report of the result of their judgment. Authors are at liberty to sit with committees so appointed, if they incline to do so.[104]

The invariable practice of 1802 had become a recommendation from the Yearly Meeting. The arrangement was changed in 1835 so that manuscripts were first presented to the Morning Meeting which could deal with them itself or pass them on to the committee.[105]

The prominent evangelical Friend J.J. Gurney had a pamphlet, *Brief Remarks on Impartiality in the Interpretation of Scripture*, rejected by the Meeting but went ahead with a printing for private circulation in 1836.[106] On the other hand the American Friend John Wilbur was reprimanded by some New England Friends for not submitting to the Meeting his *Letters to a Friend* 1832. As his *Journal* later indicated this was quite unfair:

...returned to Warrington, where I met with my dear friend Charles Osborn, from my own country, with whom we conferred about the publication of the letters, of which he fully approved, and so I proposed going to London, to lay them before the Morning Meeting for adjudication; but was informed that such was not the usage now in England; which, though well known, George Crosfield, thought best to have official information of from London, and wrote to William Manly [*sic*] for correct information.... He informed my friend George Crosfield, by letter, that it was not the practice of Friends in England to commit the inspection of manuscripts for publication to the Morning Meeting, as had been heretofore the case; and so I left the disposal of them to George Crosfield and other friends, to do as they thought best with the letters.[107]

In the 1820s the Meeting continued to consider occasional manuscripts, by then averaging only one a year, and continued too to make much the same sort of observations and alterations as in earlier years. By the 1830s it was clearly becoming redundant and works published in the name of the Society and financed by it were dealt with by one of the committees set up by the Meeting for Sufferings. It continued to read manuscripts until 1860 but on the publication of the next edition of the Society's rules in 1861 the only formal advice on publishing was that:

It is agreed that the Meeting for Sufferings be at liberty to print or purchase, and distribute in such manner as it may deem proper, such works as that meeting may think desirable; it being distinctly understood that the Society of Friends is not thereby committed to everything contained in such books.[108]

There are two possible, though both extreme, interpretations of the place and work of the Morning Meeting in the history of English Quaker publishing. On the one hand the view of an authoritarian, negative Morning Meeting, suppressing or embroidering the truth according to those who criticised it, repressive, ironing out individuality and literary qualities; on the other hand a view of a positive — almost creative — body, protecting the Society of Friends, sustaining its reputation and spiritual life, offering tender guidance, filtering out the irrational, fanatical, repetitive, illiterate or untruthful from the varied manuscripts submitted to it. I would argue that the answer is somewhere between the extremes and is influenced by one's view of the nature of Quakerism as well as the evidence for the movement's publishing history.

References

1. Quoted from *Journal of the Friends Historical Society*, vol.xxi, 1912, p.12. Robert Dring was a linen draper in Moorfield, and early London Friends' meetings were held at his house.

2. Some account of the 17th-century background can be found in D.F. McKenzie, *The London Book Trade in the later seventeenth century*, Sandars Lectures, 1976, n.p., and in Luella M. Wright, *The Literary Life of the Early Friends*, New York, 1932, especially ch.VIII.

3. Figures derived from Wilmer G. Mason, 'The Annual Output of Wing-Listed Titles 1649-1684', *The Library*, 5th series, vol.XXIX, no.2, June 1974, pp.219-20 and David Runyon, 'Types of Quaker Writings by Year 1650-1700' in Hugh Barbour and Arthur Roberts, eds, *Early Quaker Writings 1650-1700*, Grand Rapids, Michigan, 1973, pp.567-76.

4. W.C. Braithwaite, *The Beginning of Quakerism*, second edn, Cambridge, 1955, p.304.

5. *ibid.*, p.134 and see Barbour and Roberts, *op.cit.* p.42.

6. Stephen C. Morland, ed., *The Somersetshire Quarterly Meeting of the Society of Friends 1668-1699*, Somerset Record Society, n.p., 1978, p.52.

7. For an account of both sides of the story in the early period see Thomas P. O'Malley, 'The Press and Quakerism, 1653-1659', *Journal of the Friends Historical Society*, vol.54, no.4, 1979, pp.169-84 and for the hostile literature see the listing in Joseph Smith, *Bibliotheca Anti-Quakeriana*, London, 1873.

8. J.S.T. Hetet, *A Literary Underground in Restoration England*, Cambridge University PhD dissertation, 1987, p.132.

9. *ibid.*, p.117.

10. Thomas O'Malley, '"Defying the Powers and Tempering the Spirit" A Review of Quaker Control over their Publications 1672-1689', *Journal of Ecclesiastical History*, vol.33, no.1, January 1982, pp.72-88.

11. W.C. Braithwaite, *The Second Period of Quakerism*, second edn, Cambridge, 1961, p.280.

12. O'Malley, 'Defying the Powers ...', p.78.

13. Minutes of the Morning Meeting 15th of 7th month (i.e. September) 1673. Quotations from the records of the Society of Friends at Friends House, London are by kind permission of the Librarian to the Meeting for Sufferings. I have used the typed transcripts of the minutes up to 1699 and the originals thereafter. Morning Meeting Minutes are subsequently cited as MMM.

14. MMM 24th 9th month 1673; 21st 7th month 1674.

15. Minutes of the Meeting for Sufferings (subsequently cited as MMS), vol. 22nd of 3rd month 1679, pp.11-12. A.S. was Andrew Sowle, B.C. Benjamin Clark, E.H. Ellis Hookes, the Society's Recording Clerk.

16. MMM 27th 1st month (i.e. March) 1699.

17. MMM vol.3, p.45.

18. MMM vol.3, p.74.

19. *Extracts from the Minutes and Advices of the Yearly Meeting of Friends ...*, London, 1783, p.167.

20. Minutes of the Yearly Meeting (subsequently cited as YMM), vol.IX, pp.99, 162.

21. O'Malley, 'Defying the Powers ...', pp.75-6; Fox is quoted from Braithwaite, *Second Period ...*, p.280.

22. [Charles Leslie], *The Snake in the Grass*, London, 1696, p.cclxx.

23. Charles Leslie, *A Defence of a Book intituled the Snake in the Grass*, London, 1700 pursues the theme of Quaker editing and alleged deliberate misquotation at length.

24. London, 1698, p.72.

25. *ibid.*, pp.73-4.

26. McKenzie, *op.cit.*, p.33.

27. Two volumes, London, 1867; *Supplement ...*, London, 1893; Smith's *Bibliotheca Anti-Quakeriana* also contains details of the replies to adverse books.

28. Rufus M. Jones, *The Later Periods of Quakerism*, two volumes, London, 1921, p.112.

29. Wright, *op.cit.*, pp.104, 102.

30. W. Arnold Lloyd, *Quaker Social History 1669-1738*, London, 1950, p.151.

31. Based on Runyon, *op.cit.*, there is a valuable breakdown by category of literature.

32. MMM 7th of 8th month 1689, the printer was nevertheless Andrew Sowle.

33. *The works of the Long-Mournful and Sorely-Distressed Isaac Penington ...*, London: Printed by Samuel Clark, for John and Thomas Kendal, Booksellers in Colchester.

34. MMM vol.6, p.11; Smith, *Descriptive Catalogue*, vol.1, pp.511-12.

35. MMM 9th of 12th month (i.e. February) 1675/6. Probably *A Relation of A Man's Return and his Travaills out of a long and sore Captivity*, 1677?

36. MMM vol.6, p.29, by William Shewen, reprints included Dublin 1771 and Salem, 1793.

37. *ibid.*, pp.162, 172, 178.

38. *ibid.*, pp.83-4. The actual title is *A Description of the Qualifications Necessary to a Gospel Minister, containing Advices to Ministers and Elders ...*

39. *ibid.*, p.92.

40. *ibid.*, p.127.

41. Smith, *Descriptive Catalogue*, vol.1, p.135; *National Union Catalogue* also records a contemporary manuscript in the Boston Public Library. The title is *Some account of the fore-part of the Life of Elizabeth Ashbridge*.

42. See Edwin B. Bronner and David Fraser, *William Penn's Published Writings 1660-1726*, University of Pennsylvania Press, n.p., 1986, no.119.

43. MMM 30th of 9th month, 1674.

44. MMM 12th of 5th month, 1675.

45. MMM 31st of 11th month, 1680/81.

46. MMM 30th of 5th month, 1677. Bugg, *op.cit*, p.88 gives an account of two other works by her, withdrawn (he says) after printing on the orders of the London Monthly Meeting.

47. Norman Penney, 'George Fox's writings and the Morning Meeting', *Friends Quarterly*

Examiner, vol.xxxvi, 1902, pp.63-72; Henry J. Cadbury, 'The Editio Princeps of Fox's Journal', *Journal of the Friends Historical Society*, vol.53, 1974, pp.197-218; introductions to *The Journal of George Fox*, ed. Norman Penney, two volumes, Cambridge, 1911.

48. See Henry J. Cadbury, *George Fox's 'Book of Miracles'*, Cambridge, 1948; Braithwaite, *Second Period*, p.487.

49. Cadbury, *Fox's Book of Miracles*, pp.92-3.

50. *ibid.*

51. William I. Hull, *Eight First Biographies of William Penn*, Swarthmore College Monographs on Quaker History, no.3, n.p., 1936, p.10.

52. London, 1722 (Dutch original, Amsterdam, 1717), 2nd edn corrected, London, 1725; William I. Hull, *Willem Sewel of Amsterdam 1653-1720 The First Quaker Historian of Quakerism*, Swarthmore College Monographs on Quaker History, no.1, n.p., 1933, pp.174-82.

53. Hull, *Willem Sewel*, pp.188-90.

54. Smith, *Descriptive Catalogue*, vol.1, pp.182-4. The first edition is *Theologie Vere Christianae Apologia*, London, Rotterdam and Frankfurt, 1676.

55. Smith, *Descriptive Catalogue*, vol.1, p.176. The first English edition is n.p., [1673].

56. London, 1694. Smith, *Descriptive Catalogue*, vol.2, p.314.

57. MMM 13th of 10th month, 1675.

58. MMM vol.5, p.189. The original is London, 1682; there were also versions in Dutch, 1687, French, 1746 and 1793 and later in German, 1825. Smith, *Descriptive Catalogue*, vol.2, p.301.

59. MMM vol.5, pp.67-70.

60. MMM vol.5, p.71. This makes it quite clear that part of the purpose of the translation at least was educational, to provide pious rather than pagan texts to teach Latin from.

61. See James C. Dybikowski, 'Edmond Philip Bridel's Translations of Quaker Writings for French Quakers', *Quaker History*, vol.77, Fall 1988, pp.110-21.

62. MMM 20th of 10th month 1675; titles from Smith, *Descriptive Catalogue*, vol.2, p.878.

63. Rufus M. Jones, *The Quakers in the Americn Colonies*, London, 1923, pp.103-4.

64. MMM 19th of 1st month (i.e. March) 1682/3.

65. MMM 13th of 1st month 1681/2.

66. *ibid.*

67. MMM 16th of 4th month 1690, not the prolific William Smith of Besthorp, Notts. but perhaps William Smith of Market Harborough, Leics.

68. MMM 22nd of 8th month 1688.

69. MMS vol.xxx, p.497. The quotation is from the report of the committee appointed to consider the manuscript, interestingly by the Meeting for Sufferings, not the Morning Meeting.

70. MMM 2nd of 9th month 1674.

71. See Braithwaite, *Second Period*, p.25; John Ormerod Greenwood, *Signs of Life*, London, 1978, p.12.

72. MMM vol.3, pp.58-9.

73. MMM 2nd of 2nd month 1683.

74. MMM vol.6, p.36.

75. Rachel Labouchere, *Abiah Darby 1716-1793 of Coalbrookdale*, York, 1988, p.142.

76. Smith, *Descriptive Catalogue*, vol.1, p.511.

77. MMM vol.6, pp.116-17.
78. Smith, *Descriptive Catalogue*, vol.1, p.925.
79. Stephen Allott, *Friends in York*, York, 1978.
80. W. Pearson Thistlethwaite, *Yorkshire Quarterly Meeting*, Harrogate, 1979, p.292.
81. *ibid.*, pp.279-80. Boulby appears in Wing STC as Boulbie, in Smith as Bowlbie and in the catalogue of the Library at Friends' House as Bowlby. Her submissions clearly took up much of the Morning Meeting's time, see Wright, *op.cit.*, pp.104-6.
82. Thistlethwaite, *op.cit.*, gives no title for the Myers text; it would appear to be *To all our Friends and Brethren at the several Monthly and particular meetings in the County of York*, [1690]. Robert Mainforth appears in neither Wing nor Smith.
83. Neither Wing nor Smith has a Hebden title of appropriate date.
84. Thistlethwaite, *op.cit.*, p.283 suggests the existence of a Leeds printing of Watson which I have not traced.
85. *ibid.*, p.281.
86. Smith, *Descriptive Catalogue*, vol.1, pp.965-7. The printings in English are London except for Leeds 1737 and 1744, Bristol 1738, 1745, and 1747 and Dublin 1784.
87. Thistlethwaite, *op.cit.*, p.283; Smith, *Descriptive Catalogue*, vol.2, p.75.
88. MMM 27th of 1st month 1699.
89. Quoted from Russell Mortimer, ed., *Minute Book of the Men's Meeting of the Society of Friends in Bristol 1686-1704*, Bristol Record Society, n.p., 1977, p.146.
90. This account is largely based on the late Nevill H. Newhouse's presidential address to the Friends Historical Society in November 1991 'Seeking God's will: a monthly meeting at work in 1804' which it is to be hoped will be published in the Society's *Journal*.
91. David J. Hall, 'A Collection of Testimonies, 1760: a bibliographical note', *Journal of the Friends Historical Society*, vol.54, no.7, 1982, pp.313-14.
92. Quoted from Lucia K. Beamish, *Quaker Ministry 1691 to 1834*, privately published, 1967, p.99. I owe this reference to the kindness of Edward H. Milligan.
93. The manuscript of Jenkins's observations is in the Library at Friends' House and quotations are by permission of the Librarian to the Meeting for Sufferings. However page references are given to the valuable annotated transcript published by J. William Frost: *The Records and Recollection of James Jenkins*, New York, 1984.
94. *ibid.*, p.578, John Richardson, *An Account of the Life of that Ancient Servant of Jesus Christ John Richardson*, London, 1757, reprinted 1758, 1774, 1791 etc.
95. Jenkins, *op.cit.*, pp.298-9.
96. *ibid.*, p.94 and see Smith, *Descriptive Catalogue*, vol.1, pp.853-4.
97. Jenkins, *op.cit.*, p.234; Obed Cook, *A Small Tribute of O. Cook to the memory of his beloved wife, Elizabeth*, n.p., 1784.
98. Jenkins, *op.cit.*, pp.563-5.
99. Rathbone, *Narrative of Events*, Liverpool, 1804, p.152; Turford first published London 1702, there are at least 25 18th-century printings, with imprints including Bristol, Newcastle-upon-Tyne, Whitby, Hartford Conn. and Philadelphia.
100. *Extracts* ..., 1802, p.12; Rathbone, *op.cit.*, p.171. The difference between rules, judgment and advice does not need to be explored here though I feel that Rathbone's argument is perhaps at variance with the general contemporary Quaker interpretation.
101. MMS, vol.31, pp.129, 145.
102. MMS, vol.43, p.545.
103. MMS, vol.44, pp.181-3.

104. *Rules of Discipline of the Religious Society of Friends with Advices*, London, 1834, pp.170-1.

105. *Supplement to the Rules of Discipline ...*, London, 1849, p.370. *Journal of the Life of John Wilbur*, Providence, 1859, p.140.

106. Jones, *Later Periods*, p.505.

107. Wilbur, *Journal*, pp.566, 140. I am grateful to Edward H. Milligan for drawing my attention to this passage. New England Friends may of course have been influenced in this by their own prevailing system. One example of that can be found in the introduction by John Comly to *The Works of that eminent minister of the Gospel Job Scott*, 2 vols, Philadelphia, 1831, where both the Meeting for Sufferings in New England in editing the original published in 1797 and the Philadelphia Yearly Meeting's equivalent committee in approving Comly's additions exercised a role similar to that of the Morning Meeting. This reached the attention of James Jenkins in England, see Jenkins, *op.cit.*, p.251, note 26 and p.254. Scott had earlier had problems with both the New England and New York Meetings for Sufferings, these are described by Arthur J. Worrall, *Quakers in the Colonial Northeast*, Hanover, New Hampshire, 1980, pp.177-80. Worrall describes another earlier instance where the New England Meeting for Sufferings administered the Society's imprimatur for a publication, see pp.142-3. The Pennsylvania system is described by J. William Forst in 'Quaker Books in Colonial Pennsylvania', *Quaker History*, vol.80, no.1, Spring 1991, pp.1-23.

108. *Extracts from the Minutes and Epistles of the Yearly Meeting ... relating to Christian Doctrine, Practice and Discipline*, London, 1861, p.204.

The Absolutism of Taste:
Journalists as censors in
18th-century Paris[1]

ANNE GOLDGAR

SCHOLARS AND WRITERS in the 18th century were, inevitably, citizens of real countries, ones which appeared on maps, levied taxes, fought wars, and — usually — censored books. But these writers all considered themselves equally citizens of another, imaginary place, known variously as the Empire of Knowledge, the Commonwealth of Learning, and (most commonly) the Republic of Letters. And this Republic did not necessarily operate by the laws of more tangible nations. Instead, it had its own rules and standards, such as determining status more by merit and usefulness to the community than through the traditional birth or property.[2] Although 18th-century scholars and writers were of course bound by the standards and laws of the society and nations in which they lived, a dominant ethos of their lives was that of scholarly society.

One of these special standards of the Republic of Letters was the endorsement of freedom of expression. 'Parnassus,' according to Boileau, 'is always a free country';[3] Adrien Baillet said that 'if the commerce of Letters is a true Republic, as its name says, it seems that its true character must be liberty.'[4] Far from limiting discussion — as governments and churches in this period often sought to do — this community believed that, as Jean Le Clerc wrote, 'natural Equity requires that it be permitted that those who have different opinions should be allowed to support what they believe to be true, & to attack what they consider to be false.' Even if you think you are right, he said, to deny this liberty to others would be 'a very great injustice'.[5] (Of course, this freedom might go too far, as the cynic Johann Burchard Mencke wrote: 'Here, Messieurs, is what they call the Liberty of the Republic of Letters: complete Liberty, Liberty without limits, Liberty to attack with impunity, & to insult whomever one likes, on the slightest pretext ....')[6]

These ideals about freedom of opinion were borne out in action. Like academia today, this was a society founded on communication. Its structures

87

were built on ideas about exchange, and principally exchange of information; writers established or reinforced bonds by exchanging books, letters, gossip, and valuable news about their work and the output of the press. Some learned men travelled around Europe, meeting with their fellows in other cities, and not only spread information as they made their journeys, but sometimes published it, as Charles-Etienne Jordan did with his *Histoire d'un voyage littéraire* of 1735.[7] Other scholars conducted elaborate *commerces de lettres* – purely literary correspondences, often between strangers – in which they would enjoy the mutual provision of information about anything concerning their world.

The institutionalisation of these sorts of contacts was the appearance of the literary or book-review journal, which first began in 1665 with the foundation of the Parisian *Journal des sçavans*, and took off with a flurry of new journals which started to appear in the Netherlands in the 1680s. Like the community whose values it crystallised, the journal's purpose was to inform. The *Journal des sçavans* explained this in its first issue: 'the goal of the journal [is] to let people know what has been going on in the Republic of Letters.'[8] The standard format of such journals provided several types of information. The bulk of the contents would consist of a series of anonymous book reviews, or *extraits*, as they were called. This was followed by a shorter section of *nouvelles littéraires*, or literary news, which usually was a compilation of details about books in progress or in press. Both sections of the journals increased by many times the amount of information and opinion that learned readers had available. Among the sorts of readers journalists thought they would benefit were those too poor to afford the books they discussed, too isolated – even in major cities – to see books from all corners of Europe, and those with too little time to read every book that came off the European presses.

To communicate, to disseminate information, to inform: these, then, were the aims of the Republic of Letters and its journals. In apparently direct opposition to this communicative ethos, however, we find in the first half of the 18th century a government censorship system in France rapidly developing in scope, if not in effectiveness. Before the mid-17th century, censorship had been the province of the church, the *parlements*, and the university, but from 1629, when an ordinance gave the chancellor the right to appoint censors, the crown increasingly took over these functions. In the 18th century the number of censors increased rapidly. From four in 1658, their numbers grew to 41 in 1727, 73 in 1745, 82 in 1751, 119 in 1760, 128 in 1763, and 178 in 1789.[9] Every manuscript intended for the press and every book going into a new edition had to be presented to the chancellor's office to be read by a censor. These censors were intended to look for anything in the works they read which might be dangerous for the state, the church, or good morals; only if they found the works free of these taints, or if the authors were willing to change them, were books granted one of a variety of permissions or tolerations. But whether it was university, church, or state which practised this censorship, it still ran afoul of scholarly ideals about communication. As the *Journal littéraire* wrote in a 1715 review of a Jansenist work, 'The Parlement of Paris condemned this Book by an Arrêt of February 21, 1715: but, as no sovereign Authority is recognized in the Republic of Letters, & because a Book, although condemned by Arrêt, can be good, we will make an Extrait of this one ....'[10]

Most writing about French censorship has endorsed this view of an 18th-century literary society in firm opposition to control of the press. Freedom of thought — obviously the cause for which we are to cheer — is seen as the goal for which the *philosophes* fought. Albert Bachman set the tone in his book, *Censorship in France from 1715 to 1750: Voltaire's Opposition*, whose title alone gives his position away. It begins, 'The history of censorship in the first half of the eighteenth century is really an episode of the struggle between the monarchical and religious conservatism, on the one hand, and the progressive *philosophic spirit*, on the other.'[11] Although scholarship on this subject has become more nuanced since Bachman's book appeared in 1934, stressing, for example, the system's increasing ineffectiveness and the possibility of bargaining with censors, it has mostly dealt with the technicalities of censorship and the means writers found of avoiding it. 'Voltaire's opposition', as Bachman expressed it in his title, actually turns out to be Voltaire's clever avoidance of publishing in France, rather than any vocal opposition; and the same characterisation could be made of Robert Darnton's work on clandestine publishing and the Société Typographique de Neuchâtel. The story of the triumph of Enlightenment remains a story of successful evasion of a system, which, although corrupt and ineffective, placed censors in opposition to authors. Although the boundaries separating the Republic of Letters and the absolutist state have over the years grown rather fuzzier, Bachman's view of their oppressive relationship remains largely unchanged.

How, then, are we to deal with the news that these worlds were actually mixed? That censors and the writers they censored were the same people? Indeed, that censors and *journalists* were the same people? For the ranks of the French censors were permeated with citizens of the Republic of Letters.

According to research carried out by Catherine Blangonnet, in the 1750s nearly 40 per cent of censors were members of one of the major Parisian academies. Thirty per cent were associated with the University of Paris or other teaching institutions. And, even more surprising, nearly 36 per cent were journalists, either for the *Journal des sçavans* or other journals such as the *Mercure de France*.[12] At the beginning of the century, the Abbé Bignon, librarian of the Bibliothèque du Roi, director of the *Journal des sçavans*, and known as the great protector of letters, was also director of censorship; and the same paradox is presented in the 1750s by Malesherbes, writer for the *Journal*, friend to the *philosophes*, and head of the censorship system. Out of the 25 authors of the *Journal des sçavans* between 1701 and 1763, I have been able to identify at least 20 (80 per cent) as censors.[13] In 1757, nine of the ten authors of the *Journal des sçavans* were also censors.[14]

One way to reconcile these conflicting details might be to point to the common governmental control over both the censorship system and the *Journal des sçavans*. The journal had always been under government patronage, and in 1701 the chancellor's office – the same office that supervised censorship – took over its operations and finances.[15] The chancellor chose the director of the journal, as he chose the *directeur de la librairie*, and in the 1740s the chancellor d'Aguesseau presided over the staff's weekly meetings.[16] Catherine Blangonnet, who has provided us with our figures about the professional connection of censors, makes sense of this through the argument of creeping absolutism. 'The participation of censors in the editing of gazettes and journals,' she writes, 'is no doubt the indication of an attempt of the government to control and orient, through the mediation of members of its administration, the sectors of public opinion touched by periodicals.'[17]

This argument helps to explain the presence of censors on the staffs of journals. But citing absolutism as an explanation does not address the fundamental question of attitude. The *Journal des sçavans*, though at times more subdued and more conservative than some of its counterparts,[18] shared many of the same values: the values of the Republic of Letters. And in order to understand the interpenetration of these two apparently conflicting worlds, we cannot look only at issues of politics and structure. We must also look precisely at this question of values. We must ask: how did journalists think like censors? And how did censors think like journalists? In this essay I will examine these two questions in turn.

The words *censer*, *censure*, and *censeur* came into French, as they came into English, from the Latin 'censor'. In ancient Rome, the Censors were two officials who drew up a census of the citizens but who also took charge of public morals.[19] In French, as in English, the word and its linguistic relatives took on more general meanings of judgement. Medieval French used the verb 'censer' to mean think, consider, believe,[20] and variations such as *censé, censorin, censorien,* and *censeur* by the 16th century took on connotations both of approving and especially of blaming or censuring.[21] These uses − reflected in the fact that *censure* means both censorship and censure in French − predated the administrative use of the word *censeur*, which appeared only in the 17th century.[22]

The issue of *censure*, then, was not merely one of government powers, but also of judgement. Any critic, particularly one who was severe, could be called a *censeur*, and, as with our word 'censorious', this judgement could be applied to behaviour as well as to writing. Anyone who tried to speak authoritatively over these issues could informally be called a censor. Literary journals fit well into this image of the censor. They used their position of power in the Republic of Letters, at the centre of a network of scholars, to direct scholarship, both by approving or disapproving of certain books, and by encouraging writers in their projects through the publication of research plans or even exhortations to complete unfinished work. The stature of journals also made them arbiters of scholarly etiquette. Their protestations that they would not discuss 'bitter and personal disputes', as the *Bibliothèque italique* expressed it, were not only to gain themselves credit in the scholarly world, but also to dictate its behaviour. This extended to reproof of specific people or practices. François Bruys, whose *Critique désintéressée des journaux* was admittedly *outrée*, claimed that it was 'the goal of journalists to quell' the explosion of new books which actually were mediocre old ones issued under a new title. '... [T]he Public cannot be too grateful to Men of Letters who try sincerely to repress disorders,' he wrote.[23] Bruys regarded his fellow journalists harshly for failing to fulfil their duties properly; but his general view that journals could and should pronounce on questions of etiquette was shared by his colleagues. When a savant in Berlin, Maturin Veyssière La Croze, wrote an angry discourse against a fellow scholar, the brother of the journalist Henri Basnage de Beauval wrote in a letter that La Croze 'gives himself plenty of authority for an author who is just getting started. My brother is letting him know it in the extrait that he is going to publish of his French dissertations.'[24] The etiquette was for La Croze to show respect if he was low in the scholarly hierarchy; if not, he should be reproved. Journals, in performing these functions, were like the Roman censors of the Republic of Letters.

In making book reviews the centrepiece of their publications, journalists were also censors in the more modern sense of the term. That this should be so, however, is less obvious than it might at first appear. The issue of judging books was always a problematic one for journalists, because to do so carried implicit messages which ran counter to other values of the Republic of Letters. In the first place, it was impolite for journalists to criticise other scholars' books. Both authors of books and authors of journals had trouble distinguishing between the writing of a review and any other action in the Republic of Letters, a community ruled by exchange and politeness. Favourable *extraits* were acts of courtesy which were to be rewarded with gratitude, or even a favour in return. A scholar in London, Gally de Gaujac, thanked the journalist Jean Le Clerc for a kind review of his son's book, adding that 'if we can do any service for you in this city ... you have only to let us know it'.[25] In the same way, a critical review was viewed as an insult to the author. These attitudes made it difficult for journalists or their readers to feel right about voicing reservations about books.

Scholars also criticised journalists for presuming to judge books because to do so upset the hierarchy of the Republic of Letters. One thing which spurred on a journalist, according to Denis-François Camusat of the *Bibliothèque françoise*, was 'the pleasure of seeing oneself in some fashion the Arbiter of the reputation of Scholars ....'[26] Yet what qualified these people to hold such an important position? True, the *Journal des sçavans'* staff was chosen by the French government, but that did not necessarily make it qualified, and most journals were written by people who had elected themselves to that powerful position merely by negotiating with a publisher. Le Clerc, before he started his own literary journal, complained that via his journal Pierre Bayle had 'set himself up as Universal judge of all the Books which will appear from now on'.[27] This was particularly annoying for some opponents of journals (opposed because they thought they encouraged laziness and incomplete knowledge) who thought journalists naturally lower in station than original authors. After Henri Basnage de Beauval fulfilled his brother's promise to admonish Maturin Veyssière La Croze in his literary journal, a friend of La Croze's complained that Beauval 'should have dared to decry ... a person with whom he cannot be compared: for there is considerable difference between making Extraits, & publishing well-reasoned books oneself, ... whatever authors of Journals, some of whom are not competent judges, might say ....'[28]

But if it was neither polite nor socially acceptable for journalists to make judgements on books, it was also dangerous for the community. The Republic of Letters, anxious not to appear divided in a world not entirely sympathetic to its ideas, made moderation a rule of conduct. This meant that literary journals, the organs of the community, ought to remain impartial in their pronouncements on books. Some journals, such as the *Critique désintéressée des journaux*, or the *Bibliothèque impartiale*, made this stance their selling point by stressing it in their titles. But nearly all, particularly in the 17th and early 18th centuries, went out of their way to emphasise their impartiality. The very first issue of the *Journal des sçavans* declared that it would 'espouse no party' and that 'this indifference will no doubt be judged necessary, in a Work which must be both free of all sorts of prejudices and exempt from passion & partiality'.[29] This freedom from prejudice in large part meant avoiding issues of religion or politics, which were thought to lie outside the Republic of Letters, but most of the early journalists, including those of the *Journal des sçavans*, swore also to avoid making judgements about books. The Abbé Bignon, the *Journal*'s editor, wrote in a private letter in 1705 that 'to report the thoughts and the expressions' of an author, 'without approving them nor condemning them, leaving the public the liberty to make what judgement it wanted', was 'the true character of good journalists'.[30]

For all these reasons, then — questions of politeness, of hierarchy, or of moderation — journalists were wary of making censorious judgements on books. 'In my career, Neutrality is always the best policy', wrote the journalist Jacques Bernard in 1702.[31] But the constant promises of impartiality expressed in the forewords of literary journals do not bear too much comparison to the journals' actual contents. For, as the journalist Camusat pointed out, 'Prefaces by journalists are usually fairly uniform. They almost all promise the same things: the difference is in the execution ...'.[32] Almost as soon as the *Journal des sçavans* began publishing, its supposedly impartial author was dismissed for making judgements on books, and several prefaces of later journals protested their impartiality only in contrast to the lies told on this subject by competing journals.[33] Journalists could not help themselves: they had to judge books, for, despite the loud outcry at the practice, for the reasons I have stated, citizens of the Republic of Letters were even more anxious to know journalists' opinions.

The reason was that, in addition to being polite, the journal also had to be useful; and its use was to help scholars choose books. The goal of commenting impartially on everything was not, ultimately, either practical or desirable. Jean Le Clerc found this in his continuing experience as a journalist. His first journal, which began in 1686, was the *Bibliothèque universelle*: the universal library, in which he promised, as he put it, 'to talk about all works that can be found, whatever language they are written in ...'.[34] By the time he founded a new journal in 1703, he had recovered from this attitude, as the new title suggests: from the universal library he had moved to the *Bibliothèque choisie*, the selected library. In this new work, he said, 'it will not be necessary for me to read, despite myself, [books] which I do not judge to be worth the trouble, & which disturb my ordinary reading & studies too much; because I will be able to choose, & because I will commit myself only to read & to abridge what I believe to be useful.'[35]

The feelings of the author echoed those of the reader. The point of journals was *not* to inform indiscriminately: it was to choose, to judge, or, as the *Works of the Learned* put it in 1691, 'to make good Books more known, read and esteemed, by putting down an infinite number of mean ones, amongst which they are confounded'.[36] When Le Clerc had failed to judge books in the *Bibliothèque universelle*, he received complaints, such as Jacques Lenfant's report that 'people find the extraits of your biblioteque too dry ...'.[37] It was possible to make judgements without being too harsh, or taking sides in controversies, Lenfant suggested; and this is what readers wanted. The *Journal litéraire* advertised its usefulness in 1713 precisely by reminding readers how often it happened that, 'attracted by a pompous Title, we buy a Book which does not live up to our expectations, & which offers the mind only words empty of pleasure & utility'.[38] By reviewing some books badly − or by choosing not to mention them at all − journals would help readers avoid such useless material, and, as one publication said, help them 'to save both Time and Money'.[39]

Even the *Journal des sçavans*, which always swore that it would not judge books, and which rarely stated strong opinions on them, came around to this view in its statements of policy. When a new administration of the journal, headed for the second time by the Abbé Bignon, took over in 1724, the journalists declared their intention to improve the journal's waning quality.

The extraits that we give will be like the Essence of all the books .... We will try to follow the method of analysis with more exactitude than we have done in the past, so that our Journal will always continue to be a sort of abridgement of Libraries. We will apply ourselves most of all to review what we find to be the most interesting & the least common. We will read new books with attention, & we will endeavour to choose from them a part of what a man of wit & of taste would want to retain after having read them. It can be seen from this how useful the reading of Journals is. It spares you long & painful study, & makes us pay the price; you will have the advantage of nourishing yourself only with a precious pith. It is true that to do this, you will have to trust a bit in our taste, & be persuaded that we know how to choose. We will forget nothing in our attempt to inspire in the Public such a happy prejudice.[40]

Even when journals gave extended *extraits* of a book, they tended not to be very specific about why it was good or bad. Usually the format of these reviews was to present a long summary of the book's contents and then to remark on its arrangement, style, and the usefulness of its contents. But the presence of these comments suggests that standards, although not very well articulated, did exist in the minds of journalists, and that these standards tended to reflect the needs of the Republic of Letters. The *Bibliothèque raisonnée* summarised these standards in an issue of 1728.

Judging things impartially, then, what would we call a good Book? In our view, it is a Work whose subject is *important* or at least *useful*; where the Author *penetrates deeply into* his Subject, & omits nothing from it that one *wants the most* to know; where he proposes to instruct with *solidity*, rather than to say things which are simply curious; where he carefully avoids *digressions* which only serve to enlarge the Volume; & where he expresses himself with all the *clarity* of Discourse, & all the *purity of Style* that is appropriate.[41]

If we read the volumes of the *Journal des sçavans* for the 1700s and the 1750s, both periods when the staff was rife with royal censors, we can observe the same sorts of standards we have just read from the Dutch-published *Bibliothèque raisonnée*. Although officially the *Journal* liberated itself only gradually from its impartial stance, in fact the *extraits* were more violently judgemental at the beginning of the century than later on; but in both periods particular qualities of books were stressed. In the first place, journalists demanded literary merit, particularly that which aided the understanding. This included especially clarity and order. An *extrait* of a chemistry text by Macquer in 1751 praised the book because 'there is no work of this sort, in which such a shining order has been followed, & which is written with such elegance and clarity'. Although most chemistry books are far from entertaining, this one, the journal claimed, could be read with pleasure.[42] On the other hand, the *Entretiens des voyageurs sur la mer* were greeted in 1706 with the following *extrait* (in its entirety): 'These conversations already appeared a few years ago, and this is only a new

Edition of them. It can scarcely be said what this Work is. A mass of all sorts of ill-digested things are to be found in it, Religion, Gallantry, History, everything is pell-mell, with no sort of selectiveness.'[43] In both cases the reviewer was concerned with the usefulness of the works for his readers; clarity, elegance, and order made even boring subjects pleasurable, while books constructed 'pell-mell' could only with difficulty and discomfort profit the reader.

The reader's profit was the key: for literary journals concentrated on determining which books were the most useful for the world of learning. The *Journal* said that it was proper to cover more thoroughly books 'as distinguished, as vast, & as useful' as one it reviewed in 1750, than 'productions of an inferior merit, size and utility';[44] any work which expanded knowledge or provided a new method for thinking about a subject was worthy of attention. Eduardo Corsini's *Fasti Attici* was pronounced valuable because 'The Author advances entirely over those who have treated the same subject before him; he gives new clarifications, & he re-establishes the meaning of several passages of ancient Authors, of which scholars had given false interpretations to make them fit their ideas & their systems.'[45] Such works were esteemed because they were useful – a word constantly repeated in reviews – and as such were deemed 'worthy of being read'. This phrase, also much repeated, suggested again the control exercised by the journal. Only some books were actually reviewed – novels and romances, for example, were ignored by most journals – and only some of *these* earned the comment, as did Muratori's *Annali d'Italia*, that they were 'very worthy of the attention of Scholars'.[46]

As these examples make plain, the notion that control of information and thought was foreign to the Republic of Letters is a misplaced one. Indeed, many scholars of the period opposed the expanding popularity of romances and other works of literature, which they felt destroyed taste and occupied presses which would be better employed adding to knowledge of such subjects as languages or antiquities. As Anne Dacier – author of the *Causes de la Corruption du Goust* – wrote in her edition of Homer, 'Most people these days are ruined by reading so many vain & frivolous books, & cannot bear anything not in the same taste. Love, after having corrupted morals, has corrupted books.'[47] Such books were against good morals, of course, and, as one writer put it, 'corrupted youth more than one can express';[48] but a major objection to them was the simple one of taste. Charles Sorel's objections to romances stemmed not just from their licentiousness, but their absurdity;[49] and his verdict was that 'it would be just to exterminate, if one could ... Books which are either scandalous, or useless ...'.[50]

In their own way, then, scholars and writers wanted to control literary output, and journalists functioned as the censors of the Republic of Letters. Like Roman censors, they controlled the behaviour of their readers and contributors; and like censors of books, they controlled the flow of information. They may not have actually prevented information from reaching the public entirely, but they tempered the way such information was received and thus directed the tastes, interests, and activities of readers.

This was a role, in fact, which journalists fully acknowledged. Critics of journals tended to make the comparison between censors and journalists – Tanneguy Le Fèvre, criticised by the *Journal des sçavans*, responded with a piece called *Journal du Journal, ou Censure du Censure* – but the title could also be a positive one. Jean Cornand de La Crose, for example, wrote in his Frenchified English that journals ought to give 'an impartial Censure of every Book ...'.[51] Most telling, however, is the adoption of the persona of Censor in a number of literary magazines.[52] This device was most common in England, where the *Tatler* for April 22, 1710 saw Addison promising to censure morals or fashion under the title of Censor of Great Britain.[53] Addison's paper and persona were widely imitated both in England, where a magazine called *The Censor* appeared in 1717 and 1718, and abroad, where in The Hague, for example, a journal called *Le Censeur* began publication in 1714. Armand de la Chapelle translated the *Tatler* into French in the 1720s and 1730s, and both Van Effen in the Netherlands and Marivaux in France wrote imitations of the equally censorious *Spectator* in French and eventually in Dutch. In all, according to Jean Sgard, about 100 imitations of the *Tatler* and the *Spectator* appeared between 1720 and 1789 on the continent, all involving a fictional narrator who observed, who tattled, or who censored manners and morals.[54] The more modern usage of 'censor' was also well-represented in the journals. As early as 1708 we find a monthly *Censura Temporum: The Good or Ill Tendencies of Books, Sermons, Pamphlets, &c. Impartially Consider'd*, and in Fielding's *Covent-Garden Journal*, as in some of his earlier papers, the author takes on the role of 'Knight-Censor of Great Britain', whose facetious 'Court of Censorial Enquiry' deals almost solely with issues of literary taste.[55] Francophone identifications with these values included a *Censeur hebdo-madaire*, which ran in Paris from 1759-62 and at least initially limited itself to literary criticism, and a *Censeur universel anglais*, which reviewed English books from 1785-88.[56]

Even down to the title, then, literary journals and their journalists performed the office of censor in the Republic of Letters. Like their more official counterparts, their function was in large part to control the flow of information and communication within their society. But the goals of this control were, unsurprisingly, different from those of the office of the French chancellor. Journals aimed to enforce, not the laws of states and nations, but the unwritten rules of the Republic of Letters. As we have seen, they hoped to encourage writing and conduct which would benefit the community, and that meant the scholarly community; the most important thing about a scholar was that he contributed to the Republic, and for a book to be 'useful' was the quality which meant that it was 'worthy of being read'.

As one of the theoretical aims of the Republic of Letters and its journalists – impossible to achieve as it proved – was to attempt neutrality on political and religious issues, at least when acting within learned society, it is evident that the Republic's goals could clash with those of the French government. As I have noted, the government instructed its censors to look out for anything dangerous for the state, the church, or good morals. The *avocat général*, Joly de Fleury, summarised it thus in 1768:

It seems that in the matter of the censorship of books, there are five things which one must protect oneself from when it comes to authors: 1st, Things which are detrimental to religion, and 2nd things which are detrimental to the authority of the King; 3rd things which favour the corruption of morals; 4th the philosophes [or systems] that favour independence in everything, [and] tend in the most sensitive manner to belittle religion, the authority of the prince and the principles of good morals, which in an inevitable result cut the bonds of society among men; 5th those controversies argued among ministers of the Church on the subject of religion, which can trouble peace and tranquility, and on which the King has imposed silence.[57]

The instructions censors were given about this were admittedly rather vague. Each censor would be sent a piece of writing to read, along with a printed form with the blanks filled in: 'Monsieur *blank* will, please, take the trouble to examine this *blank* [either print or manuscript] with every possible attention & diligence, in order to give his judgement immediately to M. THE CHANCELLOR.'[58] The censors were then to make recommendations about whether to grant a variety of permissions to print, including the privilege, which gave exclusive copyrights and required a signed approbation from the censor, through the simple permission, which allowed publication but gave no exclusive rights, to the *permission tacite*, an anonymous permission for books the government was unwilling to acknowledge, but still would allow to be published. Of course, books could also be refused any permission, as happened in between 1/4 and 2/3 of cases.[59] The law gave no specific indication of how to make these decisions. But as censors met every Thursday to give their reports orally — much as the authors of the *Journal des sçavans* met weekly to read their *extraits* aloud[60] — they must have had plenty of opportunity to imbibe the standards upheld by their colleagues.[61] The fact was, however, that the censors' judgements which survive — either as recorded in summary in the registers of requested permissions, or in written reports from those unable to attend the Thursday meetings — tend to deviate frequently from the criteria of danger to the church, state, and morals.

Modern scholars of censorship have generally attributed this deviation to incompetence. As William Hanley expresses it: 'No proper guidelines existed for the censor .... The responsibility for interpreting the law fell on the censor without detailed instructions from his superiors .... As a result, chaotic arbitrariness reigned.'[62] But I wonder how chaotic and arbitrary this censorship really was. For when I read surviving censors' reports from the first and sixth decades of the century — the two periods when I knew that ranks of censors and authors of the *Journal* so greatly overlapped — they had a rather familiar ring. They suggested that not only did journalists, eager for control, think like censors; censors also thought like journalists.

This is not to say that censors did not look out for the requisite dangers for morals, church, and state. A large number of books were refused permission for just these reasons; in 1755, for example, a book on the state of the dead and the revived was refused because '1st, the whole Preface is Calvinist, 2nd. the pains of Hell are spoken against ... Purgatory is spoken of as if it were a chimera .... It is taught there that the Body of Jesus Christ in Heaven is not composed of bone and Flesh and that we will not be resurrected in the same body.'[63] Similarly, in 1756 a book with the title *Journal de la descente des Anglois sur la côte de Bretagne* was refused, as the censor put it, 'for the glory of the Nation'.[64] And the majority of books accepted by the censors received only the comment specified by law: 'I have examined such and such a work by order of M. the Chancellor, and I have not found anything in it which could prevent its being printed.' This is all that censors were required to say. Nevertheless, it is telling how often censors chose to write at length about their books, and how often the reasons they gave for approving or disapproving them reflected other than governmental values.

The format of censors' reports, in the first place, not only often went well beyond the simple formula required, but their style and content made them sound just like *extraits* in journals. For example, many reports, like *extraits*, gave a plan of the book and a detail of its most interesting sections: information which was totally unnecessary in a censor's report. Simon, for example, wrote of the *Mémoires historiques sur la Louisiane*, 'This manuscript contains the most memorable things that happened in this country from 1687 to 1740, with the Establishment of the French colony in this continent of north America under the Direction of the India Company; These mémoires, divided into two parts and in 40 chapters, describe the climate, the environment, and the production of this country; the origin and the Religion of the savages who inhabit it, their ways, Customs, and Ceremonies, with a detail of the Concessions, and the wars which our colonies have had with these peoples.' It went on to praise the detail and style of the work. 'I believe that it will excite the Curiosity of the public, whom it has the ability to please, and that it merits being Printed.'[65] The censor of a life of Grotius took the time to say that 'The subject whose history is given [here] is well known in the republic of letters[;] savants will be satisfied to know in detail all the productions of this great man.' The censor went on to discuss Grotius's life, his 'spirit of singularity which attracted literary combats', and how tragic his death was, having 'been surprised by death in a foreign country, and apparently having finished his days miserably'. Any mention of the manuscript's suitability for publication – 'I believed I should make many changes', the censor said – was reserved for the last line of this lengthy report.[66]

Some scholars of censorship have said that the length and tone of positive reports is a result of the approbations being published along with the name of the censor; that censors were trying to curry favour with the authors. Robert Shackleton, for example, writes that the censor Burette praised the poet Houdar de la Motte in 1713 because 'he was a nobody called Burette and La Motte was a famous man and an academician', and he cites several other instances of this type of relationship.[67] But while flattery might have been one motive of censors – and was certainly not out of the bounds of the Republic of Letters – the journal-like qualities of censors' reports show a wider identification with the goals of the Republic. It is significant that comments were added to statements of permission even when nothing could be gained from the proceeding – as when Fontenelle, who was himself illustrious, being perpetual secretary of the Academy of Sciences, added to his censor's report praise of Christiaan Huygens, whose influence was tempered by his being both foreign and dead.[68] Moreover, censors did not only add remarks when they like a book; they frequently commented at length about manuscripts they felt to be reprehensibly awful. In these cases, they hoped to keep their names secret. In the beginning of the century, the registers of permissions and reprobations recorded only that refused manuscripts were given to read 'to M. XXX'; later this practice was changed, to the distress of some censors, who complained of being harassed by authors.[69] But another reason for wishing anonymity was one of critical reputation. An approbation, though required by the government when a book received a privilege, was thought to be an endorsement of the book's contents; censors sometimes pleaded for a *permission tacite* for bad books because, as Moncrif wrote of a book whose only good quality was that it 'has nothing in it which wounds morality', 'the verses in it are so bad and most of the time the subjects of the fables so trivial that it would be ridiculous to sign the manuscript in the title of *approbateur* ....'[70] Much like journalists who preferred to write their literary magazines anonymously, censors were less than anxious to be seen publicly endorsing terrible books.

What some historians have seen as a corruption of the system of censorship, then, turns out to be another issue of the Republic of Letters. Censors felt they were being called upon to write a kind of *extrait*, a comment on the *quality* of the work, not just its potential danger to church and state. This is amply clear from the kind of standards cited in censors' reports; for they are just the same standards as those in the literary journals. Literary style, for example, was just as important for censors as for journalists. The censors in Bignon's period were particularly vehement on this point, and the registers are filled with comments like 'Refused because its style is old and filled with ridiculous turns and expressions'; 'Refused as a piece without taste'; 'Refused. There is in this poem neither rhyme nor reason nor spelling'; 'Refused because this is just an attempt of some young provincial who does not yet know what it is to write'.[71] In some cases censors specifically passed a work on its potential danger, but still refused it on grounds of style. Of one work in 1703, for example, a censor wrote, 'Refused because although there is nothing in this work which does not preach virtue, nothing could be found which was further from reasonable taste than the style and the eloquence affected by the Author.'[72] Censors at mid-century were equally interested in good writing, and were still happy to refuse a book because 'its style is miserable',[73] or it had 'a style which provokes laughter';[74] on the other hand, they might approve it because 'it appeared to me well written' or, in the case of a French-Latin textbook, 'the words and the phrases are rendered in an appropriate Latinity' with 'exact and reformed spelling'.[75] And just as for journalists, it was order and clarity — attributes which helped contribute to the understanding of the reading community — which censors particularly hoped to promote. Tercier's favourable report on Mlle de Lussan's history of the revolution of Naples in 1647 contained nothing about the ostensible objects of censorship; only that 'the causes of this event are developed with much clarity, the facts are disposed with order' and 'united with a great deal of art ...'.[76] On the other side, a work was refused in 1752 in part because it contained 'neither real divisions, nor order, nor continuity'; another because it had 'neither order nor Method'.[77]

Content was another area where censors echoed the values of journalists, rather than the law. Often, instead of protecting the state or church, they saw their role instead as one of protecting good taste. Standards of writing, particularly academic writing, had to be upheld, whether by journalists or by censors. Thus in 1704 a treatise on fortification was refused permission because the author did not know what he was talking about: 'refused because the Author is writing on a subject that he has not studied in depth, it not being his profession, so that this work is full of errors, besides being taken from a treatise of fortification by M. Sauveur'.[78] A book about the power of the king to nominate to bishoprics was criticised because it contained 'very boring digressions on the life of the saints' and because the author, besides presenting a disordered work, 'is very unfaithful in his citations, attributing to the Authors he cites terms which they did not use'.[79] Censors waxed eloquent on works which, like one by the Chevalier d'Herissant, were judged 'base, ... without vision, without design, without taste, obscure, forced, and so on. A total mishmash.'[80] Just like scholars and journalists who bemoaned the appearance of books which corrupted taste, censors considered inferior books a legitimate target for their powers. A periodical called *La forest de Marli* was refused permission in 1703 because, as the censor said, 'it is to the good of letters to stop the course of this flood of little stories & of Fairy tales which do nothing but bore people of good taste and ruin the wits of the rest'.[81]

That phrase is significant: 'to the good of letters'. For censors, as for journalists, it was the good a book could do in the Republic of Letters that made it of value. Just as *extraits* recommended books for their utility, censors' reports are littered with comments that to publish a particular book would be 'to render a service to the public'.[82] But the public that was meant was, in many cases, specifically the Republic of Letters. Journalists chose to praise books which added to the stock of knowledge of the learned community; censors were known to refuse books because they failed to do so. A set of geographic tables by Pavillon were refused in part because they are 'not as good as those by the Sieurs Sanson and others'; in the same way, in 1704 a treatise on navigation was forbidden because 'the printing of this work would be of no utility; all the material which it contains is treated better elsewhere'.[83] If a work *was* pronounced useful, it was usually not useful to the state, the church, or good morals. Works were praised because they were 'very useful for the progress of Mathematics', because 'this Work will be useful for perfecting the general History of France', because the 'work would be very useful to the progress of good architecture'.[84] Recall that the formula for censors was 'I have read this work and have found nothing in it which could prevent its being printed'. Much as this formula was used, so were comments such as 'I have found nothing in it opposed to the progress of surgery'.[85]

These examples tell us that, although naturally censors were judges, as their name suggests, in many instances they were just the same kind of judges as journalists, those metaphorical censors of the Republic of Letters. It was not the case that the ranks of journalists were infiltrated by censors in a kind of government intervention into the formation of public opinion. Although ever since there had been royal censors French absolutism had extended to exercising power over cultural expression, it is evident from the language of censors that the values they applied when censoring books — whether in 1703 or 1753 — were at least in part those of the Republic of Letters. Just like journalists, they looked not just for potential damage to the ruling powers, but very often for whether a book was '*worthy* of being printed'.[86] And the standards they used to determine this worthiness were those of their own community.

The rules of the Republic of Letters extended even to the objection to censorship. We have seen that 18th-century writers had mixed feelings about issues of control; they did not like having their works censored, but they did not approve of the free publication of terrible works. Literary journals, as we have noted, were an expression of this desire for control. And even if we look closely at the annoyance expressed by writers at government censorship, we see that its objectionable character was not so much its limitation of freedom, but rather its violation of literary hierarchy. Literary journals offended scholars because of their unelected exercise of power over the Republic of Letters. And how did Voltaire complain about censorship? 'The greatest unhappiness of a man of letters,' he wrote, 'is perhaps not to be the object of the jealousy of his colleagues, the victim of cabal, the scorn of the powerful people of the world; it is to be judged by idiots.'[87] Diderot said the list of censors contained 'a crowd of unknown names' over whom he could only shrug his shoulders.[88] And on the eve of the Revolution a denunciation of the censorship system focused not on freedom, but on hierarchy. 'Can [my readers] imagine, without bursting out laughing, Voltaire, Montesquieu, J.J. Rousseau, Buffon, Destouches, Piron, Greffet, all men of letters, of all subjects, unable to offer their ideas to the public without consulting Armenonville, Chauvelin, Héraut, Berrier, Le Noir, de Crosne, Desentelles, Villequier, Marin, Suard, and all of that sort!'[89] To be judged was not a problem; who the judges *were*, however, was.

It would be wrong, then, to maintain the traditional stereotype that censors and writers in the 18th century were in an inevitable conflict of values over freedom of the press: writers and *philosophes* for, government censors against. But nor do I wish to argue that censors were entirely citizens of the Republic of Letters, who ignored or even subverted the rule of law in France. The situation is not nearly so simple. In fact the conflict of values was one which took place inside censors themselves, and it was not on such a fundamental point. The government required one type of censorship, while the Republic of Letters suggested another; and this conflict could be resolved by appropriating literary standards for governmental censorship. But it was type of control, rather than control itself, that was at issue. Censors and journalists both made it their business to uphold the standards of literature; so that the staff of the *Journal des sçavans* probably felt little confusion about their other roles as censors. Certainly that was the case of the Abbé Geinoz, who had written for the *Journal* since 1743 and had been a censor since 1748. In 1751 he complained to Malesherbes that, despite a promise, he had not been granted a pension as a royal censor; only in exceptional cases, or after 20 years, were censors paid. In making his case for a censor's pension, he cited as a qualification *not* his experience as a censor, but his eight years of work on the journal. And his protest at losing the pension was *not* to resign as a censor, but as a journalist. 'I had hoped,' he wrote, 'that you would do more justice to my zeal for the censorship of books and for literature in general.'[90] For Geinoz and his colleagues, censorship and literature were part of the same enterprise.

References

1. I would like to thank Jack R. Censer and Bertrand A. Goldgar for their comments on earlier versions of this piece, as well as Ellen Moerman for her generous advice.
2. On these standards, see Anne Goldgar, *Gentlemen and Scholars: Conduct and*

Community in the Republic of Letters, 1680-1750 (forthcoming, Yale University Press).

3. Boileau, preface to the first ed. of his works, quoted in Des Maizeaux, *La Vie de Monsieur Boileau Despreaux* (Amsterdam: Henri Schelte, 1712), p.38.

4. Adrien Baillet, *Jugemens des savans sur les principaux ouvrages des auteurs*, ed. and contd. by B. de la Monnoye (Paris: Charles Moette et al., 1722), I, p.3.

5. Théodore Parrhase [i.e., Jean Le Clerc], *Parrhasiana, ou pensées diverses sur des matiéres de critique, d'histoire, de morale et de politique avec la défense de divers ouvrages de Mr. L.C.* (Amsterdam: Henri Schelte, 1701), II, p.4.

6. Johann Burchard Mencke, *De la Charlatanerie des savans; par Monsieur Menken: avec des remarques critiques de differens Auteurs*, trans. from Latin by David Durand (The Hague: Jean van Duren, 1721), p.95.

7. [Charles-Etienne Jordan], *Histoire d'un voyage littéraire, fait en M.DCC.XXXIII. en France, en Angleterre, et en Hollande* (The Hague: Adrien Moetjens, 1735).

8. *Journal des sçavans* (Jan. 1665), 'L'Imprimeur au lecteur'. The Paris edition is cited in all cases.

9. Nicole Hermann-Mascard, *La Censure des livres à la fin de l'Ancien Régime (1750-1789)* (Paris: Presses Universitaires de France, 1968), p.42.

10. *Journal littéraire* VI, pt.1 (1715; 1732 Gosse and Neaulme ed.), art.IX, 164.

11. Albert Bachman, *Censorship in France from 1715 to 1750: Voltaire's Opposition* (New York: Institute of French Studies, Columbia University, 1934), p.1.

12. Catherine Blangonnet, 'Recherches sur les censeurs royaux aux temps de Malesherbes (1750-1763)', *Ecole Nationale des Chartes. Positions des thèses soutenues par les élèves de la promotion de 1975* (Paris: Ecole des Chartes, 1975), p.19.

13. This figure came from comparing a list of journalists in the *Table générale des matières contenues dans le Journal des Savans, de l'édition de Paris. Depuis l'année 1665 qu'il a commencé, jusqu'en 1750.... X* (Paris: Briasson, 1764), pp.646-8, with lists of censors I compiled from entries about individual books in Bibliothèque Nationale (henceforth BN) Ms.fr.21939, 'Registre de Monsieur l'Abbé Bignon contenant les Ouvrages presentés à Mgr le Chancelier Phelypeaux' (1699-1704); BN Ms.fr.21940, 'Registre des Ouvrages Manuscrits ...' (1705-6); BN Ms.fr.21941, 'Regître des ouvrages presentéz à Mgr le Chancelier', (1707-10); A.-M. Lottin, *Catalogue chronologique des libraires et des libraires-imprimeurs de Paris, depuis l'an 1470, époque de l'établissement de l'imprimerie dans cette capitale, jusqu'à présent* (Paris: Jean-Roch Lottin, 1789), pp.177-80, which covers 1742 to 1789; *La France littéraire* (Paris: la Veuve Duchesne, 1769), I, pp.154-7; *Almanach Royal* for 1746, 1749, 1751, 1758, 1759, 1769.

14. Blangonnet, p.19.

15. On the history of the *Journal des sçavants*, see Betty Trebelle Morgan, *Histoire du Journal des Sçavans depuis 1665 jusqu'en 1701* (Paris: Presses Universitaires de France, 1928); Raymond Birn, 'Le Journal des Savants sous l'Ancien Régime', *Journal des Savants* (Jan.-Mar. 1965), pp.15-35; Jean Ehrard and Jacques Roger, 'Deux périodiques français du 18ᵉ siècle: "le Journal des Savants" et "les Mémoires de Trévoux." Essai d'une étude quantitative', in Geneviève Bollème *et al.*, *Livre et société dans la France du XVIIIᵉ siécle* I (Paris and The Hague: Mouton, 1965), pp.33-59; 'Mémoire historique' in *Table générale des matières contenues dans le Journal des Savans* X; Cyril B. O'Keefe, *Contemporary Reactions to the Enlightenment (1728-1762): A Study of Three Critical Journals: The Jesuit "Journal de Trévoux", the Jansenist "Nouvelles ecclésiastiques", and the secular "Journal des Savants"* (Paris: Champion, 1974). Except for the

contemporary account in the *Table générale*, the history of the journal's administration after about 1728 has been ignored in the scholarship.

16. *Journal des sçavans*, March 1751, p.168.

17. Blangonnet, 'Recherches sur les censeurs royaux', *Positions des thèses*, p.19.

18. On the journal's conservatism and unreceptiveness to the Enlightenment, see O'Keefe, *Contemporary Reactions*, pp.32-6, 84-8. It would be misleading to suppose, however, that the *Journal des sçavans* and the censorship bureau shared values simply because the *Journal* was particularly conservative. Journalists for less orthodox periodicals were also censors, and, moreover, some censors were notably sympathetic to Enlightenment ideas. Condillac, Lavocat, Du Resnel, and Crébillon *fils* are names William Hanley points to as 'questionable ... [w]ardens of orthodoxy' (William Hanley, 'The Policing of Thought: Censorship in Eighteenth-century France', *Studies on Voltaire and the Eighteenth Century* 183 [1980], pp.277-8), and J.-P. Belin writes that, at least toward the end of the century, 'les censeurs ne se faisaient pas aucun scrupule d'approuver ou même d'encourager les ouvrages des philosophes, qui étaient souvent leurs amis' (J.-P. Belin, *Le Commerce des livres prohibés à Paris de 1750 à 1789* [Paris: Belin frères, 1913], pp.31-2). Malesherbes himself was sympathetic to the *philosophes*, although, as Pierre Grosclaude argues, it was not the case that he used his position to favour them (Pierre Grosclaude, *Malesherbes, témoin et interprète de son temps* [Paris: Librairie Fischbacher, 1961], chapter IV). The fact that a range of attitudes existed in the community of censors suggests that the confluence of the views of censors and journalists – particularly views on taste, rather than politics – was not limited to the conservative-leaning *Journal des sçavans*.

19. 'Censor', *OED* II, p.218.

20. Frédéric Godefroy, *Dictionnaire de l'ancienne langue française et de tous ses dialectes du IXe au XVe siècle* (1883) II, p.15.

21. Edmond Huguet, *Dictionnaire de la langue française du seizième siècle* (1932) II, p.150; Oscar Bloch and O. Wartburga, *Dictionnaire etymologique de la langue française*, 4th ed. (1964), p.116.

22. Bloch and Wartburga, p.116.

23. *Critique désintéressée des journaux littéraires et des ouvrages des savans* I, preface.

24. BN Ms. fr. nouv. acq. 1216, f.173, Jacques Basnage to Nicolas Clément, March 22, [1708].

25. Universiteitsbibliotheek, Amsterdam (henceforth UBA), Ms. J 33, Gally de Gaujac to Le Clerc, London, May 4, 1726.

26. [Denis-François Camusat], *Histoire critique des journaux*, ed. Jean-Frédéric Bernard (Amsterdam: J.-F. Bernard, 1734) II, p.71.

27. UBA, Ms. N 24 ae, Jean Le Clerc to Robert Chouet, 1685, copy or draft.

28. Koninklijke Bibliotheek, The Hague, Ms. 72 H 18 #46, Gisbert Cuper to Maturin Veyssière La Croze, June 28/July 1, 1710.

29. *Journal des sçavans* I (1665; new ed. 1723), 5, 'L'Imprimeur au Lecteur'.

30. UBA, Ms. C 19 b, Jean-Paul Bignon to Jean Le Clerc, Paris, Feb. 27, 1705.

31. BN Ms.fr.19211, f.172, Jacques Bernard to Delaissement, The Hague, April 6, 1702. Copy.

32. Camusat, *Histoire critique des journaux* II, p.41.

33. See, for example, the *Bibliothèque italique* I (Jan.-April 1728), 'Preface', pp.xx-xxi: 'Ils [i.e. the journalists] sentent bien, que leur Lecteur ne sera pas entiérement rassuré par cette promesse, s'il craint quelque partialité dans leur Ouvrage. Tous les *Journalistes* leur

dira-t-on, ont pris le même engagement, & presque tous l'ont violé en quelque occasion. MM. de *Trevoux* ont promis avec *serment* de l'observer; on les accuse pourtant, assés souvent, dans le Journal de Venise, le plus retenu de tous sur leur chapitre, de ne point tenir parole. Un seul exemple comme celui-là, doit bannir pour jamais la confiance en tous les Journalistes.'

34. *Bibliothèque universelle* I (1686; 2nd ed. 1687), preface.
35. *Bibliothèque choisie* I (1703; new ed. 1718), 'Avertissement'.
36. Jean Cornand de la Crose, *Works of the Learned* (Aug. 1691), 'To the Reader'.
37. UBA, Ms. C 83 b, Jacques Lenfant to Le Clerc, Heidelberg, Jan. 4, 1687.
38. *Journal litéraire* I (May-June 1713; 2nd ed. 1715), 'Preface', vii.
39. La Crose, *Works of the Learned* (Aug. 1691), 'To the Reader'.
40. *Journal des sçavants*, January 1724, 'Avertissement'.
41. *Bibliothèque raisonnée* I, pt.2 (Oct.-Dec. 1728), p.275.
42. *Journal des sçavants*, May 1751, p.283. Extrait of Macquer, *Elemens de chymie pratique* (1751).
43. *Journal des sçavants*, June 21, 1706, p.384. Extrait of *Les Entretiens des voyageurs sur la mer* (1704).
44. *Journal des sçavants*, Feb. 1750, pp.107-8. Extrait of Bouhier, *Les Coutumes du Duché de Bourgogne*.
45. *ibid.*, Jan. 1750, p.21. Extrait of Eduardo Corsini, *Fasti Attici*.
46. *ibid.*, Sept. 1751, p.596. Extrait of Muratori, *Annali d'Italia*. Similar comments can be found in, among other places, issues for Oct. 1751, p.652, and Feb. 1752, p.104.
47. Anne Dacier, *Les Oeuvres d'Homère, traduites en françois* I (Amsterdam: Wetsteins and Smith, 1731), preface, p.iii.
48. KB, Ms. 72 G 33, Gisbert Cuper to Pierre Jurieu, June 7, 1704.
49. [Charles Sorel], *De la Connoissance des bons livres, ou Examen de plusieurs autheurs* (Paris: André Pralard, 1671), pp.103ff.
50. *ibid.*, 'Avertissement sur ce Livre'.
51. *Universal Historical Bibliotheque*, Jan. 1686, 'The Preface to the Reader'.
52. On this see Hugh Amory, 'Magistrate or Censor? The Problem of Authority in Fielding's Later Writings', *Studies in English Literature 1500-1900* XII, no.3 (summer 1972), pp.503-18.
53. Donald F. Bond, ed., *The Tatler*, no.162 (Oxford: Clarendon Press, 1987) II, pp.402-5.
54. Jean Sgard, 'La multiplication des périodiques' in Henri-Jean Martin and Roger Chartier, eds, *Histoire de l'édition française* II [Paris: Promodis, 1984], p.204. On La Chapelle's *Babillard*, see Donald F. Bond, 'Armand de la Chapelle and the First French Version of the *Tatler*', in Carroll Camden, ed., *Restoration and Eighteenth-Century Literature: Essays in Honor of Alan Dugald McKillop* (Chicago: University of Chicago Press, 1963), pp.161-84.
55. See B.A. Goldgar, ed., *The Covent-Garden Journal* (Oxford: Clarendon Press, 1988), no.3 (Jan. 11, 1752), no.7 (Jan. 25), no.9 (Feb. 1), no.10 (Feb. 4), no.12 (Feb. 11), No.15 (Feb. 22), and no.24 (Mar. 24), all 1752. See also Goldgar's 'General Introduction', pp.xxxiv-vi.
56. On these periodicals, see Jean Sgard, ed., *Dictionnaire des journaux* (Paris: Universitas, and Oxford: Voltaire Foundation, 1991) I, pp.222-3 and 224-5.
57. BN, Collection Joly de Fleury 2192, f.195, Joly de Fleury to the chancelier, Dec. 18, 1716, quoted in J.-P. Belin, *Le Commerce des livres prohibés*, p.18, and in Herrmann-

Mascard, *La Censure des livres*, p.45.

58. An example of this form is BN Ms. fr. 22139, f.117 (Coyecque #100). I use 'Coyecque' to denote the numeration given in Ernest Coyecque, *Inventaire de la Collection Anisson*, 2 vols (Paris: Ernest Leroux, 1900), because the folio numbers at the BN and the numbers in Coyecque's inventory (which are also listed on the manuscripts) differ. Coyecque enumerates by item, whereas the BN enumerates by folio.

59. See Robert Estivals, *La Statistique bibliographique de la France sous la monarchie au XVIIIe siècle* (Paris and the Hague: Mouton and Co., 1965).

60. For references to these meetings, see BN Ms.fr.22133, ff.112-112^v (Coyecque #72), Fugere to Malesherbes, Paris, May 25, 1757; *ibid.*, ff.100-100^v (Coyecque #100), draft by Malesherbes of a letter about an extrait by Lavirotte of the second volume of the *Encyclopédie*; 'Mémoire historique du Journal des Sçavans' in *Table générale* X, p.630.

61. These Thursday meetings are mentioned, among other places, in BN Ms.fr.22137, ff.140-140^v (Coyecque #125), the Abbé Graves to [Malesherbes], Arpajou le Chateau, Aug. 26, 1754; and *ibid.*, ff.110-110^v (Coyecque #98), Foucher to [Malesherbes], Dec. 20, 1755.

62. Hanley, 'The Policing of Thought', p.278.

63. BN Ms.fr.22137, ff.63-63^v (Coyecque #58), Censor's report by Cotterel on *Traité de l'état des morts et des resuscitans*, Paris, Aug. 14, 1755.

64. BN Ms.fr.22138, ff.15-15^v (Coyecque #14), the Abbé de la Ville to [Malesherbes], Fontainebleau, Oct. 17, 1756.

65. BN Ms.fr.22139, f.123 (Coyecque #106). Censor's report by Simon on *Mémoires historiques sur la Louisiane*, n.d.

66. BN Ms.fr.22138, ff.105-105^v (Coyecque #98). Censor's report by De Marcilly, Paris, May 4, 1752.

67. Robert Shackleton, 'Censure and Censorship: Impediments to Free Publication in the Age of Enlightenment', *The Library Chronicle of the University of Texas at Austin* n.s. no.6 (Dec. 1973), p.30.

68. BN Ms.fr.21939, f.29. 'Registre de Monsieur l'Abbé Bignon contenant les Ouvrages presentés à Mgr le Chancelier Phelypeaux'; record of decision of censor Fontenelle on *Le Cosmotheoros, ou nouveau traité de la pluralité des mondes, traduit du Latin de M. Hughens*. June 7, 1701.

69. For 'Donné à M. XXX', see BN Ms.fr.21939, 'Registre de Monsieur l'Abbé Bignon'. At mid-century, some censors took care to request anonymity, as De Moncrif did in a letter to Malesherbes: 'Je me flate que vous Avez la bonté de ne me point Nommer Aux auteurs quand vous me renvoyez des Ouvrages Susceptibles de quelques observations qui peuvent leur deplaire.' BN Ms.fr.22138, f.182 (Coyecque #167), De Moncrif to [Malesherbes], no date. In 1770 the censor Coqueley de Chaussepierre wrote a 'Mémoire Sur ... la Necessité que dans tous les cas, le nom du Censeur soit inconnu', saying that this 'épargneroit aux censeurs occupées d'ailleurs des visites et une perte de tems tres incommode des sollicitations fatiguantes, et souvent de complaisances dangereuses que les instances des auteurs ou de leurs amis leur arrache[nt].' BN Ms.fr.22123, ff.109-10 (Coyecque #31), Jan. 1770.

70. BN Ms.fr.22138, f.164 (Coyecque #149). Moncrif to [Malesherbes], Versailles, April 1, 1751, reporting on *Dialogues et fables allégoriques*.

71. BN Ms.fr.21940, 'Registre des ouvrages manuscrits ou imprimés presentés a Mgr Le Chancelier, 1705-7', f.26, entry on *La mere Chrestienne*, no censor listed, Feb. 5, 1705;

BN Ms.fr.21939, 'Registre de M. l'Abbé Bignon', f.48^v, entry on *Entretiens curieux sur les affaires du tems*, no censor listed, May 24, 1702; *ibid.*, f.126^v, entry on *Cantique au St Esprit*, no censor listed; *ibid.*, f.47^v, entry on de Forteville, *La Vie du cavalier religieux*, no censor listed, May 20, 1701.

72. BN Ms.fr.21939, f.69^v, 'Registre de M. l'Abbé Bignon', entry for *La Conduite de l'esprit & du coeur*, June 6, 1703.

73. BN Ms.fr.22137, f.153 (Coyecque #138), censor's report by the Abbé Guiroy on the *Almanach des plaisirs*, Nogent-sur-Marne, July 24, 1753.

74. BN Ms. fr.21939, 'Registre de M. l'Abbé Bignon', f.112^v, entry on *La Concordance des philosophes discordans*, no censor listed, July 10, 1704.

75. BN Ms.fr.22137, f.116 (Coyecque #103), censor's report by the Abbé Geinoz on the letters of De la Rivière, Paris, Nov. 24, 1750; BN Ms.fr.22138, f.43 (Coyecque #41), censor's report by Le Bret on additions to the *Apparat royal françois latin*, Paris, Oct.15, 1758.

76. BN Ms.fr.22139, f.176-176^v (Coyecque #151), Tercier to [Malesherbes], Versailles, Nov. 25, 1756.

77. BN Ms.fr.22138, f.47 (Coyecque #45), censor's report by Le Rouge on *60 Exhortations sur l'Eucharistie*, Paris, Aug. 21, 1752; BN Ms.fr.22139, f.4 (Coyecque #3), censor's report by [De Parcieux] on Bonnal's arithmetic.

78. BN Ms.fr.21939, f.109, no censor listed, June 1, 1704.

79. BN Ms.fr.21939, f.79, entry for the Abbé Faydit, *Tradition des Eglises de France sur le droit et le pouvoir de nos rois dans la nomination aux evêchés de leur royaume independamment de l'election des peuples & des bulles de Rome*, no censor listed, Oct. 27, 1703.

80. BN Ms.fr.21939, f.105, entry for the Chevalier d'Herissant, *Les Caracteres des petits maîtres avec la morale civile et politique sur chaque portrait*, no censor listed, Mar. 22, 1704.

81. BN Ms.fr.21939, f.66^v, entry for the Comtesse d'Auneuil, *La forest de Marli, nouvelles du tems*, no censor listed, Feb. 13, 1703.

82. BN Ms.fr.22139, f.15 (Coyecque #13), censor's report by Depasse on a work by De Launay on the study of Latin. No date [1750s]. Other such comments appear in *ibid.*, f.100 (Coyecque #86); *ibid.*, f.38 (Coyecque #32); Ms.fr.22137, f.145 (Coyecque #130); *ibid.*, f.136 (Coyecque #121); MS.fr.22138, f.71 (Coyecque #64); *ibid.*, f.21 (Coyecque #20); and in many other reports.

83. BN Ms.fr.21939, f.79^v, entry on Pavillon, *Tables Géographiques contenant les principales parties du monde*, no censor listed, Aug. 30, 1703; *ibid.*, f.129^v, entry on Bouguier, *Navigation par les Echelles*, no censor listed, Dec. 30, 1704.

84. BN Ms.fr.22137, f.37 (Coyecque #41), censor's report by Bouger on *La Géometrie métaphysique*, Paris, Mar. 3, 1758; *ibid.*, f.14 (Coyecque #13), censor's report by Belley on *Histoire civile et ecclésiastique de la ville d'Amiens et de sa banlieue*, Paris, Sept. 27, 1751; BN Ms.fr.22138, f.37 (Coyecque #36), censor's report by Le Blond on Blondel, *Archictecture françoise*, Versailles, July 22, 1752.

85. BN Ms.fr.22138, f.72 (Coyecque #65), censor's report by Louis on *Le temple d'amour*, Paris, July 21, 1752.

86. For this expression see, for example, BN Ms.fr.22137, f.143 (Coyecque #129); *ibid.*, f.35 (Coyecque #32); MS.fr.22138, f.23 (Coyecque #22); Ms.fr.22139, ff.62-62^v (Coyecque #55); *ibid.*, f.183 (Coyecque #158).

87. Voltaire, *Dictionnaire philosophique*, quoted in Bachman, *Censorship in France*, p.123. For further remarks of this type by Voltaire, see Hanley, 'Policing', p.277.

88. Denis Diderot, 'Lettre historique et politique adressée à un magistrat sur le commerce de la librairie', in *Oeuvres complètes*, ed. Roger Lewinter (Paris: Le Club Français du Livre, 1970) V, p.373.

89. Marie Joseph Blaise de Chénier, *Dénonciation des inquisiteurs de la pensée* (Paris: La Grange, 1789), p.19; also quoted in Belin, p.23. For similar remarks see also Louis-Sébastien Mercier's popular *L'An Deux Mille Quatre Cent Quarante* (London, 1772), pp.55-6.

90. BN Ms.fr.22133, f.138 (Coyecque #91), Geinoz to [?Malesherbes], Paris, Nov. 29, 1751.

Church censorship in the 19th century: the Index of Leo XIII

Michael J. Walsh

I WOULD LIKE to start with a personal reminiscence. I was, for 20 years, a member of the Society of Jesus. When in the Autumn of 1958 I began my philosophical studies as a young Jesuit I was introduced to the library which was at the disposal of those in the three-year course. I was immediately struck by the large letter 'L' which appeared on the spine of some of the volumes on the shelves. These books, I was told, were on the 'Index', the *Index Librorum Prohibitorum* or catalogue of works which had been banned by the Pope. Were it necessary for me to read them, then I had to seek permission from the Rector of the College.

Now the method of study was little changed from the middle ages — though the content was — and we were faced with theses to prove by syllogism, authorities to quote in support, and 'adversarii' or opponents whose views we were to demonstrate to be false. All this, I might add, was conducted orally and in Latin. Among the 'adversarii' we were thus to demolish were figures such as Thomas Hobbes, David Hume and Immanuel Kant whose books were on the Index, and therefore technically forbidden to us to read. Permission to read them was always readily given, and we were encouraged to obtain it: the only time there was any hesitation, so far as I remember, was when I wished to read certain works on Marxism by Marxists.

The Index then in force was that of 1948, which proved to be the last. The Sacred Congregation of the Index was merged with the Holy Office (formerly the Holy Roman Inquisition) in 1917. The catalogue of banned books for which it had responsibility survived for not quite half a century more, to be abolished in 1966.

Apart from those volumes marked 'L' on the open shelves, I was later to discover, there was another category of volumes locked away in a small room known as 'Hell', a term widely used for such places in Roman Catholic centres of learning. I was once shown round it, though of the books it contained I can now recall only two: Luther's Table Talk, and an edition of Rabelais with somewhat exuberant illustrations.

The point of this story is to indicate that in my experience the Index, though well enough known about in ecclesiastical circles at least, was not in the 1950s taken very seriously. It was certainly no problematic bar to the pursuit of scholarship. Ronald Knox, in his book *Difficulties*, an exchange of letters with Arnold Lunn on the hazards of conversion, remarked that though he often poked about in libraries, he had only once ever seen a copy of it.[1] This is a rather odd remark. Had he ever visited the library which I now run, which I imagine he did, for he arrived at Oxford as Roman Catholic chaplain in 1926, the same year that the Library was established 15 miles away at Heythrop Hall,[2] he would have seen a dozen or so different editions from 1597 down to that of 1948, including one in English.

Knox's view, that the Index was a thing of little importance, may have reflected a specifically English attitude. It was long held that the provisions of the Council of Trent did not apply in England because they had not been promulgated here, and this was conveniently taken to include Index legislation. On 23 October 1850 Newman wrote to Mgr George Talbot in Rome that 'I have lately had good advice from Rome that one may act as if the rule about prohibited books had not been promulgated in England'.[3] The advice he had indirectly received concluded, 'This theologian strongly dissuades you from applying to the Holy See on this subject, as then the Sacred Congregations would of course try to enforce the strict law, which in the temper of the English people would or might cause great trouble, whereas the present non-usage is sufficient to check people from reading books dangerous to them individually'.[4] Newman, it must be admitted, had his own somewhat idiosyncratic view of the Index, claiming, according to Mgr Humphrey Johnson, 'that he knew of no work which would so readily make him an infidel as [Frederick William] Faber's book, *The Blessed Sacrament*'.[5] The theologian to whom Newman was referring was right. When a 'Dubium' was eventually put to the Congregation of the Index, whether the provisions of censorship legislation applied in England or not, the Congregation responded on 23 May 1898 that they did. The English bishops continued to ignore it.

The Index had, on the other hand, received a passionate defence the previous December in the columns of the *Tablet*, the English Roman Catholic weekly:

Probably out of every hundred Englishmen or Americans who rail against the restrictions of the Index, not a tithe has any direct acquaintance with, or takes any due account of, the flood of bitterly anti-Christian literature, often infidel, immoral, and blasphemous and almost always insidiously polemical, which is poured over Italy and the continent generally, by the masonic and anti-clerical press. It is in great measure this degrading abuse of one of the noblest faculties of civilized society, and the need of duly protecting the minds of the masses, that the provisions of the Index are specially designed to meet. It is simply a measure of Catholic sanitation .... We maintain that in English-speaking countries there does not exist upon any large or popular scale such bitter and active propaganda against Christianity and Christian morality as are unhappily at work abroad, nor is there that widespread production of aggressively anti-Christian and pornographic literature which the infidel and anti-clerical press pours forth like a pestilential sewer in certain continental countries.[6]

That was one form of defence of the Index from a Catholic source. Another was equally unapologetic. Writing of the common practice of the ancient world, one Jesuit claimed,

Everywhere the books declared dangerous were cast into the fire – the simplest and most natural execution of censorship. When at Ephesus, in consequence of St Paul's preaching, the heathen were converted, they raised before the eyes of the Apostle of the Gentiles a pile in order to burn their numerous superstitious books (Acts, xix, 19). No doubt the Christians, moved by grace and the Apostolic word did so of their own accord; but all the more was their action approved by St Paul himself, and it is recorded as an example worthy of imitation by the author of the Acts of the Apostles.[7]

The composer of this apology for book-burning was Joseph Hilgers (1858-1918), a Jesuit priest and author of *Der Index der verbotenen Bücher in seiner neuen Fassung dargelegt und rechtlich-historisch gewürdigt*, published by Herder of Freiburg in 1904. While this 630-odd page volume is an unabashed defence of the use of the Index as a means of censorship, it is nonetheless the most thorough history of it available,[8] and was clearly used by George Putnam as the basis for his two-volume *The Censorship of the Church of Rome*, published in 1906.

The full title of Putnam's book is *The Censorship of the Church of Rome and Its Influence upon the Production and Distribution of Literature: A Study of the Prohibitory and Expurgatory Indexes, together with some Consideration of the Effects of Protestant Censorship and of Censorship by the State.* Speaking of the Hilgers volume he says that a reader would gather from it

a record of an administration of fatherly beneficence on the part of wise advisers, of a pleading with the perverse that they should be saved from the consequences of their own perversity; of actions furthering all scholarship that was in itself wholesome and sound, and of the discouragement simply of such perverted intellectual efforts as tended to lead men away from their duty to their Creator and to undermine the moral conduct of their own lives.[9]

Putnam's own view, not surprisingly, is wholly other:

> To the extent to which the prohibitions and restrictions of the Indexes were carried out consistently [which, one ought perhaps to interject, is a very big proviso], literary activity was checked, the production of higher literature was lessened, and the intellectual capacities of the people were stunted.
>
> It seems hardly possible that the indirect service ... that was rendered by the work of censors in emphasizing for communities, not within the control of their prohibitions, the distinctive interest and abiding importance of the prohibited books, could make an adequate offset for the sterilising influence exerted within the communities that were under thorough supervision and control.[10]

The assertion that because of the Index, 'literary activity was checked, the production of higher literature was lessened, and the intellectual capacities of the people were stunted', Putnam finds difficult to sustain.[11] He also thinks that the Protestant Reformation was just as harmful to literary activity, not because of censorship, but because the Reformers were too solemn.

Lord Acton, from the Catholic side, had an antipathy to the Index at least as strong as that of Putnam. He called it 'One of the great instruments for preventing historical scrutiny', saying that it was 'directed, not against falsehood only, but particularly against certain departments of truth. Through it an effort has been made to keep the knowledge of ecclesiastical history from the faithful, and to give currency to a fabulous and fictitious picture of the progress and action of the Church'.[12] These words are taken from an article in *The Home and Foreign Review* of April 1864, a piece which marked that journal's demise. The event which had aroused Acton's ire was the condemnation on 5 March 1857 of a book — heterodox by anyone's judgement it must be admitted — by Jakob Frohschammer on the origins of the soul. And it seems it was not so much the condemnation itself to which Acton objected, but Rome's refusal to tell Frohschammer why he had been put on the Index. This 'was a favour, he was told, sometimes extended to men whose great services to the Church deserved such consideration, but not to one who was hardly known except by the very book which had incurred the censure. This answer,' Acton concludes, 'instantly aroused the suspicion that the Roman Court was more anxious to assert its authority than to correct an alleged error, or to prevent a scandal.'[13]

Acton was, of course, himself to have direct experience of the Index when two works of his in German, *Zur Geschichte des Vaticanischen Concils* and *Sendschreiben an einen deutschen Bischof des Vaticanischen Concils*, were put on it by a decree of the Holy Office of 20 September 1871. He later determined to write a history of the book, and collected copies of the Index to that end, over 30 in all, together with a number of local versions and other related works, but the project came to nothing.[14]

I have so far been addressing the question of the Index and reactions to it in the 19th century without dwelling upon its nature and history. Historians of the book trade will know something of these from the work of Paul Grendler on *The Roman Inquisition and the Venetian Press, 1540-1605*[15] and similar studies — most of which, and there have been a good number, have been largely concerned with the 16th century. Mention of the Roman Inquisition reminds one that here is being discussed only the Index published by authority of the Holy See. In the catalogue of Indexes at present being published by the Centre for Renaissance Studies at the University of Sherbrooke in Quebec, there are 33 editions of the Index listed for the 16th century of which only five were published in Rome. Of the others, Munich, Milan and Parma published one each, Liége and Venice two, Antwerp and Louvain three, Paris six and the Portuguese Inquisition a total of seven.

The series of Roman Indexes begins with the particularly severe one of 1559, whose strictures had immediately to be modified. Five were published in the 16th century, three in the 17th, seven in the 18th and the same number again in the 19th century. To complete the tally, there were no less than a dozen produced in the present century, in fact in the first half of this century for, as I have already mentioned, that of 1948 proved to be the last.

Every historian of Church censorship begins with the example of St Paul which I have quoted above, and then usually goes on to the condemnation at the Council of Nicea in 325 of the *Thalia* of Arius, followed by the condemnation of the writings of Origen by Pope Anastasius in 400 as harmful to the ignorant though helpful to the wise.[16] From then on paths diverge. Hilgers has an interesting story that the great St Boniface sent books to Rome for judgement by Pope Zachary in 745, which were then submitted to the Roman synod. The synod ordered them burnt, but Pope Zachary instructed that they be preserved in the Apostolic Archive.[17]

The potential of the printing press was rapidly understood by the popes. In 1467 Innocent VIII instructed that all books should be examined before permission could be granted for general reading, and that the license to print be put into every one. Thus came about the 'imprimatur' still to be found in certain books by Catholics — including, at the request of the publishers who thought it would help them to sell it, one by the present writer. The first volumes that might be identifiable as 'indexes of forbidden books' were not Roman works at all, but came, in 1544, 1545, 1547, 1548, 1551 and 1556, from the Theological Faculty of the University of Paris which was in a stronger position to control the publication of books than Rome ever was.

The first Roman Index, that of 1559, was also the first to be called an 'Index'. The name was chosen because the book served as a catalogue of books condemned by the bull *In coena Domini* which listed all excommunications for offences against faith or morals.[18] By the Constitution *Licet ab initio* of 21 July 1542 Pope Paul III created the Universal (though more commonly known as the Roman) Inquisition to defend the Church from heresy. As far as the papal states were concerned it did its task with spectacular speed and success, driving the proponents of the Reform from Italy and on 12 July 1543 promulgating a decree threatening fines, loss of employment and excommunication to printers, booksellers and customs officers who failed in their duty by printing, selling, owning or permitting the entry into the papal states of heretical works. It was the Inquisition which was responsible for the 1559 Index. The volume caused enormous problems. It distinguished three categories: (1) those whose writings were condemned just because of whom the authors were; (2) individual books condemned because it was thought they presented a danger to faith or morals; and (3) anonymous or pseudonymous works which did likewise. Of the thousand or so condemnations, about half were recognisable (from Rome's perspective) heretical authors, all of whose writings were banned. The remainder were a motley, though distinguished, group of scholars and humanists such as Machiavelli, Erasmus, Rabelais and others. Sixty-one printers were banned by name, as were a number of editions of the Scriptures.

In the 18th session of the Council of Trent (1562) a Commission of bishops was established to look into the question of the control of books, but the 'Tridentine Index' of 1564 was published after the close of the Council. The Tridentine Index was particularly important because, when it was promulgated by the bull *Dominici gregis* of 24 March 1564, included in it were ten 'rules', which governed the Index until the end of the 19th century. The rules banned books by heretics, controlled bibles, especially those in the vernacular, introduced the notion that some books might be published after correction, and forbade Catholics to read obscene or magical texts.[19]

When the Congregation of the Index was established on 4 April 1571 by the Constitution *In apostolicae* as an independent office of the Holy See, it was given the task not only of publishing the Index, but of editing texts to make them suitable. In the event the Congregation undertook this task only once, publishing an *Index Librorum Expurgandorum* 'for the benefit of the studious', as it says on the title page, in 1608. Rather oddly, a facsimile of this volume was published with a preface by Richard Gibbings, by Milliken of Dublin in 1837. Though the Congregation of the Index never undertook such an exercise again, restricting itself to issuing decrees against books 'donec corrigatur' without indicating what was to be corrected, the Inquisition in other countries seems regularly to have produced such lists of amendments to texts.

Certain changes were made as time went on: a category of 'Opera omnia' was introduced in 1603, and in 1664 the three classes of banned books were done away with, so that books were henceforward listed in a single alphabetical sequence. In 1753 Benedict XIV tidied up the Index, and printed it with, as an introduction, a Constitution *Sollicita ac provida* dated 9 July. This laid down, among other things, instructions to the censors of books about their strict impartiality: there had been complaints that perfectly reputable Catholic authors had been rather hastily judged and found wanting by the Congregation. According to Benedict XIV's instructions, the Secretary of the Index, who had the title of Magister Sacri Palatii and was always a Dominican, received denunciations. He was then to examine the books himself before sending them to two consultors, each of whom was to produce a report. These reports were to go to a committee of the consultors, and then to the committee of cardinals who made up the Congregation proper. Their judgement, under the Pope, was final.

The next major reform came with Leo XIII's Constitution *Officiorum et Munerum* of 25 January 1897, which was followed by the publication of a new Index in the year 1900. The Preface to the new Index was signed by the Dominican Thomas Esser who was Secretary to the Congregation from 1900 until it was absorbed in 1917 into the Holy Office (as the Inquisition was by that time known). He makes the point that

the Decretals [he means the Constitutions of successive popes governing the Index] prohibit the greatest possible number, indeed almost all, of noxious and tainted books, the reading of which is strongly forbidden by the Natural Law itself; while the Index reviews and notes but a small part of these. By the Decretals, *genera* and classes of bad books are proscribed; by the Index, individual books each with its title and even the author's name. Hence it is plain how greatly they err who suppose that the whole question of improper books to be decided by the Index alone, as though of the innumerable perverse and pernicious books which have appeared in the course of centuries, those only are prohibited which have been condemned by special decrees and noticed in the catalogue of prohibited books.[20]

The argument here is that it is the Natural Law, not the Church's positive law, which bans books, whether heretical or obscene. This would have been the view of censors down the ages: the catalogue only names the few (in Esser's opinion) which have been drawn to the attention of the ecclesiastical authorities.

The Constitution of Pope Leo XIII is extremely interesting. It makes the point that dissatisfaction with the Index was prevalent in the time of Pope Pius IX, Leo's predecessor, and had been expressed by the bishops of France, Germany, Italy, and elsewhere, and that there was unanimous agreement that changes had to be made.

If one considers the character of the times and the condition of civil institutions and of popular morals, we must admit that these demands [of the bishops for revision] are just and reasonable .... In the rapid development of intellectual activity, there is no field of knowledge in which literature is not produced too freely, with the result of a daily accumulation of foul and dangerous books. What is still more serious is that this great evil is not only connived at by the civil law, but even secures under them a great freedom. As a result, therefore, unrestricted license is assured for reading anything whatsoever, and the minds of many are filled with religious doubts.[21]

The tone is surprising. Leo XIII had supported Pastor in his writing of the *History of the Popes* even when the German scholar tackled the difficult topic of Alexander VI. Pastor heard him say *splendore veritatis gaudet ecclesia*, 'the church delights in the splendor of truth'. One might ask, whose truth? – but in Leo's case that would, I think, be unfair. He had founded a school of palaeography attached to the Vatican Archives, and to its graduates he awarded a diploma which had as its motto, *nihil est quod ecclesiae ob inquisitione veri metuatur* – 'The Church has nothing to fear from the quest for truth'.[22]

The Constitution with its rules was incorporated into the Code of Canon Law published in 1917, but as these regulations lie outside my period I shall not discuss them here. At least, I shall not discuss the Constitution itself. The Index is a different matter, for of course it listed all condemnations from 1600 to 1900: condemnations prior to 1600 remained in force, according to the 1900 edition, but were not included in the lists. They numbered some 2,000.

Church historians would, I think, expect the Index of 1900 to reflect the greater centralisation of authority which was Rome's policy in the 19th century, and the various threats to the status of the papacy, as well as the historical criticism of the Bible of the period. In a sense their expectations are fulfilled, but the issue is not clear-cut. The number of condemnations in 50-year blocks are as follows:

1600-1649	=	469	1650-1699	=	862
1700-1749	=	723	1750-1799	=	463
1800-1849	=	576	1850-1899	=	778

and, for completeness sake,

1900-1949	=	255[23]

There were marginally more condemnations in the 19th than in the 17th century, though the largest number of condemnations occurred in the century 1650-1749 when the Pope was facing squabbles between Jesuits and Jansenists, Jesuits and Franciscans over the Chinese Rites, and Jesuits and just about everybody else over moral theology. The battle between Jesuits and Dominicans over grace had by 1650 come to an end by papal decree. In many of these instances, indeed, condemnations were intended to halt acrimonious debate.

In the 19th century the Popes used the Index repeatedly to defend their position, condemning numerous books on Italy, the administration of the papal states, and other such works, including, in 1874, Gregorovius's *Geschichte der Stadt Rom*. In the 25 years from 1851 to 1875 the papacy was politically at its most vulnerable – Rome fell to Victor Emmanuel's troops in September 1870 – and theologically at its most controversial with acrimonious debate about the pope's primacy and infallibility: the Vatican Council's assertion of these, also in 1870, did not put an end to the argument. During that period no less than 470 works were condemned – more, indeed, because that figure takes no account of the authors whose total output was consigned to the Index, no less than six of them in 1864 alone.[24] That year was something of an *annus mirabilis* for the inquisitors. Not only did Pope Pius IX attempt wholescale rejection of the modern world in his 'Syllabus of Errors', together with the six authors condemned *in toto* there were 41 individual works condemned. In 1852 and again in 1857 there were 31 condemnations, including in the first of those years the complete works of Proudhon and Gioberti, as well as the *fabulae amatoriae* of Eugène Sue.

There are, in the lists for the years 1851 to 1875, some surprising omissions: works on socialism rarely occur, for example. It is not always easy to spot why volumes were picked out. Sometimes, of course, there were personal reasons: a vendetta against a particular German prelate led rather curiously to Laurence Sterne's *Sentimental Journey Through France and Italy* being put on the Index in 1819. In the period under review books on French history figure largely because they upheld the privileges of the 'Gallican' church which were thought to undermine papal authority. Works by the orientalist-turned-exegate Ernest Renan are frequently banned, and so are sundry lives of Christ including Renan's own, but in this quarter of a century biblical studies were clearly not seen as posing a significant threat. Rather more prominent in the lists are works on 'animal magnetism' which entailed a belief in the existence of a 'vital fluid'. The influence of the fluid, it was thought, accounted for the phenomenon of hypnotism. At its more eccentric this belief tailed off into astrology and spiritualism, thus incurring the displeasure of the Roman authorities.

Two philosophical theologians figure prominently in the list of books condemned over this period, Anton Günther and Jakob Frohschammer, both for fundamentally the same reason: they appeared to teach that the human mind could comprehend the mysteries of the Catholic faith. Whether or not they ought to have been put on the Index, at least theirs were the kinds of books for which the Index had been created. However, the books most constantly declared unorthodox during the period before and after the Vatican Council were not of this sort. They were works which either implicitly or explicitly criticised papal pretensions. This is especially obvious in the years immediately following Vatican I: practically all of the 14 condemned in 1871 related directly or indirectly to the papal theme. While the Index did during this period perform its more general function of safeguarding the faith and morals of members of the Church, its primary role was one of bolstering papal pretensions both political and, more significantly, theological.

The debate surrounding infallibility produced, naturally, its crop of denunciations, including the two works by Acton I have already mentioned and in 1868 Peter Renouf's *The condemnation of Pope Honorius*. Renouf, who ended his professional life as Keeper of Egyptian Antiquities at the British Museum, was a convert to Catholicism and a close friend of Newman. Indeed, Newman had encouraged him to write his pamphlet on the supposed heretical Pope Honorius, and was with reason extremely embarrassed by the affair.[25]

One surprising absentee from the list of the condemned is Charles Darwin, though a book by his grandfather Erasmus is there early in the century. The Church in the 19th century was particularly sensitive to questions of the relationship between science and religion, and on religious philosophy: St George Mivart's 'Happiness in Hell', an article in *The Nineteenth Century*, was put on the Index in 1893, though he managed to remain on relatively good terms with the Church for some time afterwards. Some of Bentham and Mill is on, and Andrew Lang on *Myth, Ritual and Religion*.

Of 19th century novels only one major English work was put on — Laurence Sterne's *Sentimental Journey*, mentioned above. But there are a host of French novelists damned in bulk for their *fabulae amatoriae* — all of Dumas, both father and son, all of George Sand, all of Balzac, all of Feydeau, all of Eugène Sue, the author of *The Wandering Jew*. Flaubert's *Madame Bovary* was put on the Index in 1864, as was Victor Hugo's *Les Misérables*. F.D. Maurice's *Theological Essays* was put on the Index in 1854. (It is a curious turn of fate that the F.D. Maurice chair of social and moral theology at King's College, London, is now held by a Jesuit.)

Nicholas Hiley remarks in his contribution to this volume that the evidence for the success of censorship was counter-factual. If I understand him correctly, he is saying that we do not know if it has been successful because we do not know what the world would have been like without it. The Catholic Church has always preferred prior censorship, the 'imprimatur' or 'nihil obstat', to the Index. But ecclesiastical control goes back further than that. For a time I was editor of the Jesuit journal *The Month*, best known for having been the first to print *The Dream of Gerontius* and the first to turn down *The Wreck of the Deutschland*. As editor I was subject to censorship. It never caused problems, partly at least because I knew how much I could get away with, and pitched my sights accordingly. That, I think, is serious censorship, and it is self-imposed. The Index is a catalogue of the books which evaded such self-restraint, at least when they were written by Catholics. In that sense it is a list of the ones that got away, and a monument not to the success, but to the failure, of the Inquisition.

References

1. Ronald Knox, *Difficulties*, (London, 1952), p.202.
2. Knox was chaplain from 1926 to 1939; the library was at Heythrop Hall from 1926 to 1970.
3. *Letters and Diaries*, (London, Thomas Nelson, 1963), vol.XIV, p.111.
4. *ibid.*, p.112.

5. Humphrey J.T. Johnson, 'The Roman Index of Forbidden Books', *The Downside Review*, vol.72 (1955), p.173.

6. *Tablet*, 18 December 1897, vol.90, pp.961-2.

7. *The Catholic Encyclopaedia*, (London, 1908), vol.III, s.v. 'Censorship'.

8. While it is true that the two-volume study of the Index by Franz Heinrich Reusch is generally regarded as the most thorough of the available histories, it was completed in 1885, before the revisions of the Index undertaken by Leo XIII. Reusch, who was a close associate of Döllinger and an opponent of the Vatican Council of 1869-70, also published a study of the indexes of the 16th century.

9. George Putnam, *The Censorship of the Church of Rome*, (London and New York; G.P. Putnam, 1906), vol.II, p.209.

10. *ibid.*, vol.I, pp.42-3.

11. *ibid.*, vol.I, pp.48-9.

12. *Essays on Freedom and Power by Lord Acton*, selected by Gertrude Himmelfarb, (Glencoe, IL; The Free Press, 1948), p.278.

13. *ibid.*, p.283.

14. They are now in the Cambridge University Library, and I am grateful to Mr David Hall of that Library for supplying details of its holdings.

15. Paul Grendler, *The Roman Inquisition and the Venetian Press, 1540-1605*, (Princeton: Princeton University Press, 1977).

16. See, for example, Ch. Lefebvre, s.v. 'Index' in *Catholicisme*, vol.V, col.1494-1503.

17. In his full-length study Hilgers records Boniface's action, though not the Pope's. He gives as his authority G.D. Mansi, XII, 380.

18. The bull was called *In coena Domini* because it was read from pulpits on Maundy Thursday. Though meant originally for Rome, its use was gradually extended.

19. The rules may be most easily found in H.J.D. Denzinger-A. Schönmetzer, *Enchiridion Symbolorum*, (Barcinone, 1965), pp.422-5.

20. *Index Librorum Prohibitorum*, (Rome, Typis Vaticanis, 1900), pp.xi-xii. The translation is taken from Putnam, *op. cit.*, vol.II, p.383.

21. Index of 1900, pp.5-6, translation from Putnam, *op. cit.*, vol.II, p.392.

22. Owen Chadwick, *Catholicism and History*, (Cambridge: Cambridge University Press, 1978), pp.134 and 143.

23. Redmond A. Burke, *What is the Index?* (Milwaukee: The Bruce Publishing Company, 1952), p.52.

24. These were, however, condemned not for their theological writings but for their *fabulae amatoriae* or 'love stories'.

25. *Letters and Diaries XXIV*, pp.180-1 and p.189. The affair of Pope Honorius (625-638) had just come to light, cf. Chadwick, *op. cit.*, pp.72-5.

'Can't you find me something nasty?': circulating libraries and literary censorship in Britain from the 1890s to the 1910s

NICHOLAS HILEY

THE DEBATE OVER literary censorship in Britain between the 1890s and the 1910s has traditionally revolved around the growth of the so-called 'new fiction', and the development of a style of writing that professed to address modern social issues in a naturalistic way. However, what I want to examine is not the changing style and content of contemporary novels, but rather the changing reactions of the public and of the book trade to these developments, and the different strategies that evolved for containing them within the existing structures. In particular I want to examine the background to the establishment in 1909 of a centralised censorship of novels under the confidential Selecting Committee of the Circulating Libraries Association, a trade organisation with considerable influence on the British book trade.

I

The circulating libraries of the 19th and early 20th centuries were private companies that offered a lending service to paying subscribers. The largest and most powerful of them was Mudie's Select Library, which had been founded in London in the 1840s and which by the 1860s was a limited company with a large headquarters in New Oxford Street. In the early 1890s Mudie's employed more than 250 people at its London headquarters, where it maintained a stock of some 3.5 million volumes. Its subscribers were divided into different classes according to the amount they were prepared to pay. At the bottom of the scale a subscriber could pay a guinea a year to borrow one book at a time from Mudie's in New Oxford Street, but if he rose to the top of the scale he could pay five guineas to have a parcel of books sent to his house every fortnight for a year, either selected according to his instructions or chosen for him by the library. There was a considerable demand for this postal service, and each day the company dispatched

123

5,000 or 6,000 volumes from its London headquarters to its 25,000 provincial and overseas subscribers.[1]

Mudie's Select Library was not the only such establishment operating in Britain in the early 1890s, but, as one contemporary observed, the W.H. Smith library was the only other library 'worth speaking of'. The library branch of W.H. Smith and Son had been established in imitation of Mudie's during the 1860s, and in some ways it had grown to be superior to its model, for it was noted that:

> W.H. Smith and Son's is much more national than Mudie's, for W.H. Smith and Son have not only their great central depôt in the Strand, which corresponds to Messrs. Mudie's library in Oxford Street, but they have also six hundred agents throughout the length and breadth of the land. It is this which allows them to be in much closer touch with the reading public than Mudie.[2]

The network of bookstalls through which W.H. Smith ran its library indeed made it less centralised than Mudie's Select Library. Mudie's might accurately claim that its 25,000 subscribers reflected the reading habits of 'London Society and the London middle classes', but W.H. Smith was quick to observe that its 15,000 subscribers were more evenly distributed 'between Berwick-on-Tweed in the north and Penzance in the south'. The decentralisation of the W.H. Smith library was in fact reflected in its organisation and management, for although in 1895 its stock numbered just 300,000 volumes covering 12,000 different works, only about two-thirds of these were stored at its central depôt in London. The remaining volumes, 'mostly of recent publication', were either on display at the bookstalls or out on loan. In these circumstances it was vital for the central depôt to keep in close contact with the bookstalls, and it was no coincidence that in the 1890s W.H. Smith's chief librarian, William Faux, had previously been employed as inspector of bookstalls on the South-Western Line. Faux ensured that the most popular books were kept in constant motion throughout the system, and, as he informed one observer, his staff could keep him appraised of any changes in demand, and 'can tell from our daily orders as they come in from the stalls what effect is produced by articles in newspapers'.[3]

By the end of the 1890s the W.H. Smith library had a turnover of almost £70,000 a year, and its profits were sufficient to bring other companies into the market. In 1900, encouraged by the success of W.H. Smith's operation, Jesse Boot founded the Boots Book-Lovers Library to work through his national chain of chemist's shops. As with W.H. Smith's station bookstalls, a subscriber to the Book-Lovers Library could borrow books from any Boots branch and return them to any other, for the whole operation was co-ordinated from a central depôt in Nottingham by a former employee of Mudie's. In 1901 the main depôt moved to London, and the venture was such a success that within two years it was supplying books to library counters in 141 of Boot's shops, equal to almost half of his national chain. Yet this was not the only new library venture, for in 1905, as part of a desperate attempt to raise its circulation, the *3d Times* also co-operated in the launch of a circulating library known as the Times Book Club. In this scheme registered subscribers to *The Times* were offered free loans from the Book Club headquarters in Oxford Street, along with free delivery and collection in the London area, and the opportunity of buying surplus library stock at much reduced rates. Such a service would naturally conflict with Mudie's, but *The Times* planned to give its Book Club an advantage not only by paying it a subsidy for each new subscriber to the paper, but also by allowing the wholesale division of W.H. Smith to have favourable rates on distributing the newspaper, thus guaranteeing its support.[4]

In terms of readership, however, the circulating libraries remained very restricted. In 1894 they were believed to cover some 60,000 upper and middle class households, representing only some 240,000 individual readers, and it is important to realise just how small a percentage of the population this represented. In 1895 the economist Alfred Marshall declared that once a household had reached the income tax threshold of £150 a year it possessed 'the material conditions of a complete life', and from contemporary tax assessments it would seem that the incomes of some 850,000 individuals were at or above this level. If we take this as indicating some 850,000 prosperous families we can see that even among their target audience the circulating libraries reached fewer than one household in 15. To put it another way, in a country containing 26 million people aged 15 or over, the proportion using the circulating libraries represented about one per cent of the total.[5]

The narrowness of the library readership was reflected in its tastes. Subscribers tended to order between three and six volumes a week in the 1890s and 1900s, and nine out of ten borrowings were of fiction, by an upper and middle class readership whose tastes were rather indiscriminate. According to one contemporary, 'they read the latest topical favourite, follow the craze of Society, must be up to date with the latest neurotic story, simply because it is the fashion to read such books in such circles', and they seemed to demand 'little else of a novel than that it should be not more than three months old'. The expansion of the library system did little to open out the audience. In the 1910s it was felt that the new income tax threshold of

£160 a year had been fixed 'near the upper limit of ordinary manual earnings', and the returns suggested that more than a million households now lay above this limit. Even if Mudie's, W.H. Smith, and the Times Book Club had doubled the number of upper and middle class subscribers over the preceding 20 years they are unlikely to have reached more than one in ten of their target audience, and although the creation of the Boots Book-Lovers Library had probably added a number of lower middle class subscribers, it is clear that on the eve of war the libraries cannot have reached more than a tiny fraction of even their target readership.[6]

The circulating library readership of the 1890s and 1900s was thus far from representative. Mudie's Select Library and the Times Book Club undoubtedly gained a heavy London bias from their centralised distribution, although W.H. Smith and the Boots Book-Lovers Library probably reached a larger provincial audience through their bookstalls and shops. The library audience was also unusual in having a strong bias towards women. William Faux characterised the principal customers of the W.H. Smith library as 'a general class of readers, who include a large number of women', and the popular novelist Annie S. Swan supported this view, declaring that 'statistics have long since proved to us that it is women readers who devour library fiction, and any librarian will tell you that very, very few ask for anything else'. The library audience of the 1890s and 1900s was also distinguished by its age, for subscribers were said to be of 'middle and advanced age', and one patron argued that the majority was over 60, being 'persons ... whose eyesight is therefore, not what it once was, but who, having leisure time and a taste for reading, like to borrow books which are legible and handy, and which their limited means forbid them to purchase'.[7]

The circulating libraries of the 1890s and 1900s were indeed of greatest benefit to that large number of upper and middle class households in which the outward sign of prosperity was physical and social isolation, and where not only wives and daughters, but also elderly and infirm relatives, faced long periods of intense boredom. The libraries' large stock of three-volume novels was believed to have an especial attraction for the bedridden, and it was argued that they required 'that form of reading which demands no thought and not much attention; which diverts the mind without fatigue; which transports the reader to another and a more pleasant atmosphere, with a book easy to hold, light, and in large print'. The connection between physical weakness and the library novel indeed became fixed in the middle class mind, and the *Lancet* repeatedly alerted doctors to the danger 'of conveying infection by means of books lent out by circulating libraries'. In the early 1890s it was noted that one local library kept a record 'of all infected houses in the surrounding streets', and the *Lancet* thus proposed a system whereby all libraries would insist on being informed of any cases of infectious disease among borrowers, would disinfect all books returned by their families, and would in general require a subscriber 'to guarantee the freedom of his household from infection'.[8]

The circulating libraries of the 1890s thus served a small and unrepresentative sector, but its purchasing power nevertheless allowed them to dominate the British book market. The most obvious example of this came in their deliberate commitment to the three-volume novel. Three-volume production was expensive, and, as a writer in *The Times* observed, 'few private persons, we imagine, ever dream of paying 31*s*. 6*d*., even with a liberal discount, for a new novel, so that the circulating libraries are apparently solely responsible for encouraging this fancy price'. The standard print run for a three-volume library novel was no more than 500 copies, the majority of which were destined to go straight to Mudie's for the use of its subscribers. As the Society of Authors acknowledged, the system was thus a highly artificial one in which 'novelists positively do not offer their books to the world at all, but only to the limited number of those who subscribe to the libraries — perhaps 60,000 in all'.[9]

The purchasing power of the libraries indeed permitted them to dominate the British book market. To support its non-fiction sections we thus know that in 1883 Mudie's bought 1,500 copies of Anthony Trollope's *Autobiography*, and that in 1890 the library not only bought 3,000 copies of H.M. Stanley's *In Darkest Africa*, but also ordered 1,000 copies of William Booth's *In Darkest England*. Orders of this size could cover the publishing costs of a book, and the same was true of fiction, where it was noted that 'many novels ... have no circulation at all save through the libraries'. A popular novel with a total print-run of 50,000 copies might sell as many as 10,000 of them to the libraries. To satisfy the enormous demand from its subscribers Mudie's had to buy 3,500 copies of Hall Caine's novel *The Christian* in 1897, followed by some 3,000 copies of Marie Corelli's novel *The Master-Christian* in 1900, and over 3,200 copies of Mrs Humphrey Ward's novel *The Marriage of William Ashe* on its publication in 1905. For many authors the circulating libraries were thus a vital channel of distribution, and it was said that without their help a novelist would reach only 'a few hundred out of the hundreds of thousands of readers of fiction'. When Bernard Shaw's play *John Bull's Other Island* was published in 1907, the Times Book Club submitted an order for 2,000 copies, and two years later the novelist Arnold Bennett acknowledged that 'without the patronage of the circulating libraries I should either have to live on sixpence a day or starve'.[10]

Their bulk buying gave the libraries considerable power, and they actively intervened to censor any works they believed might offend their readers. Charles Mudie had determined that 'no book that was worthless or morally tainted would be placed on his list', and it was claimed that 'the fate of many a book, if not the reputation of many an author was largely influenced by the number of copies "subscribed" by Mudie'. This careful vetting was a feature of all the major libraries, and any book considered too controversial for subscribers was subjected to a practice known as 'stocking it, but not listing it', where a suspect book would neither be publicised nor supplied to subscribers without a special request. The method of selection was largely a matter of taste. William Faux of W.H. Smith claimed to work by 'instinct born of experience', and admitted that he made his choice of new books even before the publishers had sent them out for review. When George Moore published his novel *Esther Waters* in 1894, Faux thus decided on his own initiative that it was 'not suitable to our library', and gave instructions to stock it but not list it. The book was duly prevented from being sent out to W.H. Smith's bookstalls, although as Faux informed one interviewer, 'if anybody likes to order the book from us we gladly supply it, because in that case it is fair to presume that the person ordering knows what he or she is asking for'.[11]

The power of the circulating libraries could indeed be quite arbitrarily used. In 1894, finding the three-volume format too expensive even for their limited market, Mudie's and W.H. Smith decided to force publishers to end the production of such novels. The prevailing retail price was 15s for a three-volume set, or 5s a volume, but on 27 June 1894 the libraries simply refused to continue paying this sum for their novels. As Mudie's stated in a circular to publishers, it had decided:

(i)   That, after December 31, 1894, the charge to the library for works of fiction shall not be higher than 4s per volume, less the discount now given, and with the odd copy as before.

(ii) That the publishers shall agree not to issue cheaper editions of novels and of other books, which have been taken for library circulation, within twelve months from the date of publication.

The libraries did not seriously expect that three-volume novels would in future be published at 12s, for their intention was simply to kill them off by making them unprofitable, and in this they were triumphantly successful.

Thomas Palmer and William Faux at W.H. Smith and Son's London headquarters, soon before the latter's retirement in 1903. Faux is shown 'estimating the demand for a new book' by casting a suspicious eye over Richard Savage's novel *The Golden Rapids of High Life*, and the picture was originally captioned 'How many copies shall we order?' [Reproduced from *The World's Work*, vol.2 (1903), p.484.]

The packing room at W.H. Smith and Son's London headquarters, where crates of books were loaded and dispatched to branches of the circulating library. By 1905 the library was operating through eight hundred stalls and shops, and kept some 500,000 volumes in circulation. [Reproduced from *The World's Work*, vol.2 (1903), p.483.]

184 three-volume novels were issued in 1894, but in 1895 this fell to 52, and the number continued to decline, to just 25 in 1896 and to only four in 1897. Three years after the libraries made their demands the three-volume novel was thus quite dead.[12]

However, if the libraries' action in suppressing the three-volume novel had seemed dictatorial, their action 15 years later was even more drastic. In 1909 the circulating libraries were concerned over the growing trend of social comment in modern literature, and decided that it was time to act. On 30 November a meeting of representatives from all the major circulating libraries was thus convened at W.H. Smith's London headquarters, and it was decided to form a Circulating Libraries Association. Alfred Acland of W.H. Smith then produced a draft circular to the trade which the members passed for release on 1 December 1909. The circular announced bluntly that:

In order to protect our interests, and also, as far as possible, to satisfy the wishes of our clients, we have determined in future that we will not place in circulation any book which, by reason of the personally scandalous, libellous, immoral, or otherwise disagreeable nature of its contents, is in our opinion likely to prove offensive to any considerable section of our subscribers. We have decided to request that in future you will submit to us copies of all novels, and any book about the character of which there can possibly be any question, at least one clear week before the date of publication.[13]

This was not the full extent of the scheme, however, for the meeting also decided to establish a centralised censorship of books, to be exercised by the members of a confidential Selecting Committee to whom all questionable books could be referred. As the Circulating Libraries Association explained to the trade:

It was agreed to classify all books as (a) satisfactory, (b) doubtful, and (c) objectionable, and that the libraries concerned should be bound by the following rules:
  (1) They will not circulate any novel until it has been submitted for reading at least one week.
  (2) They will at once advise the other members of any doubtful or objectionable book.
  (3) That they will not circulate or sell any book considered objectionable by any three members of the association.
  (4) That they will do their best to make the distribution of any book considered doubtful by three members of the Association as small as possible.[14]

The impact of these measures on book publication was considerable. As one novelist explained, a book in class (a) would remain free from interference, but 'if a book is put into class (c) it is altogether banned, in other words, not stocked or procured at all; if put into class (b) it is stocked, but not sent out on the library's own initiative, and not freely displayed or fairly put forward in libraries or the shops that belong to them'. The records of the Selecting Committee have not survived, but we can trace its activities in a number of specific bans. In October 1910 it would seem that John Trevena's novel *Bracken* was placed in class (c), and thus banned completely, whilst in January 1912, after objections from W.H. Smith, Compton Mackenzie's novel *Carnival* was placed in class (b) and thus prevented from circulating freely. In July 1913 Hall Caine was similarly informed that the Selecting Committee had placed his novel *The Woman Thou Gavest Me* in class (b), and that the libraries had reduced their orders for the book on the grounds that it was 'not suitable for general circulation'. He immediately called on the chairman of the Circulating Libraries Association, Alfred Acland of W.H. Smith, and demanded to know if he had actually read the book. Acland said he had not, but nevertheless understood that it contained passages 'not suitable for the reading of young women and girls', and that for this reason its circulation had been restricted. Hall Caine refused to allow his publisher to supply the libraries with any copies of his book until the matter was reconsidered, but a second meeting simply confirmed the earlier decision to limit its circulation.[15]

The Circulating Libraries Association seems to have intervened quite frequently to ban contentious books. In September 1913, when Compton Mackenzie's novel *Sinister Street* was published, Acland once again decided to restrict its circulation. Mudie's and the Times Book Club had already placed large orders for the novel, but as W.H. Smith and Boots both objected to its free distribution the Selecting Committee was eventually persuaded to place it in class (b). As Mackenzie recalled, Mudie's and the Times Book Club were obliged to accept the Selecting Committee's decision, 'and at once cancelled their large subscription for a very much smaller one'. Later that same month the Selecting Committee also placed William Maxwell's novel *The Devil's Garden* in class (b), prompting the novelist John Galsworthy to write to *The Times* and warn that 'if something is not done there will not be a dog's chance in this country for any outspoken work of art in five or ten years' time'.[16]

II

The imposition of a centralised censorship can be seen as yet another demonstration of the circulating libraries' power over the book trade, and this was indeed how many regarded it at the time. Yet by concentrating on the libraries we are in danger of underestimating the power of the reading public to censor the material it was offered. To take just one example, in the 1900s the novelist Eden Phillpotts published at least one book a year, and a few days after the publication of each one he would receive an unstamped letter through the post, containing nothing but the title-page across which was written:

Thank Heaven, I have destroyed another of your abominable books. Pay the twopence yourself.[17]

There cannot have been many individual readers prepared to take such direct action, but a large number of people were prepared to take some stand against what they saw as the decline of literature. The rate-supported public libraries indeed found it necessary to maintain a censorship of books that was at least equal to that of the circulating libraries, and Ernest Baker, the librarian of the Woolwich Public Library, went so far as to declare that 'the public library ... stands *in loco parentis* towards its very miscellaneous body of readers'. About two-thirds of the borrowings from a typical public library were of fiction, and in 1907 Baker attempted to purge the shelves of questionable books by dividing novels into three categories. In the first he placed the works of authors such as Dickens which 'should all be well represented in every public library': in the second he placed those by authors such as Mrs Henry Wood and Marie Corelli, which 'may be labelled as popular mediocrities and doubtful cases': and in the third he placed those by authors such as Guy Boothby and William Le Queux, which were 'decidedly below the standard admissible in a rate supported library, if there is no undue surrender to popular demands of a frivolous nature'. The duty of the public librarian was to the rate-payers rather than to the borrowers, and the public libraries patrolled their shelves with a vengeance.[18]

A sharp distinction thus came to be made between the public libraries, which presented themselves as guardians of the nation's morals, and the circulating libraries, whose commercialism was considered fatal to any didactic purpose. In 1907, when the ½d *Daily Chronicle* mounted a campaign against what it called 'SORDID FICTION', a reporter asked Jesse Boot for his comments on the growing frankness of modern novels and the need for censorship. Boot gave a cautious reply through his chief librarian, admitting that the tendency was unfortunate and that 'the bulk of the readers ... don't like these books', but still daring to suggest that those subscribers who wished to read them 'have to be taken into consideration'. Boot's attitude to censorship was indeed somewhat ambivalent, but as his librarian reported:

He thinks, however, that a satisfactory censorship could be established if Mudie's, Smith's, and himself — in fact all the big libraries — were to combine, and say definitely that this sort of literature would not be supplied by them under any circumstances.[19]

The circulating libraries were indeed caught by a groundswell of opinion against the new realism. In March 1908 the question of 'indecent literature and pictures' was included in the terms of reference of the Joint Select Committee on Lotteries and Indecent Advertisements, and when the committee reported four months later it advocated new legislation to permit concerted action against such works. By the following year the circulating libraries were not only receiving 'constant complaints of the unwholesome character of certain books which have been put into circulation', but in November 1909 the 6d *Spectator* also entered the battle against what it called 'POISONOUS LITERATURE' by publishing an utter condemnation of H.G. Wells's new novel *Ann Veronica*. In the following week it returned to the attack by giving prominence to the suggestion of one clergyman that if the police would not act against such offensive literature, a fighting fund would have to be established to support private prosecutions. The editor of the *Spectator*, St Loe Strachey, in fact devoted an editorial to the proposed fund, suggesting that it should be administered by a committee of 'men of the world', including one or two lawyers and a few clergymen, who would be authorised to take action whenever offensive literature was referred to them. Outraged readers quickly pledged some hundreds of pounds to the fighting fund, and by the beginning of December 1909 the trade had become alarmed by the gathering momentum of the campaign. As a former librarian recalled, the formation of a committee seemed decisive, for 'it had been known for some time to those in the book trade and to persons behind the scenes in library management that ... a determined attempt would be made to set up some sort of censorship of literature'.[20]

The question of literary censorship finally came to a head over the publication of Lady Cardigan's *Memoirs*. Lady Cardigan was an elderly widow with a fund of racy stories about Victorian society, and in 1909 the

hack novelist William Le Queux managed to persuade her to dictate some
of these to a professional ghost writer named Maude Ffoulkes. According
to Le Queux 'the blue pencil had to be exercised very freely' before these
stories were considered fit for publication, and even after this process was
complete they still possessed the power to shock. On their publication in
September 1909 Lady Cardigan's *Memoirs* were indeed widely criticised for
their 'frankness and indiscretion', and, according to Maude Ffoulkes, one
aggrieved family directed its complaints to the King himself, who was
'begged to exercise his prerogative and command the withdrawal of Lady
Cardigan's book from circulation'.[21]

However, it was not so much the publication of the book as its
distribution through the circulating libraries that caused the greatest trouble.
The circulating libraries had always specialised in travel and biography as
well as in fiction, and towards the end of 1909 a copy of Lady Cardigan's
book was included in a parcel destined for the daughter of 'a woman socially
prominent in the governing classes'. There were various rumours as to what
happened next, but in each of them the results were much the same.
According to one version 'the girl returned this particular book to her
mother, and the mother, after reading it, promptly forwarded it to Scotland
Yard', who then reminded the libraries of their legal responsibilities.
However, the novelist Arnold Bennett heard a more dramatic variant in
which:

The woman went directly to an extremely exalted member of the Cabinet, being a
friend of his; and she kicked up a tremendous storm and dust. The result was that
'certain machinery' was set in motion, and 'certain representations' were made to the
libraries; indeed, the libraries were given to understand that unless they did
something themselves 'certain steps' would be taken.

According to contemporary rumour it was thus the pressure of public feeling
that forced the libraries to form the Circulating Libraries Association in
November 1909, and it is significant that its first list of restricted books
included H.G. Wells's *Ann Veronica*, against which the *Spectator* had
originally spoken out.[22]

The circulating libraries indeed became a focus of action for moralists
opposed to the modern trend in fiction. In January 1910 a meeting of the
'Representatives of London Societies interested in Public Morality' publicly
thanked the Circulating Libraries Association 'for combining to prevent the
circulation of immoral, objectionable, and unhealthy books professedly
treating of the sex problem', but the disease theory of circulating libraries
had grown too strong for this to satisfy their opponents. Just as there had

always been a belief that the circulating libraries could introduce physical disease to respectable households, there were now strong fears that they could also transmit the intellectual diseases of modernity. In the debate on literary censorship the questionable books supplied by the circulating libraries were not simply described as unpleasant but were denounced as 'poisonous' and 'unhealthy', and as 'carriers' of moral disease, and it is hardly surprising in these circumstances that library subscribers began to believe that they might succumb to some dreadful corruption if they did not control the books that entered their houses.[23]

The campaign against the libraries thus continued. In March 1911 the ½d *Daily Mail* published a letter signed by the Chief Constable of Manchester, the wife of the Archbishop of Canterbury, and numerous headmasters and society figures, urging the many societies concerned with 'debasing and demoralising' literature to amalgamate in a single powerful association. There was little doubt that Mudie's and W.H. Smith were once again the target, for it was proposed that the association should contain a powerful 'advisory council' that would not only pronounce upon objectionable literature but would also bring pressure to bear 'on publishers, circulating libraries, and bookstalls'. The aim was to obtain legislation along the lines of that recommended by the Select Committee on Lotteries and Indecent Advertisements, but this was only one of a number of determined attempts to force the government to take action. In January 1912 the National Council of Public Morals thus organised a deputation of publishers, librarians, and booksellers to press the Home Secretary for more determined action to be taken against what was called 'poisonous and demoralizing' literature. The deputation was led by the editor of the *Spectator*, St Loe Strachey, who urged the Home Secretary to introduce legislation that would enable the police to take action against literature which, although falling outside the technical definition of 'obscene', was nevertheless indecent:

Anticipating the objection that this involved a police censorship, he suggested that the objection might be met by the police being willing to receive from societies or individuals complaints as to specific books and then to refer such books to a competent adviser. If they were advised that the books were bad, they might then issue the necessary warning, to be followed, if the warning were not listened to, by a prosecution.[24]

The secretary of the Circulating Libraries Association supported Strachey's arguments, reminding the Home Secretary of the libraries's own efforts in this respect, and urging that its members were 'entitled to the support of the law' in their censorship campaign. In his reply the Home

Secretary carefully avoided the question of an official censor of literature, and, after muttering some platitudes about public opinion, thanked the deputation for its support of the existing draft Bill. He confidently informed it that 'there should not be any very great difficulty in getting it through the House of Commons', but not surprisingly this was the last to be heard of such an obviously contentious measure.[25]

III

We thus have two different interpretations of the circulating library censorship. On the one hand it appears to have been a deliberate attempt by the libraries to become guardians of morality, and yet on the other hand it seems to have been a measure forced upon them by public outrage at their irresponsible behaviour. Yet there is still a third interpretation, in which the libraries seem to be brought to censorship by the changed economics of the British book trade, and forced to oppose the new fiction of the 1890s simply to protect their business.

The circulating libraries were indeed less concerned for the content of the books they stocked than for the balance between their cost and the likely demand. As William Faux admitted in the early 1890s, it was their ability to balance the high cost of the three-volume novel with its relatively short demand 'which largely gives Mudie and ourselves our exceptional position':

Cheaper books the local libraries will take, but it is only the large firms which can afford to pay 18s for a book, the life of which is only nine months. They are evanescent, are novels, and we do not reckon that we can keep them in circulation more than nine months. Some last longer, of course, and others a shorter period; but taking an average, they only remain in circulation for nine months.[26]

The whole structure of the circulating library was in fact determined by the balance of cost and demand. As Faux told another interviewer, the time which a book remained in circulation was vital to the libraries, and the librarian's job involved 'increasing care, forethought, and discrimination, else shelves and rooms might be piled with unreadable and unsaleable stock':

Many people imagine ... that it pays us best to circulate inferior three-volume novels, and light literature generally, whereas the facts are entirely the other way. We like books that will read for six months or a year, and not lose their value in six weeks. In short, the best books are the best books for us.

The threat from reduced demand was uncomfortably real, and one visitor to Mudie's in 1894 was shown a basement room that contained 'piles upon piles, shelf above shelf, case after case' of one popular novel, that had cost the library over £3,600 to buy but was now only fit for burning or pulping.[27]

The duration of demand was in fact the key to the prosperity of the circulating library, for if a book remained popular the libraries could not only keep it in circulation for several months, but could afterwards sell it second-hand to reduce their costs. By the 1890s it was indeed being noted that the prosperity of the circulating libraries 'more than anything else, depends on their facilities for selling surplus copies at fair prices', and in the 1900s the founder of the Times Book Club, Horace Hooper, claimed that 'it's not what you buy that matters, it's what you can sell'. The purchasing policy of the circulating libraries thus revolved around the projected second-hand value of new books, whilst their economics demanded that the popularity of all their books should endure for six months or a year.[28]

Yet by the end of the 19th century the whole economic basis of the libraries was under threat. The first challenge came from the sheer volume of fiction being published in Britain, for although in 1883 this amounted to only some 350 new books, by 1893 it had risen to 1,150 new books without any sign of slowing down. The circulating libraries found it very difficult to cope with this rapid increase, for not only was the number of novels increasing much faster than the number of subscribers, but competition had forced the value of each new subscription to a dangerously low level. The second challenge came from a range of new publishing strategies built around the new concept of the 'best-seller', a book whose price was low and whose sales were large, but whose demand might last for only three or four months. The best-seller was part of a deliberate attempt to widen the market for book publishing by appealing to the mass market, but many critics saw nothing but instability in so dangerous a procedure. 'The public,' observed the *Publishers' Circular* in disgust, 'is influenced by fashion, has no particular standard of taste, and likes to be thought abreast of the time.' If left to its own devices 'it fastens on a work − inferior, it may well be, to many other works in its class ... and lo! that lucky book has a boom', but the problem for the trade was that these 'booms' often collapsed as rapidly as they had arisen, and were no guarantee of future demand.[29]

The circulating libraries were thus under threat from a new form of publishing, which increased the number of books that the libraries had to buy at the same time as reducing their returns both from borrowing and

In the Catacombs.

The lower levels of Mudie's New Oxford Street headquarters held thousands of books for which therre was no longer any demand, and staff referred to this maze of storerooms as 'the catacombs'. By 1894, when this sketch was made, they were piled high with unwanted novels.
[Reproduced from *Good Words*, October 1894, p.669.]

resale. A number of desperate attempts were made to defend the libraries against this considerable danger. It was, for instance, argued that the libraries' patronage allowed the publication of many serious works 'that could not otherwise be printed', and that such novels would reach as large a public through the circulating libraries as they would if issued directly to the public in a cheaper form. Contemporaries argued that during its short career a library novel would reach 'from ten to twenty readers, counting each family as one reader', and that each of these families contained an average of four readers. As the circulating libraries bought sufficient copies of a popular library novel to keep '750 copies going slowly round in this island', it was thus possible that, over its six or nine months of circulation, an expensive three-volume novel would reach as many as 60,000 individuals in 15,000 households, and that its total readership would be close to that of a cheap novel produced in France or the United States.[30]

The libraries were indeed attractive to the publishers of small editions. If a publisher allied himself to the circulating libraries he could spend just £90 in producing a small edition of a three-volume novel, and recover the costs of production even if the librarians took only 130 copies at 14s each. This naturally made the library edition an attractive way of launching new authors, but with popular and established writers the economics were quite different. If a publisher issued a popular novel in a one-volume edition that retailed at 3s 6d, he would have to devote about £100 to producing and advertising 1,000 copies, and would need to sell 600 copies to get a return on his investment. But this was not difficult to achieve with a popular author. When Chatto and Windus launched its series of 6d reprints in 1893 it confidently issued Charles Reade's *The Cloister and the Hearth* in a run of 50,000 copies, and when the cheap edition of George Du Maurier's 1894 novel *Trilby* was launched it sold 80,000 copies in three months. At this level of demand it was inevitable that publishers would try to bypass the circulating libraries in their efforts to reach a larger public.[31]

It is thus hardly surprising that although by 1894 the publication of expensive three-volume novels was virtually static, the cheap single-volume format was advancing rapidly. In the 12 months to June 1893 British publishers issued some 101 three-volume and 344 one-volume novels, but in the 12 months to June 1894 this had risen to some 107 three-volume and 482 single-volume novels, showing an increase of 40 per cent in the publication of cheap editions. The *Publishers' Circular* warned that although hundreds of works of fiction were published in 1894 only a minority would sell more than 2,000 copies, and only half a dozen were likely to reach sales of more than 20,000 copies; but even this level of sales was enough to make cheap publication an attractive proposition. Any novelist who could sell a thousand copies could now be published in a single volume, and for a handful of really popular authors it was essential to publish in this form in order to reach a mass audience.[32]

British publishers thus began to turn from expensive three-deckers in small editions to cheap single volumes with long print-runs and huge advertising, but the shortening of demand which this produced put the circulating libraries in an awkward position. As W.H. Smith explained in its circular to the trade in June 1894:

> For some time past we have noted with concern a great and increasing demand, on the part of the subscribers to our library, for novels in sets of two and three volumes. To meet their requisitions we are committed to an expenditure much out of proportion to the outlay for other kinds of literature. Most of the novels are ephemeral in their interest, and the few with an enduring character are published in cheap editions so soon after the first issue that the market we formerly had for the disposal of the surplus stock in sets is almost lost.

The libraries were indeed alarmed less by the content of the new fiction than by the strategies for its distribution. In July 1894 the Edinburgh circulating library of Douglas and Foulis confirmed the national spread of the problem by acknowledging that, although its orders for novels were undoubtedly increasing, this demand 'lasts only for a short time' and was soon killed off by cheap reprints.[33]

By July 1894 popular authors had indeed begun to turn away from the patronage of the circulating libraries and towards the mass market. The three-volume novel was killed as much by the shift in fiction publishing towards monthly magazines and single-volume editions as by the actions of the libraries. As the novelist Henry Rider-Haggard admitted, the book market was rapidly moving away from the expensive library editions and towards these cheap printings. He acknowledged that 'the rich folk who subscribe to libraries are not as a rule the chief purchasers of light literature':

> Many novelists of repute would be able to show ... that their true *clientèle* is to be found among people of small means — clerks, and even intelligent working men, who out of their savings buy the books of those writers whose works they chance to admire. It is, therefore, to the advantage and wishes of the book buyer — not to those of the book borrower — that the author should look, and doubtless the book buyer is best served by the primary production of a novel at a nominal price of 6*s* and a net price of 4*s* 8*d*.

Rider-Haggard argued that novelists would have to abandon the circulating libraries if they wished to survive, for rather than extending the readership of a popular novel the libraries could easily halve its sales.[34]

Rider-Haggard was not the only contemporary to observe the dilemma facing the circulating libraries. The *Publishers' Circular* noted in 1894 that the libraries's attempt to kill off the three-volume novel could easily backfire, for the most popular authors had already developed their own readership and once their work was cheaply available 'the public will forsake the libraries and flock to the booksellers'. A writer in the 1*d Pall Mall Gazette* confirmed the vulnerability of the libraries, observing that they were now offering publishers less than 4*s* a volume for new novels, at a time when the public was effectively offering up to 6*s* a volume for its favourite authors. The libraries' action thus seemed certain to bring 'the end of the three-volume novel and the circulating library together':

> This conclusion is inevitable, because the library companies have now put three shillings and eightpence farthing, their price, side by side with the six shillings[,] and three shillings and sixpence[,] that the public actually spends in thousands of cases at the bookstalls. The library companies are actually forcing the publishers to take the last plunge, and, passing them, go direct to the public with their new books.[35]

The circulating libraries were thus under threat from a shift in publishing away from the prosperous audience around which they were constructed, towards a mass market whose purchasing power was even greater but whose tastes were less easily predicted. They were forced to choose between protecting their existing market and attempting to expand their operations to absorb the new publishing strategies. Yet the only way that the libraries could have contained the cheap best-seller, with its short demand and low second-hand value, would have been to increase their subscriptions to an uneconomic level, and they thus resorted to a series of measures designed to protect their traditional market. The first of these was the decision not to purchase any more expensive three-volume novels, and further to restrict the number of copies of new novels bought. The inevitable result, noted one critic in the 1900s, was that whenever a popular book was published the circulating libraries 'bought a number of copies quite inadequate for the number of their subscribers':

> Consequently a man might put it at the head of his list week after week for many weeks without getting a copy to read. Thus one copy was made to do duty for a great many subscribers. Not only so, but after its vogue was past it went on doing duty by being foisted upon people who asked for some newer book which was denied them.[36]

By the 1900s the libraries were thus already intervening both to restrict their initial purchase of new novels and to extend the pattern of demand, but it became clear that any further interventions would require the moral support of their audience. It was here that the Selecting Committee of the Circulating Libraries Association was of tremendous economic importance, and as one employee of the Times Book Club recalled, its formation was intimately linked to 'commercial considerations'. When Lord Northcliffe became chief proprietor of the 3d *Times* in 1908 he placed his colleague Kennedy Jones in charge of the Book Club with the idea of reconstructing it as a purely commercial undertaking. Jones was a hard-headed businessman who was convinced that the libraries would have to combine to protect their commercial interests, and it is no surprise to learn that in 1909 he was a prominent figure in the movement to create a Circulating Libraries' Association.[37]

The formation of the Selecting Committee was indeed designed to contain the economic threat of modern publishing rather than its moral threat. Arnold Bennett was convinced that this moral crusade 'would certainly not have occurred had not the libraries perceived ... the chance of effecting economies', and other contemporaries regarded the Selecting Committee in much the same light. As early as December 1909 the critic Clement Shorter observed in the 6d *Sphere* that the formation of the Selecting Committee seemed to have an economic as well as a moral function:

It is suggested in some quarters that the libraries were very much annoyed at the demand for Lady Cardigan's *Memoirs*; 17,000 copies of this book were sold at 10s 6d, and a very large proportion of these must have been taken by the libraries. The libraries do not like buying large quantities of a high-priced book, and this was particularly the case with Lady Cardigan's *Memoirs*, which was not a book that many people would wish to preserve permanently in their libraries.

The libraries were indeed forced to buy the majority of the first printing of Lady Cardigan's *Memoirs*, and this placed them in a difficult situation. As a writer in the 1d *Observer* noted, they found themselves buying 12,000 copies of a sensational book that not only cost twice as much as a novel, but was also guaranteed to make a very poor showing on the second-hand market.[38]

This economic interpretation is confirmed by the pattern of bans, which shows quite clearly that the censorship policy of the libraries was never allowed to interfere with their economic performance. This was in fact noted by contemporaries, and in 1910 the librarian of Battersea Public Library stated quite bluntly that the members of the Circulating Libraries' Association were animated 'not so much by solicitude for the morals of their customers as by the dread of losing their subscriptions'. As he explained, 'there seems every reason to believe that their leading principle, in the future as in the past, will be to consult the requirements of subscribers, and no results of any consequence need be looked for'. The moral results of the censorship were thus of little consequence, for the number of books against which the Selecting Committee took action was remarkably small. Of almost 8,500 new books published in Britain in 1909, including over 1,800 new works of fiction, the Selecting Committee decided to place only seven of them in class (c), thus banning them completely. The following year saw an equal number of new books launched on to the British market, and yet the Selecting Committee placed only six of them in class (c), with only another 17 or 18 in class (b).[39]

The moral impact of the Selecting Committee was in fact much less than even the pattern of bans would suggest. When the Selecting Committee placed Hall Caine's novel *The Woman Thou Gavest Me* in class (b) in July 1913, its author protested that this action 'greatly reduced' the number of copies which the libraries ordered from his publisher, and yet they still bought several thousand copies and presumably worked them as hard as they could. The same pattern occurred in September 1913, when the Selecting Committee placed William Maxwell's novel *The Devil's Garden* in class (b). Despite their apparent objection to its contents the circulating libraries still managed to satisfy the demand from their customers, and were said to be 'handing out his novel in large quantities daily to his admirers, who refuse to take no for an answer'. After 1909 the process of placing a book in class (b) in fact meant little more than keeping the advanced orders to a minimum, and, as the chairman of the Circulating Libraries' Association admitted, ensuring that future orders were tailored to 'the demand from the public'.[40]

The circulating libraries' efforts to control the book market were indeed economic rather than moral. The libraries first intervened in 1894, after they had suffered a sharp decline in both membership and use during 1893-4, and it is no surprise to find that their intervention in 1909 was preceded by a similar crisis during 1904-6. The formation of the Selecting Committee was little more than an attempt to gain moral authority for an attempt to stabilise the library market, and the pattern of bans imposed by the Circulating Libraries' Association must be seen in this light. The economic basis of the censorship was indeed clear to some contemporaries, and Compton

Mackenzie blamed Herbert Morgan of W.H. Smith for the decision to place *The Woman Thou Gavest Me* in class (b), stating bluntly that his firm 'was much more concerned to keep down their subscription order for a popular favourite than for its moral effect upon their respectable clients'.[41]

It is indeed difficult to identify anything other than commercial morality at work in the operations of the circulating libraries. In the 1890s William Faux of W.H. Smith apparently kept a top shelf in his office 'from which he would take a "censored" novel as a gift', and although after 1909 the libraries were supposed to destroy all works that were banned by the Selecting Committee, at least one book withdrawn from the Times Book Club is known to have been sold second-hand from the private address of a member of staff. Even in the 1910s it was noted that 'men send their office-boys to Mudie's for stories with stir and "go" in them, and sometimes, maybe, for others, not always "in stock"', and subscribers knew that if they wished to obtain a small selection of less reputable books an effort would always be made to accommodate them. As one female subscriber was heard to say to an assistant at the Times Book Club, 'I feel a little low today; can't you find me something nasty?'.[42]

References

1. O.B. Bunce, 'English and American Book Markets', *North American Review*, April 1890, p.473: *Publishers' Circular* [hereafter given as *PC*], 1 Nov. 1890, p.1418, 'Mr. Charles Edward Mudie': W.C. Preston, 'Mudie's Library', *Good Words*, Oct. 1894, p.675. For the growth of Mudie's Select Library see also G.L. Griest, *Mudie's Circulating Library and the Victorian Novel* (Newton Abbot, 1970), pp.17-27.

2. W.T. Stead, 'The Reading Public and the Press', *Review of Reviews Annual 1893* (London, 1893), supplement p.18: C. Wilson, *First with the News: The history of W.H. Smith 1792-1972* (London, 1985), pp.355-9.

3. *PC*, 11 April 1891, pp.379-80, 'A Representative Librarian: Mr. W. Faux'; 5 May 1894, pp.464-5, 'Mr. George Moore's New Novel': Stead 'Reading Public', p.18: W.C. Preston, 'Messrs. W.H. Smith and Son's Bookstalls and Library', *Good Words*, July 1895, pp.477-8: *Unwin's Chap Book 1899-1900* (London, 1899), p.55, 'A Prime Minister of Circulating Libraries': J. Milne '"Mudie's": The Diamond Jubilee of a great library', *Strand Magazine*, Aug. 1919, p.138.

4. F.H. Kitchen, *Moberly Bell and His Times: An unofficial narrative* (London, 1925), pp.184-6: J. Milne, 'A Library of To-day', *Cornhill Magazine*, Oct. 1934, pp.443-4: *The History of The Times Vol.III: The twentieth century test 1884-1912* (London, 1947), pp.447-8: S.D. Chapman, *Jesse Boot of Boots the Chemists* (London, 1974), p.88: Wilson, *First with the News*, p.362.

5. A. Marshall, *Principles of Economics* (3rd ed., London, 1895), p.2: J.C. Stamp, *British Incomes and Property: The application of official statistics to economic problems* (London, 1916), p.448.
6. *The Times*, 25 July 1894, p.10 col.1 [leading article]: W. Besant, 'London Free Libraries', *Author*, 1 Aug. 1894, p.78: A.L. Bowley, 'The British Super-Tax and the Distribution of Income', *Quarterly Journal of Economics*, Feb. 1914, p.261: A.L. Bowley, *The Division of the Product of Industry: An analysis of National Income before the war* (Oxford, 1919), p.12: J.E. Courtney, *Recollected in Tranquillity* (London, 1926), p.182: Q.D. Leavis, *Fiction and the Reading Public* (London, 1932), p.14.
7. *PC*, 5 May 1894, pp.464-5, 'Mr. George Moore's New Novel'; 18 Aug. 1894, p.171, 'The Three-Volume Novel': *Woman at Home*, Oct. 1896, p.31, 'What Should Women Read?': Milne, '"Mudie's"'; p.138.
8. *Lancet*, 24 May 1890, p.1135, 'Public Libraries and Contagion': *Author*, 1 Aug. 1894, p.64, 'Literary Property': *PC*, 16 March 1895, p.305, 'The Three-Volume Novel'.
9. Bunce, 'English and American Book Markets', p.472: *The Times*, 25 July 1894, p.10 col.1 [leading article]: *Author*, 1 Aug. 1894, p.63, 'Literary Property'.
10. Bunce, 'English and American Book Markets', p.472: *PC*, 1 Nov. 1890, p.1418, 'Mr. Charles Edward Mudie'; 17 Jan. 1891, p.59, 'Notes and Announcements'; 8 Oct. 1898, p.423 [leading article]: *All the Year Round*, 26 May 1894, p.488, 'Circulating Libraries': [*The Times*], *The History of the Book War: Fair book prices versus publishers' trust prices* (London, 1907), p.48: *Observer*, 16 Jan. 1910, p.7 col.6, 'The Library Censorship': A. Bennett, *Books and Persons: Being comments on a past epoch 1908-1911* (London, 1917), p.88: Milne, '"Mudie's"', p.142.
11. *PC*, 1 Nov. 1890, p.1418, 'Mr Charles Edward Mudie'; 5 May 1894, pp.464-5, 'Mr. George Moore's New Novel': Stead, 'Reading Public', p.18: Preston, 'Mudie's Library', p.669: Preston, 'W.H. Smith's', p.478: *Daily Chronicle*, 9 July 1907, p.6 col.3, 'Sordid Fiction': G. Moore, *A Communication to My Friends* (London, 1933), p.75.
12. *PC*, 7 July 1894, p.7, 'The Circulating Libraries and Three-Volume Novels'; 15 Oct. 1910, p.566, 'The Issue of Fiction': R.A. Gettmann, *A Victorian Publisher: A study of the Bentley Papers* (Cambridge, 1960), p.260.
13. *The Times*, 2 Dec. 1909, p.12 col.3, 'Circulating Libraries Association': *PC*, 4 Dec. 1909, p.827, 'The Circulating Libraries Association'.
14. *PC*, 4 Dec. 1909, pp.827-8, 'The Circulating Libraries Association'.
15. *Author*, 1 Dec. 1910, p.78, 'Libraries' Censorship': *Daily Telegraph*, 2 Aug. 1913, p.10 col.6, 'Mr. Hall Caine's New Novel'; 7 Aug. 1913, p.9 cols.1-7, 'Mr. Hall Caine's New Novel': *The Times*, 3 Oct. 1913, p.9 cols.4-5, 'Library Censorship' [letter from John Galsworthy]: C. Mackenzie, *My Life and Times: Octave four 1907-1915* (London, 1965), p.194. The banning of books from the library bookshops was a considerable extra penalty, for they were said to control two out of three retail outlets in London: S. Hynes, *The Edwardian Turn of Mind* (Princeton, 1968), p.297.
16. Mackenzie, *Life and Times: Octave four*, pp.192-3, 196: *The Times*, 15 Sept. 1913, p.9 col.2, 'The Library Censorship'; 3 Oct. 1913, p.9 cols.4-5, 'Library Censorship'.
17. *PC*, 24 Jan. 1914, p.77, 'A Private Censor'.
18. *The Reader's Index: The bi-monthly magazine of the Croydon public libraries*, vol.ix (1907), pp.4, 33, 59, 115, 144: E.A. Baker, 'The Standard of Fiction in Public Libraries', *Library Association Record*, Feb. 1907, pp.72-3: E.A. Baker, 'The "Poisonous Literature" Scare', *Library Association Record*, 15 Jan. 1910, p.2.

19. *Daily Chronicle*, 9 July 1907, p.6 col.3, 'Sordid Fiction. / Modern tendency suggests need of censorship'.

20. *Sessional Papers 1908*, 'Report ... on Lotteries and Indecent Advertisements' [29 July 1908], pp.vii-viii: *Spectator*, 20 Nov. 1909, pp.846-7, 'A Poisonous Book'; 27 Nov. 1909, pp.876, 881-2, 'Poisonous Literature'; 4 Dec. 1909, p.945, 'The Guarantee Fund': *PC*, 12 Feb. 1910, p.181, 'The Libraries Censorship': *The Times*, 12 Sept. 1913, p.4 col.1, 'The Library Censorship'. The fund eventually stood at £721, but only £34 of this was in cash: *Spectator*, 25 Dec. 1909, p.1100, 'The Guarantee Fund'.

21. *Observer*, 5 Dec. 1909, p.11 col.4, 'Morals or Money / A sequel to Lady Cardigan's book': M. Ffoulkes, *My Own Past* (London, 1915), p.239: W. Le Queux, *Things I Know about Kings, Celebrities, and Crooks* (London, 1923), pp.132-4.

22. *PC*, 11 April 1891, p.380, 'A Representative Librarian: Mr. W. Faux': 'Jacob Tonson' [Arnold Bennett] 'Books and Persons', *New Age*, 23 Dec. 1909, p.184: *Daily Express*, 9 Aug. 1913, p.4 col.4, 'The Boom Thou Gavest Me': Courtney, *Recollected in Tranquillity*, pp.182, 197.

23. Hynes, *Edwardian Turn of Mind*, pp.293, 301.

24. *Daily Mail*, 22 March 1911, p.7 col.6, 'Impure Fiction. / Project to Suppress its Circulation': *The Times*, 24 Jan. 1912, p.10 col.4, 'Demoralising Literature. / Deputation to the Home Secretary'.

25. *The Times*, ibid.

26. Stead, 'Reading Public', p.19.

27. *PC*, 11 April 1891, pp.379-80, 'A Representative Librarian: Mr. W. Faux': Preston, 'Mudie's Library', p.671.

28. *PC*, 14 July 1894, p.34, 'Libraries and Three-Volume Novels': Courtney, *Recollected in Tranquillity*, p.192.

29. *PC*, 31 Dec. 1883, p.1430, 'Analytical Table'; 6 Jan. 1894, p.8, 'Analytical Table'; 21 July 1894, p.57, 'London Booksellers and the Libraries' Circular'; 28 Sept. 1895, p.333 [leading article]: Milne, 'Library of To-day', pp.447-8: N.N. Feltes, *Modes of Production of Victorian Novels* (Chicago,1986), p.98.

30. Bunce, 'English and American Book Markets', pp.472-3; *PC*, 28 July 1894, p.80, 'The Incorporated Society of Authors and the Three-Volume Novel'.

31. *Author*, 1 Aug. 1894, p.63, 'Literary Property': *PC*, 26 Oct. 1895, p.472: *Sixpenny Wonderfuls: 6d. gems from the past* (London, 1985), p.8.

32. *Author*, 1 Oct. 1894, p.128, 'Fiction: Comparative Lists': *PC*, 28 July 1894, p.80, 'The Incorporated Society of Authors and the Three-Volume Novel'; 15 June 1895, p.657 [leading article].

33. *PC*, 7 July 1894, p.7, 'The Circulating Libraries and Three-Volume Novels'; 21 July 1894, p.57, 'London Booksellers and the Libraries' Circular'.

34. *The Times*, 27 July 1894, p.11 col.6, 'The Three-Volume Novel': C. Mackenzie, *Literature in My Time* (London, 1933), pp.109-10: Feltes, *Modes of Production*, pp.78-80.

35. *PC*, 7 July 1894, p.5 [leading article]: *Pall Mall Gazette*, 11 July 1894, p.3 col.3, 'The Circulating Libraries and Publishers'.

36. [*The Times*] *History of the Book War*, p.24.

37. Courtney, *Recollected in Tranquillity*, pp.187, 193, 195.

38. *Observer*, 5 Dec. 1909, p.11 col.4, 'Morals or Money / A sequel to Lady Cardigan's book': C.K. S[horter], 'A Literary Letter', *Sphere*, 18 Dec. 1909, p.268: 'Books and Persons' by 'Jacob Tonson' [Arnold Bennett] in *New Age*, 23 Dec. 1909, p.184, and 13

Jan. 1910, p.254.

39. L. Inkster, '"Poisonous Books"', *Library Association Record*, 15 Jan. 1910, p.3: *PC*, 12 Feb. 1910, p.181, 'The Libraries Censorship'; 7 Jan. 1911, 'Books of the Year'; 18 Feb. 1911, p.207, 'Books and the National Council of Public Morals'.

40. *Daily Telegraph*, 2 Aug. 1913, p.10 col.6,'Mr Hall Caine's New Novel'; 7 Aug. 1913, p.9 col.4, 'Mr Hall Caine's New Novel': *Daily Express*, 9 Aug. 1913, p.4 col.5, 'The Boom Thou Gavest Me': *The Times*, 15 Sept. 1913, p.9 col.2, 'The Library Censorship'.

41. Wilson, *First With the News*, p.363: J. Feather, *A History of British Publishing* (London, 1988), p.154.

42. *PC*, 12 Feb. 1910, p.181, 'The Libraries Censorship': Courtney, *Recollected in Tranquillity*, pp.178, 195-6: J. Milne, 'A Great Circulating Library', *Cornhill Magazine*, April 1935, p.452: Mackenzie, *Life and Times: Octave four*, p.192.

Index